Frameworks for Practice in Educational Psychology

of related interest

Nurture Groups in School and at Home
Connecting with Children with Social, Emotional and Behavioural Difficulties
Paul Cooper and Yonca Tiknaz
ISBN 978 1 84310 528 2

Promoting Resilience in the Classroom
A Guide to Developing Pupils' Emotional and Cognitive Skills
Carmel Cefai
Foreword by Paul Cooper
ISBN 978 1 84310 565 7

Cool Connections with Cognitive Behavioural Therapy
Encouraging Self-esteem, Resilience and Well-being in Children and Young People Using CBT Approaches
Laurie Seiler
ISBN 978 1 84310 618 0

Understanding School Refusal
A Handbook for Professionals in Education, Health and Social Care
M.S. Thambirajah, Karen J. Grandison and Louise De-Hayes
ISBN 978 1 84310 567 1

Listening to Children
A Practitioner's Guide
Alison McLeod
ISBN 978 1 84310 549 7

Reaching and Teaching the Child with Autism Spectrum Disorder
Using Learning Preferences and Strengths
Heather MacKenzie
ISBN 978 1 84310 623 4

Psychological Processes in Deaf Children with Complex Needs
An Evidence-Based Practical Guide
Lindsey Edwards and Susan Crocker
ISBN 978 1 84310 414 8

Frameworks for Practice in Educational Psychology

A Textbook for Trainees and Practitioners

Edited by Barbara Kelly, Lisa Woolfson and James Boyle

Jessica Kingsley Publishers
London and Philadelphia

| 6 | The Woolfson *et al.* Integrated Framework: An Executive Framework for Service-Wide Delivery | 121 |

Dr Lisa Woolfson, Reader in Psychology and Director of the Doctorate in Educational Psychology Programme, University of Strathclyde

Part Four: Frameworks for Practice with Therapeutic Roots — 137

| 7 | Consultation as a Framework for Practice | 139 |

Patsy Wagner, Principal Educational Psychologist and Lead Practitioner, Kensington and Chelsea Education Psychology Consultation Service

| 8 | A Systemic Solution-Oriented Model | 162 |

Ioan Rees, Sycol Foundation

Part Five: Frameworks for Practice for Psychological Theory and Research — 183

| 9 | Positive Psychology as a Framework For Practice | 185 |

Professor Stephen Joseph, Centre for Trauma Resilience and Growth, School of Sociology and Social Policy, University of Nottingham

| 10 | Activity Theory and the Professional Practice of Educational Psychology | 197 |

Jane Leadbetter, Associate Tutor, MEd Educational Psychology Programme, University of Birmingham

| 11 | Illuminative Evaluation | 218 |

Professor Bob Burden, School of Education, University of Exeter

| | Appendix to Chapter 11: The SPARE Wheel Model | 231 |

Part Six: Developing an Integrated Methodology for Training and Practice — 235

| 12 | Developing a System of Complementary Frameworks | 237 |

Barbara Kelly and Lisa Woolfson

| | INDEX | 251 |

List of Figures and Tables

Figures

Figure 4.1:	Problem-solving frameworks	72
Figure 4.2:	The 2008 and 1998 problem-analysis frameworks	82
Figure 4.3:	Interactive Factors Framework diagram for A, aged six years, whose teacher consulted an EP on account of 'Difficulty initiating and sustaining verbal interaction with adults and peers in a range of social interactions'	89
Figure 5.1:	Visual representation of COMOIRA (first published in Gameson *et al.* 2003)	95
Figure 6.1:	The Integrated Framework	124
Figure 6.2:	Phase 3 problem-analysis	130
Figure 7.1:	Framework for a meeting in a joint school–family Consultation	151
Figure 7.2:	A framework for use in multi-agency meetings	153
Figure 7.3:	Questions for use in annual review and evaluation of Consultation	156
Figure 8.1:	The Solution-Oriented Systemic model	180
Figure 8.2:	The three stages of Solution-Oriented Systemic Development	181
Figure 10.1:	First-generation Activity Theory model	199
Figure 10.2:	Second-generation Activity Theory model	200
Figure 10.3:	Third-generation Activity Theory model	201
Figure 10.4:	Activity System showing a learning programme	204
Figure 10.5:	Activity System showing pupil views of transition at the end of Year 7	207
Figure 10.6:	Activity System showing teacher views of transition at the end of Year 7	207
Figure 10.7:	Questions used to facilitate Developmental Work Research workshops	211
Figure 10.8:	Multi-agency working viewed as an Activity System	212
Figure 10.9:	Consultation meetings between EPs and teachers viewed as an Activity System	214
Figure 12.1:	Key parameters of the frameworks discussed in this book	247

Tables

Table 6.1:	Phase 2/3 summary proforma	127
Table 6.2:	Summary of Phase 3 problem dimensions	129
Table 6.3:	Phase 4 action plan proforma	132
Table 6.4:	Phase 5 summary proforma	134
Table 10.1:	Summary of Activity Theory contradiction surrounding pupil transition from Year 6 to Year 7	208

Acknowledgements

We would like to thank trainees, practice tutors and practitioners for their comments, reflections and contributions to the development of training in the MSc and Doctorate in Educational Psychology programmes at Strathclyde University. We would also like to thank Dr Harry Rafferty and Andrew Richards for their advice on historical perspectives and legislation in England and Ireland. Last, but not least, our thanks to Richard Cotter, Dr Richard Woolfson and Dr Liz Boyle for their help and support.

Foreword

This book is edited by Barbara Kelly, Lisa Woolfson and James Boyle, all of whom are tutors at the University of Strathclyde who contribute to the development of the profession of educational psychology through both the initial postgraduate professional training of educational psychologists (EPs), and the post-qualification research doctoral programme for practising EPs, in parallel with maintaining their own expertise as practitioners.

The responsibilities and long-standing experience of the editorial team within these roles have given a sustained impetus to their very careful consideration of questions central to the development of the educational psychology profession, amongst which they identify as a fundamental challenge, the need 'to develop the means to express (and to experience) more coherently, and with justifiable conviction, what it is actually doing and why' (p.241).

It is generally recognised at a surface level both within the profession of educational psychology and by our employers and service users, that one of the distinctive dimensions that EPs bring to the multi-agency children's workforce is the application of psychological knowledge and skills. However, quite how distinctive these applications of psychology are is brought into question by the observation by Farrell *et al.* 2006 that the majority of school-based respondents to their survey, and about half of the EPs, had indicated that alternative providers may have been equally well qualified and able to fulfil tasks undertaken by EPs.

Against a context then in which it appears that it is not what EPs do, or even the fact that they apply psychology in fulfilling their responsibilities toward children and young people and other service users, which form distinctive components of EPs' professional identity and practice, the current text sets out to fulfil an ambitious purpose: 'the development of a coherent approach to assimilating, understanding and applying necessarily complex theoretical perspectives with equally complex practice methodology' (p.241).

At the outset, Kelly makes explicit the primary aim of this new text: 'to allow trainee EPs and practitioners to access the concepts behind emerging and established practice frameworks and to become familiar with their relative characteristics and usefulness'. She adds her claim that, in addressing this broad aim, the text fills a void, since 'few texts attempt systematically to address the question of how practitioners should go about applying theory in educational contexts' (p. 15).

The various frameworks presented in this edited text provide a comprehensive range of procedural/executive and conceptual models through which EPs can bring rigour and coherence to their unique, situation-specific applications of psychological theory and research, within the dynamic 'real world' contexts in which they work, and approach the practitioner-scientist ideal with confidence.

In relation to our profession's claims toward evidence-based practice, the editorial team and contributing authors go further than previous texts devoted to educational psychology practice and service delivery, by giving careful consideration to the epistemological foundations of the 'science' or 'sciences' upon which we draw.

Kelly and her colleagues argue persuasively for the central role of critical realism (a position that maintains that there exists an objectively knowable, mind-independent reality, whilst acknowledging the role of subjective experience, mediated by perception and cognition, in providing access to this objective reality), arguing that it offers 'the necessary scaffolding for the growth of professional educational psychology, ... forming a base from which contemporary knowledge, skills and theories can root and flourish' (p. 248).

This attention to philosophical, as well as theoretical and research bases for the practice of applied psychology is based upon the editing team's appreciation of EPs' need for a 'clear view of where and how the underlying psychological theory and philosophy of science functions and affects their day-to-day work' (p. 246). Moreover, the approach has considerable value both in positioning the ecological and Social Constructionist theoretical paradigms upon which EPs draw in their search 'for dynamic and transactional models of shared or negotiated meaning' (p. 21).

The position of the editing team as academics and leading members of the profession ensures that they have been able to develop an elegant and coherent conceptual framework within which to position and integrate the contributions of a number of recognised experts from the fields of educational psychology training and practice, whose work has had a major role in supporting the development of the profession over recent decades.

Overall, this text provides a very rich resource for those of us who seek to ensure that we do indeed offer clients a distinctive contribution as psychologists – one that is different from the involvement of education administrators, teachers and social workers.... It offers a very judicious balance between conceptual complexity and more pragmatic considerations.

I would anticipate that this book will form a core text recommended on reading lists for prospective EPs, trainee EPs and for EP service libraries, in addition to forming a very useful reference resource for colleagues working in Children's Services and in higher education institutions.

Sue Morris
Educational Psychology Programme Director
University of Birmingham

References

Farrell, P., Woods, K., Lewis, S., Rooney, S., Squires, G. and O'Connor, M. (2006) *A review of the functions and contribution of educational psychologists in England and Wales in light of 'Every Child Matters: Change for Children'*. London: DfES Publications

PART ONE
Perspectives on Applying Educational Psychology

CHAPTER 1

Frameworks for Practice in Educational Psychology: Coherent Perspectives for a Developing Profession

Barbara Kelly

Key themes: Social Constructionism, the perception of professional change and creating flexible tools to address complexity

Introduction

The primary reason for writing this textbook is to allow trainee educational psychologists (EPs) and practitioners to access the concepts behind emerging and established practice frameworks and to become familiar with their relative characteristics and usefulness. It is hoped that it will engage educational psychologists in a dynamic and creative process of critical reflection on the shape and direction of the profession.

In examining its theoretical basis, we find the profession to date has few textbooks attempting to systematically address the problem of *how* the practitioner should go about applying theory in educational contexts. In contrast, analysis of *processes of change* within the profession itself has assumed rhetorical dominance in the literature; change, growth and professional esteem and effectiveness – or rather, a disconcerting lament over the lack of these – is considered to be of extraordinary importance. In-depth study of this 'change' literature reveals a narrow and unsettling focus on the apparent role confusion and perceived ineffectiveness of the contemporary practitioner (Stobie 2002). This confusion is identified as being linked almost exclusively to practitioners' apparent collective failure to adopt a Constructionist theoretical model and perspectives. However, a wider, more complete view – which includes an understanding of the conceptual and practice implications of Social Constructionist Theory alongside the study of practitioner reaction to it – gives a more balanced and helpful picture of the profession's development and status. To help locate practice frameworks in terms of their sources and their objectives, we have included a brief analysis of the impact, contemporary influences and potential of Social Constructionism for educational psychology.

Practice frameworks are potentially a very significant and urgently needed professional resource, enabling a long overdue clarification and articulation of the profession's complex theory, methodology and objectives. In addition, some more recent frameworks present an innovative, systematic approach to clarifying professional objectives and evaluating outcomes of professional involvement. The Monsen *et al.* and Woolfson *et al.* frameworks are the two clearest examples of this type. They might be described as 'overarching' or 'executive' frameworks, which would enable a practitioner or trainee to elucidate and articulate their reasoning and justify interventions. This type of framework in particular may be able to play a central role in bringing a much needed clarity and cohesion to the very complex relationship between theory and practice. Executive frameworks include a series of systematic steps, ensuring that theory is clearly and appropriately accessed. They guide, but do not prescribe, the content and style of eventual professional intervention, ensuring that these are most likely to be effective and that guidelines for best practice are adhered to.

Exploring the role of training frameworks in professional development

This book arose largely through striving to answer questions from trainees and their field tutors about the usefulness of training frameworks – in particular the Monsen *et al.* Problem-Solving Framework (Monsen *et al.* 1998), the Integrated Professional Framework (Woolfson *et al.* 2003) and the COMOIRA (Constructionist Model of Informed and Reasoned Action) Framework (Gameson *et al.* 2003).

These frameworks have been used for some time in university training contexts to develop and support robust and accountable professional methodology. Naturally, the frameworks have been both endorsed and challenged. However, some common questions did suggest that their perceived role has often been misunderstood and their significance underestimated. These particular frameworks have been described as both 'prescriptive' and 'restricting' and other frameworks have been suggested as alternatives. For example, Solution-Focused approaches were suggested by some field tutors and trainees as alternatives to the Monsen *et al.* Problem-Solving training approach. These two approaches are derived from different sources and support different types of work. They might, however, be used in a complementary way to support a range of objectives.

The point raised by trainees and tutors is a major one, highlighting the range of perspectives and approaches that characterise contemporary educational psychology. Currently there is no coherent discussion of the range of practice undertaken by educational psychologists and the very different perspectives it may represent. Considering this major point, it also becomes clear that that there is no obviously common and distinctive professional language or agreed conceptual or theoretical understanding of practice frameworks, training or otherwise. It was this lack of clarity and disagreement that prompted us to explore the concept of frameworks in some depth.

We set out to clarify both the conceptual, theoretical and practical aspects of practice and training frameworks. In addition, we set out to assess their usefulness against a contemporary professional backdrop with its emphases on professional accountability, a drive for greater transparency in psychological processes and decision-making, rigorous evaluation of effectiveness and an increasingly central role for collaboration and joint decision-making. In carrying out this exploration of existing frameworks, we found that they were indeed highly differentiated in both a theoretical and applied sense. They derived from very different sources and had an array of conceptual, theoretical and applied functions. Considered as a whole they offered a clear articulation of the very wide-ranging social, psychological and sociological theory currently underpinning educational psychology and resulting practice responses.

Frameworks in practice

Each of the chapters in this book offers the trainee, field practitioner and stakeholder in educational psychology some mechanisms whereby psychological theories and other relevant sources and systems might be used to guide and support practice. First of all, however, it is essential to clarify what we mean by the various terms used to refer to theory and practice; what is a framework, what is a model, what is the difference between a practice framework and a theoretical model? Currently, there is little or no comparative commentary on the role of frameworks in educational psychology literature and no clear agreement on definitions. In training contexts, frameworks designed to offer an array of theoretical perspectives on analysis of contexts have been available for some time. These include the work of Apter (1982), Checkland (1981) and Frederickson, Webster and Wright (1991). These frameworks illustrate how specific aspects of Constructionist Theory might be applied in practice.

However, other approaches exist that offer similar stages, steps or actions whereby values, theories or standards are applied but these have not necessarily been identified as practice frameworks. These relate to the application of, for example, therapeutic approaches as a protocol for psychological service delivery or values and ethics as a framework ensuring accountability and client protection. Introducing the idea of frameworks for practice to a range of issues and theories impinging on practice clarifies their role and potential in the field. We have therefore proposed a set of definitions and terms that seem most appropriate to educational psychology.

A framework may be conceptualised as a structure involving a set of parts that sit or work together. Clearly the term 'framework' can be applied to both theory and practice. The distinction between *theoretical models* and *practice frameworks* is central to this book. In reality, however, the role and application of theories and frameworks is not so clear-cut. For example, some contemporary practice frameworks can be seen to derive from and apply to one theoretical model. The Consultation model and the Solution-Focused model, as discussed in this book, are drawn from therapeutic theory and practice and are seen by many practitioners to cover the requirements of a service-delivery policy as well as providing a theoretical model for practitioners. We would argue that close examination of each of these approaches using key criteria allows us to differentiate their role and impact from other more executive-based frameworks. This, in turn, allows us to use them more appropriately, with a clearer understanding of the professional gaps left by adopting therapeutic – or, indeed, executive – frameworks as a service-delivery policy.

A 'theoretical framework' we prefer to describe as a 'model' and define a theoretical model as a prototype describing *how* a theory works or may be applied. Theoretical models relevant to educational psychology might bring together a range of theories to create wider or more specific meanings and applications. Social Constructionism is a good example of a complex, wide-ranging, theoretical model with fundamental relevance to educational psychology theory and practice. Ecological theory is derived from Social Constructionism and is familiar in educational psychology practice, drawing as it does on complex, social, transactional theory involving hypotheses about the pathways and outcomes of individual development in specific contexts.

In contrast to theoretical models, we have chosen to define a 'practice framework' as a series of steps, stages or actions that support the application of a theoretical model or models. In educational psychology the practice framework bridges the gap between theoretical models and the effective application of these in the applied context. The ideal practice model is informed by statutory and professional requirements and by the broad demands of contemporary good practice, as well as by the need to apply psychology effectively. In training educational psychologists, the same definitions apply.

The relationship between theory and practice in educational psychology

The chapters in this book cover work we have identified as key contemporary frameworks, theories and models currently being used in the academic training of educational psychologists or as part of service delivery in educational psychology. Their source, range and field of impact differ widely. They draw on rationalist, humanistic, therapeutic and psychological/psycho-social roots. The Monsen *et al.* Problem-Solving Framework (Monsen *et al.* 1998) addresses the complexity of the issues presented to the educational psychologist via processes of disconfirming hypotheses derived from a widespread evidence base. The Monsen *et al.* framework is in the executive mould, and aims to ensure that interventions are focused and effective. The appropriate psychological models or theories for use in specific situations emerge *from* the use of this framework and are not prescribed directly *by* the framework itself.

Humanistic models linked to therapeutic movements or to humanistic psychology have given rise to Solution-Oriented, Consultation and Positive Psychology frameworks for practice. They offer good examples of a contemporary movement towards the systemic use of approaches derived from an individual, therapeutic or well-being perspective. These approaches have a powerful appeal but are, in fact, very different from each other and need to be assessed and understood by trainees and practitioners in relation to their paradigms, their value system, their field of impact and their effectiveness.

Frameworks derived from psychological or psycho-social theory apply key approaches from both these disciplines. Activity Theory, for example, is derived from a dynamic model of both learning and socio-cultural theory aiming to facilitate positive, individual and systemic change. Others are based on Social Research Theory and practice, offering a systematic approach to tackling the elements and consequences of perceptions and constructions and of values systems and ethical considerations that impinge on and shape professional roles.

All of the frameworks discussed here represent familiar or emerging value systems and contain many theoretical, scientific, socio-political and ethical tensions. They reflect a range of interests but currently lack cohesion and clarity as a body of knowledge – applied or otherwise – especially in terms of how they relate to each other and how appropriate, valuable and effective they may be for the practitioner. That educational psychology practice has emerged in this way reflects a historic lack of cohesion between theory and practice and a parallel, consuming professional focus on why professional development and practitioner change are so difficult to evidence. The backdrop to the development of applied practice frameworks might have been expected to derive more obviously from

Social Constructionism, which has provided the major impetus for professional change in the past 30 years. Certainly, before an innovative methodology can be laid out, it is essential to consider the nature and impact of its precursors. To understand the processes underlying professional development and perceptions about the nature of change, it is worth exploring the role of Social Constructionism in some depth.

Social Constructionism and divergence in professional debate

It is fundamental to the development of the profession to ask why change or improvement is needed and what will actually be achieved. In this context an examination of the influence and role of Constructionist Theory is revealing. An exploration of the broader basis of the relationship between theory and practice in educational psychology suggests reasons for underlying and enduring core uncertainties in the profession. These key assumptions and omissions can be seen to relate to a large extent to failure to develop historically timely and appropriately detailed conceptual, theoretical and applied training for educational psychologists. In fact, the primary difficulty of devising and describing sound relationships between theory and practice has been a major, if underlying and hidden, concern in the development of educational psychology.

Role confusion and problems in identifying desirable changes in educational psychology practice may be primarily linked to an academic failure to describe and articulate complex and progressive theoretical models and to demonstrate how to apply them effectively. As noted at the beginning of the chapter change has become a focal point for ongoing debate and soul-searching on the apparent failure of educational psychology to transform or revolutionise itself in desired directions. Arguably, though, the change the profession has sought to achieve has been very ambitious indeed and is, for very good reasons, difficult to mobilise in the field.

The major theory implicated in the change problem is that of Social Constructionism. Since the 1970s and the publication of Gillham's (1978) key collection of papers in *Reconstructing Educational Psychology*, the profession has been committed to a move away from a predominantly child-deficit professional focus and, perhaps unwittingly, towards an immensely challenging new one. This new focus involved dealing with educational issues and problems via sociological and social psychological theories that were newly emerging in the 1960s, for which the collective term is 'Social Constructionism'. This theoretical model is immensely broad and complex, deriving initially not from psychology but from the sociological theory of knowledge.

Within Constructionist thought, a social construction (or social construct) is a concept or practice that may appear to be natural, objective and valid to those who accept it, but which, in reality, is an invention or artefact of a particular culture or society (Berger and Luckmann 1967). Social Constructionism is about dynamic and transactional models of shared, or negotiable, meaning – as opposed to static and objective models – of social and interpersonal experience.

The catalysts to the move towards this theoretical perspective for educational psychology in particular are found in the Summerfield Report of 1968 (DES 1968). It reflects very clearly a downward shift in tolerance amongst educational psychologists. Educational psychologists were unwilling to continue to apply a range of procedures that they themselves had identified as having no clear rationale and as causing academic and professional embarrassment. Theoretical developments in sociology and in social and cognitive psychology made their traditional role untenable. Gillham (1978) pointed out that EPs in the 1970s were emerging from a period of already makeshift professionalism. A degree in psychology or in teaching had not created confident, applied practitioners nor provided effective, applied perspectives. Postgraduate courses in educational psychology were still concerned to a large extent with assessment of individual child deficit and treatment of disorders and learning difficulties, while social and psychological theory was emerging in parallel with an inescapable relevance for applied psychology. It was impossible for professional development to ignore the crucial role of educational and other social and cultural contexts in individual developmental trajectories. However, there were no course texts in the 1970s offering applied frameworks for constructionist theoretical models. The practical response of the profession was captured largely by a swing to *Systemic* work, arguing that the social systems and organisations in education were the more appropriate focus for psychological intervention than the individual child.

The facts that the change debate continues and Systemic work has not proved to be the panacea to role confusion for educational psychologists suggests that Social Constructionism offered more profound challenges than at first suspected. Social Constructionism seems to have been adopted initially as a value system or ideology, radically changing the emphasis for the practitioner about the nature of difficulties, problems or solutions. As it stood, however, it offered little help to the practitioner beyond a description of how perspectives influence the meaning and manufacture of difficulties. In addition, it generated its own minefield of conflicts about role focus and about the relationship of educational psychology to education.

Concerns about effectiveness and uneasiness about accountability, although dominant in contemporary literature, are not new. Gillham (1978) tells us that early ideas about applying Social Constructionism were characterised, first, by an emphasis on the need for educational psychology to influence and educate systems – moving schools away from pseudo-clinical conceptualisation and from a professional focus on the child. Its emphases would be preventative work, screening processes and general encouragement for teachers and parents to become involved in carrying out their own applied psychology.

At the point of writing, Gillham had considerable insight about the task at hand, suggesting that educational psychology was becoming clear about what it had to do – even if there were problems in implementation. There were, indeed, very major problems in implementation which, had they been given more careful examination – ideologically, theoretically and practically – might have led to the anticipation of the complexity of the related professional role. This did not happen in any particularly obvious way and, as a result, the development of educational psychology has been more organic and reactive than systematic.

Critically, though, after the early re-constructionist phase in the late 1970s, the discussion of the way forward for educational psychology became bifurcated. Two separate elements, the need for restructuring professional practice itself and the need for new theoretical and applied frameworks to implement change, became separate issues. The former, the need for and struggle to achieve professional change, somehow gained dominance. This situation might be attributed to a great extent to the discontinuity or delay in the emergence of academic developments that both reflected Social Constructionist Theory and could be applied with clarity and confidence in the practice field. This delay, of course, also affected cohesion in instruction and practice in field contexts. The result is a very lop-sided progression in educational psychology with, if one listens to the 'no change' rhetoric, little to offer in terms of conceptual and theoretical developments relevant to the job and no coherent development of applied paradigms and frameworks (Thompson 1998; Stobie 2002). That this situation was the basis for a growing and immensely complex, challenging profession is scarcely believable unless one understands and takes into account the fact that the impact of Social Constructionism was first of all largely ideological and rhetorical. Transforming practice could never have happened overnight as the required developments were far from obvious.

This lack of developmental cohesion in both academic and practice spheres continues to assume a high profile in contemporary literature – despite, for example, the Currie Report (Scottish Executive 2002) in Scotland, which itemises the role of the educational psychologist very fully. Practitioner journals continue to this day to ruminate over basic issues relating to the role and, of course, value of educational psychology. Fortunately though there are now more constructive and detailed responses (Ashton and Roberts 2006; Cameron 2006). Nevertheless, it is still asserted that many educational psychologists experience professional identity crises, the themes of which are all too familiar – the erstwhile traditional practice model and the value of educational psychology (Cameron and Monsen 2005). Perhaps the impact of a call to Constructionist Theory and related practice needs a little more unpicking before it can be fully appreciated and understood.

Was Social Constructionism right for educational psychology?
Social Constructionism is remarkably sound and has a powerful evidence-base but it is, at the same time, extremely challenging in application and requires a receptive, background ideology or value system in order to support change. Constructionist Theory was highlighted both as an explanation for the failure of the more traditional, medical or individual-deficit paradigm and as a way forward. In order to address psychological and social problems, it was argued that the dynamic interaction of biology, ideology, values, systems, attitudes, behaviour and resources had to be taken into account. As we know, Social Constructionism holds that development, responses and outcomes, whether individual or organisational, are a product of a complex system of transactions and interactions. Problems, issues and difficulties are a *product* of this complex web of perceptions and responses and therefore lack the essential, objective sway associated with the traditional, child-deficit paradigm where the problem is incontrovertibly in the child. The research evidence for an alternative, Constructionist interpretation of many issues defined as 'external' or 'objective' problems in the educational context is more than convincing. Gillham quoted Power, Benn and Morris (1967) for example, who pointed out that investigation of individual pupils does not help us understand why two schools, which are apparently matched closely for external characteristics, nevertheless show widely differing rates of delinquency or criminal court appearance.

It is useful to ask the question 'How does social science itself cope with the implications of Social Constructionist Theory?', as social science underpins academic and applied psychology. Taken at face value, the theory allows a range of actions and interpretations about and upon reality, but crucially, it negates the *positivist* scientific approach and its evidence-base. It is not difficult to see therefore why educational psychology faces a problem of role confusion when the processes which it seeks to influence are fluid, negotiable, subject to interpretation, without firm objective evidence and inevitably vulnerable to social control and power differentials. However, if we look at developments in Social Constructionist Theory and analysis, we can draw helpful and illuminating parallels with contemporary trends, responses and requirements in educational psychology.

Social Constructionism: Implications for professional frameworks for practice
Social Constructionism has continued to develop and differentiate as theory and as a basis for applied research. On the way it has offered considerable opposition to positivist theory, which to some extent supported the assumptions and actions of early child-deficit approaches in educational psychology. The tensions currently affecting educational psychology are also reflected in contemporary

concepts, definitions and debates relating to the nature of all scientific knowledge, not just in the social sciences. Robson (2002) explored the topic in some depth, summarising positivist and relativist scientific positions.

Positivism is very familiar to most of us since it represents what Robson (2002, p.19) described as the standard view of science. Positivism deals with objectivity, separates facts from values, is based on quantitative data and explores facts via hypotheses. Its focus is causal relationships and causality demonstrated through 'empirical regularities'. It is rarely possible to use this framework with confidence in the social or 'real' world context where people and processes are the subject of study and, as Robson points out, this difficulty has led some to believe that positivist methodology has no rightful role in social science.

Positivism has been subject to intense scrutiny and severe criticism by philosophers as well as social scientists. The details of these critiques are covered elsewhere (see for example Chalmers 1982; Outhwaite 1987) but, to summarise briefly, positivism holds that all observers can be demonstrated to share a congruent view of an objective reality. This overlooks the reliable and demonstrable role and effects of perspective, which can be seen to confound the positivist reality. In contrast, relativism is a philosophical and social scientific position that discards the objectivity and measurability of positivism and argues instead for reality as represented through the eyes of the participants. This position negates the role of any independent reality that can be accurately reflected in our beliefs, theories and concepts.

Currently, natural science and social science theory and research methodology reflect a mixed approach to understanding and investigating reality. Contemporary positivism accepts that values and perspectives do in fact influence what is observed. Relativism, on the other hand, has become Social Constructionism. Constructionism is one of many labels used to describe relativist thinking. Robson (2002) cites Tesch (1990) as offering 26 different labels for Constructionist approaches. Arguably, the approach of most immediate relevance to educational psychology is scientific or, more specifically, Critical Realism. In academic contexts, realism provides a model of scientific explanation relevant to the social sciences and offers significant resolution of the difficulties presented by both positivism and relativism (Bhaskar 1986). 'Critical Realism' is also seen as offering robust and appropriate methodology in the practice- and value-based professions (Anastas 1998). For the trainee educational psychologist and the practitioner, realist approaches and in particular Critical Realism are of crucial importance in explaining and understanding how educational psychology works and in helping to clarify and articulate the various processes underlying educational psychologists' values, concepts and practices in effecting change.

Critical Realism represents an integration of positivist and relativist positions and is a relatively recent development in scientific thinking. It is carefully described in Robson (2002) and involves using qualitative and quantitative approaches alongside each other. Working together, these two approaches agree:

- on the role of values in enquiry
- on the theoretical nature of facts
- that reality is complex, multiple and constructed, and
- that any particular set of data is explicable by more than one theory.

This approach also includes what is described as 'emancipatory' research – work that questions the value systems and interpretations of reality exposed by Critical Realism and furthers social progress and individual development by linking results to ethical systems and political and social action. Examples of this type of approach are found in the exploration of gender imbalances and racial inequality (Mertens *et al.* 1994).

The relevance of Critical Realism for the educational psychologist is in providing the wider theoretical framework and the practice rationale for analysing and acting in the complexity of social and educational contexts. In highlighting the study of the impact of values and beliefs, and in including ethics, welfare and emancipation in the equation, Critical Realism guides and facilitates highly reasoned, reflective and coherent actions in bringing about positive change.

Whilst you as a reader may be able to appreciate that the contemporary educational psychologist's role can be seen to be derived from a relativist position and to reflect the substance of Critical Realism, this understanding and transparency is generally lacking or fragmented in the professional literature. Debate about role and effectiveness from within the profession itself reflects the tensions articulated in social science theory but suggests a lack of familiarity with advanced Social Constructionist models and research frameworks that help to inform and explain existing and emerging practice frameworks. Social Constructionism or, more specifically, Critical Realism provides an overarching theoretical model by which to create and evaluate practice frameworks. Critical Realism has been found to be particularly useful in a very wide range of research in practice- and value-based professional contexts such as social work (Anastas 1998). In educational psychology, there is pressure to demonstrate effectiveness, to be accountable and to make use of appropriate evidence-bases in working with clients. Critical Realism allows us to tackle these issues with confidence, drawing on extended philosophical and social-scientific theory.

As Social Constructionism has come of age it now offers sophisticated, theoretical models from which professional practice frameworks can be derived. There is, however, a continuing tendency to look for positivist effects or cures in a profession which is more appropriately seen as complex and value-based with its own forms of emancipatory social practice. In exploring and emphasising the nature and impact of Critical Realism, we are now in a position to create a stronger and more theoretically grounded profession. From this perspective we might expect a range of frameworks to emerge in educational psychology derived from different sources and traditions but measurable in terms of their ethics, political affiliations, underlying values and received impact. This is more realistic, important and scientifically sound in educational contexts than to try to cure the problem child in isolation.

Recognisable Social Constructionism in educational psychology

The Ecological model is an example of a more familiar but less far-reaching, specific, Constructionist theoretical model. It supports some of the conceptual underpinnings of contemporary educational psychology in the UK, at least at the level of academic training, and it is represented in a number of the practice frameworks reviewed in this book (British Psycologcal Society 2006). It is based largely on the work of Bronfenbrenner (1979) who postulated the idea of an eco-system to explain complex processes contributing to differentiated, developmental outcomes. The model looks at levels or spheres of influence, moving from, and including, a child's individual characteristics to the characteristics, processes, values and beliefs associated with the home, school and community. The interaction of characteristics, factors, processes and values is described as 'transactional', meaning that the child and his or her responses, characteristics and developmental outcomes contribute to and are influenced and modified by dynamic, interactive processes. Potentially, the child influences the eco-system as much as it influences him or her. For example, one child in a family or class may be neglected by peers or bullied by siblings. The same outcome may not arise if that child had experienced different family characteristics, class dynamics or value systems.

Ecological Theory has powerful, explanatory value and its validity is not in doubt, but it represents an ambitious, applied theoretical stance. Although it reflected contemporary trends in academic theory and social ideology in the late 1970s, it was not necessarily a good fit, as it stood, for engaging educational systems in the process of self-reflection and positive development. It was instead, undoubtedly, seen as profoundly threatening by educationalists and by practitioners. Moreover, in the 1970s, in terms of legislative frameworks affecting education and children with exceptional educational needs, these were still firmly focused on the child as an objective entity, not on the quality of the educational experience. Nowadays, Social Constructionism and Ecological Theory have moved into the contemporary, political value system and are endorsed as powerful descriptors of social and developmental processes in education as well as in other contexts. They are reflected in current legislative and ethical frameworks in the UK, which evidence a more sophisticated understanding of the complex, causal webs contributing to individual development and educational processes. This can be seen as a belated but welcome endorsement of the Constructionist perspective adopted by educational psychology 30 years ago.

The application of Eco-Systemic Theory

To apply Eco-Systemic Theory as part of professional practice requires an array of sophisticated tools and approaches. Early Constructionist educational psychologists needed to engage clients in a collaborative process of exploration and change that was considerably challenging and demanding. Related professions sharing the educational-psychology client group have not been so quick to grasp the complex and intricate eco-systemic nettle. Clinical psychology does now venture into the school context in diagnosing and dealing with individual child problems whilst holding onto its more clinical and case-based identity. However, child and adolescent psychiatric practice tends not to acknowledge the determining potential of the wider context so overtly, but will readily focus on skewed dynamics of the family as the root of many apparently child-centred problems. In these professions, however, the child generally remains the focus of referral, investigation and intervention although change in family or school systems might be the intervention required and even recommended.

To summarise, early Constructionist Theory placed an emphasis on the centrality and complexity of social processes as a dominant, professional focus for educational psychology. From an academic perspective, the contemporary professional and training focus appears to have moved very far from a theoretical stance endorsing child-deficit work, towards a much subtler, conceptual and practice role aimed at assessing and influencing contexts as well as individuals. This, in turn, suggests that there are ideological, theoretical and practice frameworks for understanding and carrying out this type of psychological work. However, investigators insist there was, and is, little evidence of change. Contemporary 'change' literature insists that educational psychologists do what they always did and this is taken as evidence that nothing has actually changed. In considerable contrast to these assertions, professional journals and current academic training for educational psychology reflect very significant developments in the multi-dimensional, Constructionist analysis of issues and complex, matched multi-stranded interventions that exemplify Critical Realism in action. Historically, the developmental processes in Social Constructionism and in wider scientific theory have taken considerable time to emerge and to be recognisable in influencing professional practice frameworks. Arguably, a related lack of continuity in academic and practice training, difficulty in articulating the complexity of the emerging role and the somewhat random and organic evolution of tools have contributed to difficulty in discerning and building on positive change (Gray and Lunt 1990). The training of educational psychologists has developed quite radically in the past ten to fifteen years, devising and developing Constructionist frameworks that have altered the emphases and impact of teaching. These have influenced practitioner responses to questions about the nature of their role and the objectives and processes of change (Kelly 2006). They are perhaps slower to influence the practice and views of already established practitioners and psychological services. Evidence of professional clarity and development is, however, long overdue.

The plan of this book

The chapters presented in this book will cover a range of approaches to various aspects of educational psychology. Pulling them together allows an understanding to emerge of both the individual characteristics of each framework and their relative and collective contribution, both theoretically and in relation to practice. The role of effectiveness is related to underlying theoretical assumptions and to external expectations. This, in turn, has to be measured against a backdrop of contemporary understanding of the nature of psychology as a science and the role of Critical Realism in guiding theoretical models, practice frameworks and the imperatives of ethics, values and political forces.

The chapters are organised to reflect the frameworks' most obvious spheres of influence, from a broader, executive role to the more intrinsic and contextual approaches. None of the terms – executive or intrinsic – is exclusive and the degree of flexibility and applicability of the range of frameworks described is significant. Interestingly, all answer to the call to Constructionism to some extent, either in descriptive and analytical terms or more radically in attempting to address the immediate and more remote demands of Critical Realism. Some might interlock and support each other, reflecting the complexity of the role of educational psychology. The chapters on the historical and statutory contexts (Chapter 2) and on ethics and values (Chapter 3) create powerful frameworks for practice in their own right and they represent shifting and highly influential sources of pressure for particular professional responses.

Current training frameworks (described in Chapters 4 and 5) offer a long-overdue account of the conceptual and applied advances in the academic contexts. The Integrated Framework for Practitioners, outlined in Chapter 6, combines constructionist, ecological theory and problem-solving in an innovative, collaborative framework for practitioners.

Frameworks derived from therapeutic roots are outlined and explored in Chapters 7 and 8 by Wagner and Rees, who have developed and applied these approaches as part of wider psychological service delivery policy. In Chapter 9 Joseph explores the potential of the Positive Psychology movement as a framework for practice in educational psychology. He considers and questions the central role of the familiar paradigms, values and beliefs that underpin contemporary, applied psychology, using Constructionism as a critical and analytical tool to explore its underlying value systems.

Activity Theory is explained in Chapter 10, which draws directly on cognitive, learning and socio-cultural theory in describing a Constructionist system for enabling individual and organisational change. In Chapter 11, Burden explores realist research paradigms to elaborate on the hidden factors and processes that impact on the educational psychologist's attempts to bring about change in organisations. Illuminative Evaluation is a research-based practice framework that guides the practitioner through complex, embedded and difficult contextual and Constructionist problems. The frameworks discussed here are only a selection of those used by academic and practitioner psychologists at present.

In the final chapter, Chapter 12, we explore the various frameworks described, pulling together themes and points of contact. We look at the potential of each framework to shape and inform different areas of practice, considering what is offered in teaching and developing educational psychology and in terms of service delivery. In this way we hope to inform and support the clearer, and more confident, articulation of the role of educational psychologist as scientist and practitioner

References

Anastas, J.W. (1998) 'Reaffirming the real: A philosophy of science.' *European Evaluation Society Annual Conference.* Rome, 29–31 Oct.

Apter, S. J. (1982) *Troubled Systems, Troubled Children.* New York: Pergamon.

Ashton, R. and Roberts, E. (2006) 'What is valuable and unique about educational psychology?' *Educational Psychology in Practice 22,* 2, 111–123.

Bhasker, R. (1986) *Scientific Realism and Human Emancipation.* London: Verso.

Berger, P.L. and Luckmann, T. (1967) *The Social Construction of Reality: A Treatise in the Sociology of Knowledge.* Harmondsworth: Penguin.

British Psychological Society (2006) *Core Curriculum for Initial Training Courses in Educational Psychology.* Leicester: Division of Education and Child Psychology.

Bronfenbrenner, U. (1979) *The Ecology of Human Development.* Cambridge, MA: Harvard University Press.

Cameron, R.J. (2006) 'Educational psychology: The distinctive contribution.' *Educational Psychology in Practice 22,* 4, 289–304.

Cameron, R.J. and Monsen, J. (2005) 'Quality psychological advice for teachers, parents/carers and LEA decision makers with respect to children and young people with special needs.' *Educational Psychology in Practice 21,* 4, 283–306.

Chalmers, A.F.K. (1982) *What is This Thing Called Science?* (2nd edn). Milton Keynes: Open University Press.

Checkland, P. (1981) *Systems Thinking, Systems Practice.* Chichester: John Wiley.

Department of Education and Science (1968) *Psychologists in Education Services* (The Summerfield Report). London: HMSO.

Frederickson, N., Webster, A. and Wright, A. (1991) 'Psychological assessment: A change of emphasis.' *Educational Psychology in Practice 7*, 1, 20–29.

Gameson, J., Rhydderch, G., Ellis, D. and Carroll, T. (2003) 'Constructing a flexible model of integrated professional practice. Part 1: Conceptual and theoretical issues.' *Educational and Child Psychology 20*, 4, 97–116.

Gillham, B. (1978) *Reconstructing Educational Psychology.* London: Croom Helm.

Gray, P. and Lunt, I. (eds) (1990) 'Training for professional practice.' *Educational and Child Psychology 7*, 3.

Kelly, B. (2006) 'Exploring the usefulness of the Monsen Problem-Solving Framework for applied practitioners.' *Educational Psychology in Practice 22*, 1, 1–17.

Mertons, D.M., Fraley, J., Madison, A. and Singleton, P. (1994) 'Diverse voices in evaluation practice: Feminist minorities and persons with disabilities.' *Evaluation Practice 15*, 123–9.

Monsen, J., Graham, B., Frederickson, N. and Cameron, R.J. (1998) 'Problem analysis and professional training in educational psychology: An accountable model of practice.' *Educational Psychology in Practice 13*, 4, 234–249.

Outhwaite, W. (1987) *New Philosophy of Social Science: Realism Hermeneutics and Critical Theory.* London: MacMillan.

Power, M.J., Benn, R.T. and Morris, J.N. (1967) 'Delinquent schools?' *New Society*, 16 October.

Robson, C. (2002) *Real World Research.* Oxford: Blackwell.

Scottish Executive (2002) *Review of the Provision of Educational Psychology in Scotland* (The Currie Report). Edinburgh: Scottish Government Publication.

Stobie, I. (2002) 'Processes of change and continuity in educational psychology, Part 1.' *Educational Psychology in Practice 18*, 3, 214–237.

Tesch, R. (1990) *Qualitative Research: Analysis Types and Software Tools.* London: Falmer.

Thompson, L. (1998) 'Searching for a niche: Future directions for educational psychologists.' *Educational Psychology in Practice 12*, 2, 99–106.

Woolfson, L., Whaling, R., Stewart, A. and Monsen, J. (2003) 'An integrated framework to guide educational psychologists' practice.' *Educational Psychology in Practice 19*, 4, 284–302.

PART TWO

History, Ethics and the Law in Educational Psychology

CHAPTER 2

The Legislative Context and Shared Practice Models

James Boyle, Tommy MacKay and Fraser Lauchlan

Introduction

The application of psychological theory to the practice of educational psychology does not take place in a political or conceptual vacuum: the duties of educational psychologists (EPs) in the UK have reflected the prevailing goals, values and understandings embedded in the legislation of the time. In turn, EPs have influenced statutes, government circulars and guidance and local education authority policy, most notably in the areas of special educational needs and social inclusion – with more recent developments reflecting the paradigm shift of the 1970s and 1980s from a medical model of assessment and intervention to a more ecological, educational approach (Gillham 1978; Kirkaldy 1997).

This chapter considers the impact of legislative and policy contexts upon the practice of educational psychology and the impact of this practice upon legislation and policy in England, Wales, Northern Ireland and Scotland – the four distinctive education systems of the UK. The extent to which legislation has created contexts that have given rise to shared models of practice within these systems – and may thus be regarded as a framework in its own right for such practice – will also be discussed, together with the implications for future developments in the UK. Readers interested in developments outwith the UK are referred to Jimerson, Oakland and Farrell's (2006) review of legislation, policy, organisation and EP practice in over 40 countries.

Educational psychology in the UK: A historical overview

The scientific study of children in the UK dates back to the laboratories of Francis Galton and James Sully, opened in 1884 and 1896 respectively (see MacKay 1996, 2008 for a review). Sully's experimental work with 'difficult' children, in particular, represents an intriguing link between the decline of the 'Child Study' movement of the 19th Century (with its emphasis on eugenics, 'social Darwinism' and ethnographic approaches) and the development of professional educational psychology (see Wooldridge 1994 for a discussion).

Kagan (2005) notes that the first recorded use of the term 'school psychologist' in English was by Hugo Munsterberg (1863–1916), the German-born psychologist who established the department of psychology in Harvard University at the end of the 19th Century. Munsterberg's 'job specification' for educational psychologists (published during his term of office as President of the American Psychological Association in 1898) is in marked contrast to the 'clinical' approaches of contemporaries such as Witmer (1907) and Stern (1911), which emphasised the study of individual children with handicapping conditions.

Munsterberg located the 'consulting school psychologist' (1898, pp.131–32) within the classroom with a remit that might encompass all learners. He further highlighted the importance of applied research and evidence-based practice (a counter to the Child Study approach) with an emphasis upon classroom organisation, teaching and the curriculum that resonates even today:

> When in the quiet experimental working place of the psycho-educational scholar, through the steady co-operation of specialists, a real system of acknowledged facts is secured, then the practical attempts of the consulting school psychologist and of the leader of experimental classrooms have a safer basis, and their work will help again the theoretical scholar until the co-operation of all these agents produces a practical education which the teacher will accept without his own experimenting. (Munsterberg 1898, pp.131–32)

The first 'educational psychologist' was Cyril Burt, who was appointed to the half-time post of psychologist to the London County Council (LCC) in 1913, a post he combined with academic positions. Scotland followed shortly thereafter, with the appointment of Douglas Kennedy Fraser by the Glasgow Education Committee in 1923 as a 'psychological adviser' and the establishment of a child psychology service by the City of Glasgow in 1937.

Growth in the numbers of EPs employed by local education authorities (LEAs) was hindered by three factors in the early years of the profession (Wooldridge 1994):

- financial constraints
- a belief on the part of education officials that the psychology input into teacher-training courses would enable teachers to deal with all but the most severe difficulties; and
- the fact that school medical officers had the statutory responsibility for the examination and ascertainment of the 'mentally deficient'.

But by the late 1920s, the numbers of educational psychologists working in LEAs across the UK had increased, with additional impetus provided by the arrival, in 1927, of the Child Guidance model of practice from the US in England, and in Scotland in 1931 (Kerr 1952; McCallum 1952; Sampson 1980).

These developments shifted the focus of educational psychology from the province of psychometrics, individual differences and classification to incorporate a psychodynamic approach to the treatment of 'maladjustment' by a multi-disciplinary team comprising educational psychologists, psychiatrists and social workers. This heady combination of psychodynamic and psychometric approaches helped to define the practice of educational psychologists in the UK for a further 40 years and beyond (MacKay 1996, 2008).

The first professional EPs working in education authorities and in Child Guidance Clinics felt the indifference of, on the one hand, their academic colleagues with higher academic qualifications based in teacher-training colleges and in universities and, on the other, of school medical officers. But Hearnshaw (1979) and Wooldridge (1994) argue that the years between 1924 and 1944 represent a high-water mark for the influence of EPs on government policy-making in England and Wales, most notably in the advice given to the Board of Education's Consultative Committee (the precursor to the later Ministry of Education) by Burt and other leading EPs of the day. A series of influential reports published by the Consultative Committee under the chairmanship first of Sir Henry Hadow (Board of Education 1924, 1926, 1931, 1933) and then of Mr (later Sir) Will Spens (Board of Education 1938) and others (see Board of Education 1929) argued for ideas that were considered radical and undeniably meritocratic. These called for:

- a more objective, 'scientific' approach to academic selection and streaming through the use of 'psychological' tests
- the introduction of a universal 11-plus examination, and
- an overhaul of the secondary school curriculum and provision of different types of secondary schools to ensure that each pupil received an education appropriate to his or her ability.

But Burt did not always win the argument. He was scathing of the Norwood Report, *Curriculum and Examinations in Secondary Schools* (Board of Education 1943), which defended the traditional curriculum and the status quo of teacher selection of pupils into their 'natural divisions' based on aptitudes, and the view that IQ tests should only be used with 'full consciousness of their experimental nature and their proper application' (*ibid.* 1943, p.17) (see Burt 1943).

Much of the thinking of prominent EPs of the time informed the wartime 1944 Education Act, which formalised the principle that pupils should be educated according to their age, ability and aptitude and which led to the development of grammar schools (for the most able), secondary technical schools (for those with a scientific or technical aptitude) and secondary modern schools (for the majority), with 11-plus examinations used to select pupils for each. The Act also formally defined no fewer than 11 categories of mental and physical handicaps, which were then used for almost 40 years – including that of 'educationally sub-normal'.

Following the recommendations of the Underwood Committee (Ministry of Education 1955) on maladjusted children and the Summerfield Report (Department of Education and Science 1968) on psychologists in the education services, there was a steady increase in training places and in the number of EPs in the UK, although unfilled posts remained a problem.

The 1970s and 1980s saw not only a rise in the use of behaviourist approaches by EPs (e.g. Miller 1979; Miller and Ellis 1980) but also the advent of the 're-constructionist' movement, which countered traditional 'within-child' deficit explanations of learning and behavioural problems and psychometric testing with a vision of the EP as an agent for change in schools informed by an understanding of ecological approaches and systems theory (Gillham 1978). However, the day-to-day realities of the work of the EP continued to be shaped and defined by statutes, as considered below.

The legislative context
England and Wales
A significant development in the legislative context for EPs in the UK was the publication of the Warnock Report (DES 1978). The recommendations outlined in the Warnock Report informed the policies of the 1981 Education Act in England and Wales, and were to provide a significant shift in attitudes towards special education. The 1981 Act resulted in a move from special education to a more global, inclusive model of special educational needs (SENs). In other words, the 1981 legislation represented a shift away from merely considering segregation of children in special school settings, and instead considered a more inclusive model of including children with particular individualised needs in mainstream settings. In essence, the legislation was an attempt to promote a more positive, inclusive view of children and young people with special educational needs.

As a result of the 1981 Act, specialist provision was no longer to be considered merely in terms of a specific location (i.e. special school), but instead, in terms of the nature of the support required, in addition to that usually provided in mainstream schools. However, an ongoing difficulty for the profession remained; how decisions were made regarding the criteria for deciding upon what constituted additional support. The gatekeeper role of the EP was still germane, and usually revolved around a framework (as outlined in Warnock) of assessing the individual strengths and weaknesses of each child. It has been argued that such an assessment was often undertaken with reference to norm-based standardised measures (Buck 1998; DfEE 1997; Leyden 1999; MacKay 2000).

The 1992 HMI Report *Getting in on the Act* (DES 1992a) tried to clarify some of these issues in recommending guidelines regarding what would warrant a need sufficient for the drafting of a 'statement' of SENs. The report also included the recommendation that statements should be specific about the targets for each child, and how and when these should be met (e.g. the provision of certain resources), rather than merely considering a move to a specific location. These recommendations led to the Green Paper on SENs (DES 1992b) and were made policy in the 1993 Education Act, and enshrined in the Code of Practice (DfE 1994, further adapted in 2001 (DfES 2001).

The introduction of the Code of Practice established effective procedures and systems for schools and EPs when dealing with children with SENs. The 1993 Act also established the concept of SEN Tribunals, a significant development that was to influence some aspects of EP practice. One frequently cited problem with the Code of Practice was that the EP's contribution was seen as beginning at Stage 4, i.e. the assessment for a Statement, preventing any consultation or preventative work by EPs at an earlier stage (Wedell 2000). Moreover, it was felt that the Code of Practice 'underlined the expectations for using "standardised tests" of "cognitive functioning" and "attainment" especially with regard to pupils who may have specific learning difficulties' (Buck 1998, p.92). It was perhaps unsurprising that Lokke *et al.* (1997) found that 65 per cent of respondents said they had significant or increased use of psychometric assessment. Buck (1998, p.98) declared that 'value continues to be placed on standardised measures of cognitive ability' when deciding on drafting statements and 'determining provision'.

The Green Paper *Excellence for All Children* (DfEE 1997), and follow-up document *Meeting Special Educational Needs: A Programme for Action* (DfEE 1998) led to a significant appraisal of the future role of the EP in 2000 (DfEE 2000). The report, *Educational Psychology Services (England): Current Role, Good Practice and Future Directions*, defined the aim of the contribution of EPs as follows:

> to promote child development and learning through the application of psychology by working with individual and groups of children, teachers and other adults in schools, families, other LEA officers, health and social services and other agencies. (DfEE 2000, p.5)

A key phrase in this definition was 'through the application of psychology', a concept that was felt to have been marginalised by the profession because of the proliferation of statutory work (Boxer *et al.* 1998), and in particular the work involved in following the Code of Practice and writing statements of SENs

(MacKay 2000). Tribunals were increasing and the amount of time spent on a tribunal (including preparation time) could often be around ten hours (Bennett 1998).

The 1997 Green Paper *Excellence for all Children* and the 2001 Special Educational Needs and Disability Act (SENDA) were intended to begin a greater commitment towards better inclusion of children with SENs within mainstream education. Norwich (2000) raised the question of whether a move towards inclusive education would result in a marginalisation of the EP role as the concepts of special education and SENs were dissolved. Norwich, instead, called for the profession to make a positive contribution to their work with children and young people, and one that revolved around the philosophy of 'professional educational psychology that goes beyond school psychology' (Norwich 2000, p.6). It was to be some years before this philosophy was realised when the *Every Child Matters* (ECM) legislation took effect in 2004.

The most significant development in recent years for the EP profession in England and Wales has been the introduction of the ECM legislation (DfES 2004a). The ECM legislation certainly represents the most major development at a national level since the DfEE (2000) report on the role of educational psychology services, even though within ECM 'the professional contribution of educational psychology receives scant attention' (Baxter and Frederickson 2005, p.89). Nevertheless, since the implementation of ECM, there have been considerable changes in the delivery of educational psychology services in England and Wales, not least the increased focus on working in a multi-agency context, working as part of integrated children's services, and with an emphasis on the community context rather than mostly being school-based. Previously, the Children Act of 1989 and 2004 was clear in highlighting the importance of multi-agency working, and outlined the need for all agencies to develop effective strategies and procedures that would improve the quality and impact of such work.

One of the consequences of the ECM legislation, in many local authorities, has been the restructuring of council departments to combine education and social services under one umbrella, commonly referred to as 'integrated children's services'. In some authorities this has resulted in shared accommodation between EPs and social services staff, and reflects the drive towards the Common Assessment Framework (CAF)[1], which is designed to lead to more consistent and integrated assessment practice across disciplines. It is important to note, however, that local authorities across England and Wales are all at different stages in regard

---

1   The Common Assessment Framework is a UK government initiative designed to provide a stardardised approach to conducting an assessment of a child's additional needs, and deciding how these needs should be met.

to the co-location of services and the development and implementation of the Common Assessment Framework.

The changes in educational psychology services, as a result of ECM, are reflective of the evolving role of EPs, and are significantly different from the nature of EP work when the DfEE (2000) report was undertaken (Farrell *et al.* 2006). It could be argued that the EP role was more school-based before, and most of the work done by EPs appeared to revolve around the statutory role of EPs, namely assessing children for statements of special educational needs. One of the recommendations following the DfEE (1997) Green Paper was to try to reduce the number of 'statemented' children to 2 per cent by 2002. In a further DfES (2004b) report, *Removing Barriers to Achievement*, the Government formally recognised that there was a need to reduce the emphasis on separate SEN structures and processes (Baxter and Frederickson 2005). Recent evidence would suggest that these objectives have been achieved (Farrell *et al.* 2006), with the result that EPs have been freed up to carry out other aspects of service delivery – for example, training, research, group-work and consultation.

Local councils in England and Wales are now intent on delivering the five ECM outcomes for children, namely, that children and young people should: (1) be healthy, (2) stay safe, (3) enjoy and achieve, (4) make a positive contribution, and (5) achieve economic well-being. Local authorities are now being inspected on whether they can meet these outcomes, and they are gradually becoming incorporated into the organisation, processes and actions of all children's services, including NHS trusts, schools, and other local authority services. Educational psychology services (EPS) have also adopted the ECM outcomes and are planning and evaluating their work according to whether they can meet these targets.

It has been argued that the *Every Child Matters* legislation endorses the execution of the United Nations Convention of the Rights of the Child, to which the UK signed up in 1995. Indeed, the five key outcomes of ECM enshrine the 40 Articles that relate explicitly to the aspired experience of children and young people (Baxter and Frederickson 2005).

One of the most detailed reports of EP service delivery in recent years was the DES report *A Review of the Functions and Contribution of Educational Psychologists in England and Wales in light of 'Every Child Matters: Change for Children'* (Farrell *et al.* 2006). The report outlined research conducted by Manchester University's School of Education on the implementation of the ECM agenda by EPS. Questionnaires were distributed to EPs, schools, parents and other professional groups, as well as local authority officials. Interviews (telephone and face to face) of pupils and 'relevant organisations', as well as site visits also took place.

The researchers found evidence of EPs' involvement in multi-agency work, and moreover, service users reported that EPs were 'making an effective contribution within such contexts' (Farrell *et al.* 2006, p.8). The range of different agencies, voluntary organisations and professional groups with which EPs engage in multi-agency work was extensive:

> social workers, education welfare officers, residential support workers, child psychiatrists, child clinical psychologists, paediatricians, a variety of CAMHS workers and therapists, speech and language therapists, YOT (Youth Offending Team) staff, Connexions workers, parent partnership workers, school teachers, specialist teachers and special educational needs coordinators, police officers, portage workers, specialist nurses, physiotherapists and occupational therapists, voluntary sector professionals. (Farrell *et al.* 2006, pp.38–39)

The research discovered evidence of a distinctive contribution by EPs within these multi-agency settings (i.e. 'the application of psychological methods, concepts, models, theories and knowledge'); a significant outcome given that another finding was that a lot of the work done by EPs could have been done by other (and on some occasions less trained, and less expensive) professional groups. Furthermore, EPs were viewed by many respondents as being well placed to coordinate some of these different agencies and to act as 'a bridge between school and community' (Farrell *et al.* 2006, p.47).

There was also evidence in the study that EPs were doing less statutory work than in the past, and instead were undertaking a greater range of 'effective SEN work'. Respondents felt that the reduction of statutory work was enabling EPs to extend their delivery of services, with the desired result of moving towards the goals of the ECM agenda. However, respondents acknowledged that EPs still have an important role to play with individual children who have severe and complex needs, and that for these children, the statutory role was still germane.

Some barriers to more effective EP practice included the limited contact time that school staff, in particular, felt EPs have with their client groups. Limited time with client groups is a common difficulty for EPs in the UK, which has undoubtedly had an impact on the nature of service delivery, such that there is more emphasis placed on systemic work and consultation (which is arguably more time efficient than working mostly with individual children).

The report concludes with recommendations for the future role and function of EPs. The most significant of these is that serious consideration should now be made about the future merger of the academic disciplines of child clinical psychology and educational psychology, given the more community-based nature of EP work, and the now assimilable three-year doctoral training programmes of the two professions. It remains to be seen whether there is widespread support for this view amongst both professions.

One of the considerations regarding the introduction of the Common Assessment Framework (CAF) is who should be the Lead Professional involved with each case.[2] The research by Farrell *et al.* (2006) indicated that respondents did not necessarily think that this should always be the EP, since it may not be the most effective use of their time. However, it was felt that there would be some circumstances where the EP might well be best placed to act as the Lead Professional (e.g. if a child has long-term, complex needs of an educational or mental health nature and where the EP has long-term involvement with the child and family). However, these issues are yet to be resolved as the CAF is only beginning to be fully implemented across the country.

The restructured initial training for EPs in England and Wales has been a key development in recent years, and some initial perceptions of its impact on the profession were made in the Farrell *et al.* (2006) report. Many EPs and Principal EPs felt that the restructured training fits well with the expanded role of the EP, and should lead to improved quality of services offered by EPS, but in particular, will lead to a more strengthened role of research in educational psychology services.

In Wales, it is important to note that EP services fall under the jurisdiction of the Welsh Assembly. In 2004 the two documents *Educational Psychology in Wales* and *Children and Young People: Rights to Action* (Welsh Assembly 2004a, 2004b) outlined an agenda for the role of EPs in meeting the needs of children and young people with SEN. Two issues were highlighted by Farrell *et al.* (2006) who also researched EPs in Wales, namely:

(i) the difficulties there are in delivering effective EP services, especially in a multi-agency context when working in small local authorities with low child populations, and

(ii) the shortage of Welsh-speaking EPs.

Northern Ireland

Although the Acts themselves are separate, education legislation in Northern Ireland largely mirrors that of England and Wales, with the Department for Education in Northern Ireland (DENI) being the body with the responsibility for education in Northern Ireland. Thus, the Education Act (Northern Ireland) 1947 followed the 1944 Education Act in England and Wales and was the first in Northern Ireland to require local authorities to assess the needs of pupils with learning difficulties and to make appropriate arrangements for their education in special schools or special classes within mainstream schools. Recent legislation includes:

---

2   The Lead Professional is the person who acts as the single point of contact for the child or young person, and his or her family, to help guide them through the assessment process.

- the Education Reform (Northern Ireland) Order 1989, which introduced the Northern Ireland statutory National Curriculum, and
- the Education (Northern Ireland) Order 1996, which together with the amendments of the Special Educational Needs and Disability (Northern Ireland) Order 2005 (SENDO), deals with special education legislation in the Province.

The Education (Northern Ireland) Order 1996 and the Education (Special Educational Needs Code of Practice) (Appointed Day) (Northern Ireland) Order 1998 established assessment and statementing procedures similar to those in England and Wales. These heightened tensions between pressures to carry out statutory assessments on the one hand, and opportunities to engage in early intervention and preventative work, on the other.

More recently, The Special Educational Needs and Disability (Northern Ireland) Order 2005 (SENDO) led to the establishment of a tribunal system similar to that in England and Wales, although it does not deal with disability discrimination because this legislation currently does not apply in Northern Ireland.

Opportunities for change for EPs in the Province are likely to come from proposed developments such as the amalgamation of existing children's services in Northern Ireland in the light of the ten-year strategy for children and young people in Northern Ireland (Northern Ireland Commissioner for Children and Young People 2006) with its parallels with ECM, interdisciplinary collaboration for the mental-health promotion strategy for children and young people (Department of Health, Social Services and Public Safety 2006), the ongoing review of special educational needs and inclusion with a proposed reduction in statutory assessments, will bring opportunities for change for EPS in the Province.

Scotland

In comparison with the rest of the UK educational psychology services in Scotland have developed in a distinctive way. Whereas in England and Wales educational psychologists worked in school psychological services provided by education authorities and in child guidance clinics that were medically led, in Scotland the functions of both services were combined in an education authority child guidance service under the direction of a principal psychologist (McKnight 1978; Sampson 1980). By the outbreak of World War II, several authorities had clinics in operation, most of them held on a Saturday morning with staff who worked on a voluntary basis.

It was in recognition of these developments that the statutory period for services began with the Education (Scotland) Act 1946. The Act empowered education authorities to provide child guidance services. It also required the Secretary of State to make regulations defining the various categories of handicapped children, and these were set out in the Special Educational Treatment (Scotland) Regulations 1954. This had important implications for psychologists, who developed a central role in determining which of these children required special education. With the passing in 1969 of the Education (Scotland) Act child guidance services became mandatory, and every education authority was required to provide, or to have access to, such a service. The Education (Mentally Handicapped Children) (Scotland) Act 1974, by bringing every child in Scotland under the care of the education authority, led to an extended role for psychologists in working with pupils with complex learning difficulties. The Education (Scotland) Act 1981 extended the psychologist's role further in relation to children and young people with pronounced, specific or complex special educational needs of a long-term nature, who required a Record of Needs. The Record was discontinued with the passing of the Education (Additional Support for Learning) (Scotland) Act 2004, but the Act made provision for children with the most complex needs by means of a Coordinated Support Plan. Parents were given a right to request psychological assessment of the needs of such children.

Educational psychology services in Scotland are built on a statutory foundation that is broader than for any other country in the world (MacKay 1996, 2008). Unlike England and Wales, where the only statutory function of the educational psychologist for many years has been the assessment for the Statement of Needs (Sheppard 1995), a much more comprehensive psychological service was envisaged in the Scottish legislation. The current statutory functions are almost identical to those set out in the 1946 Act, but with some updating to account for modern terminology and requirements of later legislation. These functions are prescribed in the Education (Scotland) Act 1980, which remains the principal Act for Scottish education, although it has been considerably amended by subsidiary legislation since then. The Act as amended states:

> It shall be the duty of every education authority to provide for their area a psychological service in clinics or elsewhere, and the functions of that service shall include – (a) the study of children with additional support needs; (b) the giving of advice to parents and teachers as to appropriate methods of education for such children; (c) in suitable cases, provision for the additional support needs of such children in clinics; (d) the giving of advice to a local authority within the meaning of the Social Work (Scotland) Act 1968 regarding the assessment of the needs of any child for the purposes of any of the provisions of that or any other enactment. (Education (Scotland) Act 1980, Section 4)

The wording reflects the anachronisms that arise in schedules of amendments, hence the continuing reference to 'clinics', despite the child guidance service with its clinics being renamed as 'education authority psychological services' as a result of the Disabled Persons (Services, Consultation and Representation) Act 1986, at which time also the age range was extended to cover the population from 0 to 19 years.

While the Scottish statutory functions will be seen as sharing much in common with the work of educational psychologists elsewhere, the main difference is that they are all mandatory and not discretionary. The wording of the statutes also embraces other important differences that have shaped the way services in Scotland have developed. Most significantly, Scottish educational psychology has not been circumscribed in legislation as a service that is exclusively concerned with narrow educational matters. Four aspects of the wording of the statute reflect this.

First, the requirement was to have 'a psychological service' as opposed to 'a school psychological service'. The view from the beginning of the statutory period, as expessed by the Advisory Council on Education in Scotland, was that 'the child guidance service is essentially a psychological service, and it should be brought to bear on all manner of problems… requiring psychological knowledge and skills' (Scottish Education Department 1952, p.22). When the services were renamed, all of the broad functions they had as child guidance services continued to be applicable.

Second, although the statutory duties were already very broad, the Act envisaged services that would be wider than what the wording required. Thus, it was stated that the functions would 'include' rather than 'comprise' the prescribed duties. This point was taken up in a key report, which noted that the Act 'states what a child guidance service must do and does not place any limit on its functions' (Principal Psychologists of Scotland, 1972, paragraph 2.2). This broad view has continued to be reflected in official documents on the work of services, and, in particular, in the national review of educational psychology in Scotland (Scottish Executive 2002).

Third, the terminology used to describe the client group of educational psychology refers to children with 'additional support needs'. This is the same client group as was described in 1946 as 'handicapped, backward and difficult children'. The definition of those who fitted this description was very broad, and included those who showed 'emotional instability or psychological disturbance'. Following the Warnock Report and the change of focus from deficits to needs, the terminology used in the Education (Scotland) Act 1981 was 'special educational needs'. This term, too, was replaced by the Education (Additional Support for Learning) (Scotland) Act 2004, which led the way in fostering inclusive and non-discriminatory educational legislation and terminology. However, the client group remained the same as it had always been, and was sufficiently broad to give Scottish educational psychologists a statutory remit to deal with the widest range of psychological problems of childhood across the domains of development, learning and behaviour.

Fourth, the wording of the statutes gives Scottish services a remit that extends far beyond the scope of education services. It includes giving advice to the local authority in relation to the Social Work (Scotland) Act 1968 or to 'any other enactment'. This was the broadest expression of statutory duties that could ever have been assigned to any service. The immediate significance of the Social Work (Scotland) Act 1968, insofar as it concerned psychological services, was the setting up of the new Scottish Children's Hearings to replace the juvenile court system and the new duty of contributing psychological reports for that purpose. However, the wording of the Act is all-embracing. It involves giving advice to the council itself (the 'local authority') and not just to the education authority. The advice can relate to any enactment: that is to say, whatever legislation is laid on a council on any subject relating to the needs of children, the psychological service has a statutory duty to respond with advice if so required. In other words, the duties are not restricted to education (far less 'schools'), and they cover every statutory purpose the council might ever require of educational psychologists.

This unique statutory breadth – supported consistently by government reports, circulars and other national documents – has provided a basis that would allow Scottish educational psychology to develop as true 'community psychology', extending well beyond the boundaries of school and education (see MacKay 2006a, p.7). This is compatible with the original vision on which the statutes were first based. Following the 1946 Act the Advisory Council on Education in Scotland provided commentary on the statutory functions in a discussion of 'relationships with the community':

> It is a mistake to think that child guidance is a self-contained service... It is important to possess psychological techniques; it is also important to be informed about such matters as the efficiency of the local youth club, how to find temporary foster-parents, what action to take when a parent deserts, where to send a child who needs a holiday, how the local gangs of adolescents are organised, what facilities exist in the neighbourhood for recreation. (Scottish Education Department 1952, p.26)

The breadth of the statutory foundations of Scottish educational psychology services has provided an ideal substrate from which to develop a comparably broad range of professional roles. MacKay (1989) sought to articulate these under five headings: consultation, assessment, intervention, training and research. These were formalised when the Scottish Government took the lead in commissioning nationally recognised performance indicators for educational psychology (MacKay 1999), with the five 'core functions' operating at three levels: the level of the individual child or family, the level of the school or establishment and the level of the local authority. This was further ratified as the basis for service delivery by the Scottish Ministers following publication of the national review of services (Scottish Executive 2002).

The inclusion of 'research' as a required core function of educational psychology in Scotland also reflects the spirit of the original legislation. The first duty laid upon services in the Act is 'to study', the object of the study being 'children with additional support needs' (Section 4). Research is therefore one of the functions that is subject to inspection as part of the cooperative arrangement reached by services with Her Majesty's Inspectorate of Education (HMIE) following the national review. To support this process, a comprehensive self-evaluation tool-kit was prepared in collaboration with representatives of several services and of the universities (HMIE 2007).

The national review of services built on the broad legislative foundations of Scottish services in two further ways:

- First, it was envisaged that educational psychologists would play a key role in supporting the Government's priorities for education in Scotland in relation to all children and young people, and not just those with additional support needs. The Standards in Scotland's Schools etc. Act 2000 required education authorities to ensure that school education was 'directed to the development of the personality, talents and mental and physical abilities of the child or young person to their fullest potential' (Section 2). The Act also made provision for the Scottish Ministers to define national priorities in education. The Education (National Priorities) (Scotland) Order 2000 defined five such priorities. This opened the way for a much more direct role for educational psychologists in influencing policy and practice at both local and national level.

    - raising standards of educational attainment, especially in the core skills of literacy and numeracy
    - supporting and developing the skills of teachers and the self-discipline of pupils, and enhancing school environments
    - promoting equality, particularly for those with additional support needs
    - working with parents to teach pupils respect for themselves and others and to promote citizenship; and
    - equipping pupils with the skills, attitudes and expectations necessary to prosper in a changing society and to encourage creativity and ambition.

- Second, the national review endorsed the recommendations made in the Beattie Report on post-school education and training of young people with special needs (Scottish Executive 1999). This proposed the development of educational psychology services for 16- to 24-year-olds, and represented a natural progression for services which already had statutory duties for the 0 to 19 age group. As a result, 12 local authorities became Pathfinders for post-school psychological services. Evaluation of this initiative (MacKay 2006b) led the Government to fund the further development of post-school services as part of the new structure of educational psychology in Scotland.

Discussion

By defining the statutory duties of EPs the prevailing legislation of the day serves as a shared model of practice. But it also functions as an external challenge and as both a barrier to, and a vector for, change (Stobie *et al.* 2002). Legislative structures determine the scope of the work of EPS, most notably in the formal requirements imposed by the burden of statutory assessments for special educational needs/additional support needs. But these structures are time-limited and evolve to reflect the values of society, and EPs in their 100 years or so of history have witnessed and contributed to marked legislative changes – from the divisive and discriminatory statutes of the 1940s to 1960s to the principles of inclusion and equality in the 21st Century.

Current developments in legislation in the UK

As we have seen, recent developments in education legislation in the UK have given rise to greater coordination of children's services, with wide-ranging implications for the practice of EPs – most notably the challenge of providing a distinctive and effective voice within multi-agency teams (Norwich 2005). Furthermore, while schools prioritise academic standards as part of the drive towards the knowledge-based economy, as Norwich (2005) notes, EPs in contrast emphasise the values of citizenship and social inclusion.

The introduction of a 'public health' perspective from the US (Meyers and Nastasi 1999) has brought with it a more positive focus for EPs, with its emphasis upon promoting mental health and quality of life, fostering learning and raising achievement for *all* children, not just those with SEN/ASN (additional special needs) (MacKay 2002; Baxter and Frederickson 2005). But these developments also raise the issue of whether the child remains the primary focus for the work of EPs (Norwich 2005).

These moves away from the narrow traditional functions linked to SEN/ASN are welcome developments, with time previously spent on statutory assessment increasingly available for consultation and research. A survey carried out in Scotland by MacKay (1997) revealed that primary head teachers strongly endorsed the importance of research by EPs, and, more recently, Boyle and MacKay (2007) provided evidence of the value of systemic models of service delivery, with research and involvement in the strategic issues facing schools regarded by primary and secondary head teachers in Scotland as being of central importance. However, the findings from the latter study also emphasised the value placed by schools on the full range of intervention services offered by EPs, including direct work with individual children and young people, and highlighted the co-existence of traditional and systematic approaches to practice.

Concluding comments

Recent taxonomies of the essential features of EP practice (Cameron 2006; Gersch 2004) pose questions about what can be regarded as distinctive about the work of EPs and how their contributions differ from those of clinical psychologists and other applied psychologists, on the one hand, and specialist teachers and professionals such as social workers who have received some training in psychology, on the other. The future of educational psychology in the UK may ultimately depend upon the evidential base for EP practice work, the strength of collaborations with parents and other professionals alike, and the quality of EP training and staff development. But legislation will continue to be of paramount importance as it both shapes and legitimises EP practice and it is still as crucial as ever before that EPs should continue to contribute a voice to the processes of legislative change.

References

Baxter, J. and Frederickson, N. (2005) 'Every Child Matters: Can educational psychology contribute to radical reform?' *Educational Psychology in Practice 21*, 2, 87–102.

Bennett, P.L. (1998) 'Special educational needs tribunals'. *Educational Psychology in Practise 14*, 3, 203–208.

Board of Education (1924) *Psychological Tests of Educational Capacity.* London: HMSO.

Board of Education (1926) *The Education of the Adolescent.* Consultative Committee Report (The Hadow Report). London: HMSO.

Board of Education (1929) *Report of the Mental Deficiency Committee* (The Wood Report) London: HMSO.

Board of Education (1931) *The Primary School.* Consultative Committee Report (The Hadow Report). London: HMSO.

Board of Education (1933) *Infant and Nursery Schools.* Consultative Committee Report (The Hadow Report). London: HMSO.

Board of Education (1938) *Secondary Education with Special Reference to Grammar Schools and Technical High Schools.* Consultative Committee Report (The Spens Report). London: HMSO.

Board of Education (1943) *Curriculum and Examinations in Secondary Schools* (The Norwood Report) London: HMSO.

Boxer, R., Foot, R., Greaves, K. and Harris, J. (1998) 'LEA criteria and the nature of EP assessment.' *Educational Psychology in Practice 14*, 2, 128–134.

Boyle, J. and MacKay, T. (2007) 'Evidence for the efficacy of systemic models of practice from a cross-sectional survey of schools' satisfaction with their educational psychologists.' *Educational Psychology in Practice 23*, 1, 19–31.

Buck, D. (1998) 'The relationship between educational psychologists' assessments and the allocation of provision to children with special educational needs.' *Educational and Child Psychology 15*, 4, 91–102.

Burt, C. (1943) 'The education of the young adolescent: The psychological implications of the Norwood Report.' *British Journal of Educational Psychology 13*, 126–140.

Cameron, R.J. (2006) 'Educational psychology: The distinctive contribution.' *Educational Psychology in Practice 22*, 4, 289–304.

Department for Education (1994) *Code of Practice on the Identification and Assessment of Special Educational Needs.* London: HMSO.

Department for Education and Employment (1997) *Excellence for All Children – Meeting Special Educational Needs. The Green Paper.* London: HMSO.

Department for Education and Employment (1998) *Meeting Special Educational Needs: A Programme for Action.* London: HMSO.

Department for Education and Employment (2000) *Educational Psychology Services (England). Current Role, Good Practice and Future Directions. Report of the Working Group.* London: HMSO.

Department for Education and Skills (2001) *Special Educational Needs Code of Practice.* London: HMSO.

Department for Education and Skills (2004a) *Every Child Matters: Change for Children.* London: HMSO.

Department for Education and Skills (2004b) *Removing Barriers to Achievement: The Government's Strategy for SEN.* London: HMSO.

Department of Education and Science (1978) *Special Educational Needs* (The Warnock Report). London: HMSO.

Department of Education and Science (1992a) *Getting in on the Act: Provision for Pupils with Special Educational Needs.* London: HMSO.

Department for Education and Science (1992b) *Special Educational Needs: Access to the System.* London: HMSO.

Department of Education and Science (1969) *Psychologists in the Education Services* (The Summerfield Report) London: HMSO.

Department of Health, Social Services and Public Safety (2006) *A Vision of a Comprehensive Child and Adolescent Mental Health Service: The Bamford Review of Mental Health and Learning Disability (Northern Ireland)* (The Bamford Report) Belfast: DHSSPS.

Farrell, P., Woods, K., Lewis, S., Rooney, S., Squires, G. and O'Connor, M. (2006) *A Review of the Functions and Contribution of Educational Psychologists in England and Wales in Light of 'Every Child Matters: Change for Children'.* London: DfES Publications.

Gersch, I. (2004) 'Educational psychology in an age of uncertainty.' *The Psychologist 17*, 3, 142–145.

Gillham, B. (ed.) (1978) *Reconstructing Educational Psychology.* London: Croom Helm.

Hearnshaw, L.S. (1979) *Cyril Burt: Psychologist.* London: Hodder and Stoughton.

HMIE (2007) *Quality Management in Local Authority Educational Psychology Services: Self-Evaluation for Quality Improvement.* Livingston: HM Inspectorate of Education.

Jimerson, S., Oakland, T. and Farrell, P. (2006) *The Handbook of International School Psychology.* Thousand Oaks, CA: Sage.

Kagan, T.K. (2005) 'Literary origins of the term "School Psychologist" revisited.' *School Psychology Review 34*, 3, 432–434.

Kerr, G. (1952) 'A history of child guidance.' *British Journal of Educational Psychology 22*, 5–29.

Kirkaldy, B. (1997) 'Contemporary tasks for psychological services in Scotland.' *Educational Psychology in Scotland 5*, 6–16.

Leyden, G. (1999) 'Time for change: The reformulation of applied psychology for LEAs and schools.' *Educational Psychology in Practice 14*, 4, 222–228.

Lokke, C., Irvine, G., M'gadzah, H. and Frederickson, N. (1997) 'The resurrection of psychometrics. Fact or fiction?' *Educational Psychology in Practice 12*, 4, 222–233.

MacKay, T. (1989) 'Special education: The post-Warnock role for the educational psychologist.' *BPS Scottish Division of Educational and Child Psychology*, Newsletter 1, 1–8.

MacKay, T. (1996) 'The statutory foundations of Scottish educational psychology services.' *Educational Psychology in Scotland 3*, 3–9.

MacKay, T. (1997) 'Psychological service delivery to primary schools: Do head teachers want research?' *Educational Psychology in Practice 13*, 165–169.

MacKay, T. (1999) *Quality Assurance in Education Authority Psychological Services: Self-evaluation using Performance Indicators*. Edinburgh: Scottish Executive Education Department.

MacKay, T. (2000) 'Educational psychology and the future of special educational needs legislation.' *Educational and Child Psychology 17*, 2, 27–35.

MacKay, T. (2002) 'Discussion Paper – The future of educational psychology.' *Educational Psychology in Practice 18*, 3, 245–253.

MacKay, T. (2006a) 'The educational psychologist as community psychologist: Holistic child psychology across home, school and community.' *Educational and Child Psychology 23*, 1, 7–13.

MacKay, T. (2006b) *The Evaluation of Post-School Psychological Services Pathfinders in Scotland (2004–2006)*. Edinburgh: Scottish Executive Department of Enterprise, Transport and Lifelong Learning.

MacKay, T. (2008) 'Psychological Services and Their Impact.' In T. Bryce and W. Humes (eds) *Scottish Education* (3rd edn). Edinburgh: Edinburgh University Press.

McCallum, M. (1952) 'Child guidance in Scotland.' *British Journal of Educational Psychology 22*, 78–89.

McKnight, R. (1978) 'The Development of Child Guidance Services.' In W. Dockrell, W. Dunn and A. Milne (eds) *Special Education in Scotland*. Edinburgh: Scottish Council for Research in Education.

Meyers, J. and Nastasi, B.K. (1999) 'Primary Prevention in School Settings.' In T.B. Gutkin and C.R. Reynolds (eds) *The Handbook of School Psychology* (3rd edn). New York: Wiley.

Miller, A. (1979) 'A classroom-based treatment programme for an extremely withdrawn six-year old boy.' *Remedial Education 14*, 138–142.

Miller, A. and Ellis, J. (1980) 'A behaviour management course for a group of mothers: The importance of the course setting for effective use of available resources.' *Child: Care, Health and Development 6*, 147–155.

Ministry of Education (1955) *Report of the Committee on Maladjusted Children* (The Underwood Report) London: HMSO.

Munsterberg, H. (1898) 'Psychology and education.' *Educational Review 16*, 105–132.

Norwich, B. (2000) 'Educational Psychology and special educational needs: How they relate and where is the relationship going?' *Educational and Child Psychology 17*, 2, 5–15.

Norwich, B. (2005) 'Future directions for professional educational psychology.' *School Psychology International 26*, 4, 387–397.

Our Children and Young People – Our Pledge: A Ten Year Strategy for Children and Young People in Northern Ireland 2006–2016 (2006) Belfast: Office of the First Minister and Deputy First Minister.

Principal Psychologists of Scotland (1972) *Child Guidance Services: The Future.* Unpublished Report of a Working Party on the Structure of the Child Guidance Service in Scotland. Aberdeen: Aberdeen County Council

Sampson, O. (1980) 'Child guidance: Its history, provenance and future.' Leicester: The British Psychological Society Division of Educational and Child Psychology, Occasional Papers, Vol. 3, No. 3.

Scottish Education Department (1952) *Pupils who are Maladjusted because of Social Handicaps.* A report of the Advisory Council on Education in Scotland. Edinburgh: HMSO.

Scottish Executive (1999) *Implementing Inclusiveness, Realising Potential* (The Beattie Committee Report). Edinburgh: Scottish Executive.

Scottish Executive (2002) *Review of Provision of Educational Psychology Services in Scotland* (The Currie Report). Edinburgh: Scottish Executive.

Sheppard, J. (1995) 'The Education Act 1993.' In British Psychological Society: *Professional Psychology Handbook.* Leicester: BPS Books.

Stern, W. (1911) 'The supernormal child II.' *Journal of Educational Psychology 2,* 181–190.

Stobie, I., Gemmell, M., Moran, E. and Randall, L. (2002) 'Challenges for educational psychologists and their services.' *School Psychology International 23,* 3, 243–265.

Wedell, K. (2000) 'Moving towards inclusion: Implications for professional psychological Services.' *Educational and Child Psychology 17,* 2, 36–45.

Welsh Assembly Government (2004a) *Educational Psychology in Wales.* Cardiff: Welsh Assembly Government Pupil Support Division.

Welsh Assembly Government (2004b) *Children and Young People: Rights to Action.* Cardiff: Welsh Assembly Government Pupil Support Division.

Witmer, L. (1907) 'Clinical Psychology.' *The Psychological Clinic 1,* 1–9.

Wooldridge, A. (1994) *Measuring the Mind: Education and Psychology in England c 1860–1990.* Cambridge: Cambridge University Press.

Relevant legislation
The Children Act 1989
The Children Act 2004
The Disabled Persons (Services, Consultation and Representation) Act 1986
The Education Act 1944
The Education Act 1981
The Education Act 1993
The Education Act (Northern Ireland) 1947
The Education (Additional Support for Learning) (Scotland) Act 2004
The Education (Mentally Handicapped Children) (Scotland) Act 1974
The Education (National Priorities) (Scotland) Order 2000
The Education (Northern Ireland) Order 1996
The Education Reform (Northern Ireland) Order 1989
The Education (Scotland) Act 1946
The Education (Scotland) Act 1969
The Education (Scotland) Act 1980
The Education (Scotland) Act 1981
The Social Work (Scotland) Act 1968
The Special Educational Needs and Disability Act (SENDA) Act 2001
The Special Educational Needs and Disability (Northern Ireland) Order 2005
The Special Educational Treatment (Scotland) Regulations 1954
The Standards in Scotland's Schools etc. Act 2000

CHAPTER 3

Ethics and Value Systems

Geoff Lindsay

Introduction

Practising educational psychology is not simply a matter of drawing upon technical knowledge and skills. The academic background of the psychology degree mainly deals with research and theory. Postgraduate training builds upon this to develop the knowledge base and to develop skills. At this stage an educational psychologist in training (EPiT) has the opportunity also to undertake the important process of integrating knowledge and skills so that each enhances the other. However, there is a further domain that is of fundamental importance: ethical practice.

In the past there has been relatively little specific and targeted discussion of ethics in educational psychology training. The British Psychological Society (BPS) code might have been presented and discussed but most impact would have come through the discussion of practice. This had the benefit of potentially embedding consideration of ethics within a real-life scenario. The disadvantage was that this did not necessarily occur. Practical matters concerned with knowledge and techniques could easily take over.

The need to consider ethical issues directly as part of educational psychology training has been stimulated by three main factors:

- First, there has been an increase in general interest in the profession with research studies of ethical dilemmas (for example, Lindsay 1996; Lindsay and Colley 1995).
- Second, universities have been required to address ethics more systematically, in particular with respect to research studies. This has required both guidance to academic staff, and protocols in decision-making systems.

- Third, there has been an increased interest in, and awareness of, the importance of values and a parallel development of requirements for practices that respect and enhance certain values – for example, equality of opportunity.

In this chapter I shall explore the role of ethics in educational psychology practice and will argue that any practice framework, as discussed in other chapters, must also include consideration of values and ethical principles.

Locating ethical practice in a practice framework

The invitation to contribute to this book came as a result of my work as external examiner to the Strathclyde postgraduate programme for the initial training of educational psychologists (EPs). In reading, as I had, samples of all EPiTs' work I was impressed by the use of the decision-making models promoted and taught by the course staff. But I was also struck by what seemed to me to be a limited connection with values and how these might influence decision-making with respect to the presenting problems. It is arguable, therefore, that decision-making models may be too 'cognitive' in the sense that they have an internal coherence but a less well-developed relationship with the context, in terms of values and ethical issues, in which practice takes place. In discussing this matter with EPiTs it was very clear that they thought a great deal about these issues and the tensions that could arise. It was less clear that the models took sufficient account of this.

Values

I take a position that psychological practice is not value free, any more than is the practice of other professions dealing with people (Lindsay 1995). Political decision-making is shaped by many factors including economics and expediency, but ideology and values are central. I shall take inclusive education as an exemplar.

Inclusive education has been a major policy-driver in the UK and many other countries for many years. Its promotion in the recent past has been based on the two main lines of argument:

- The first is that special education in 'segregated' provision denies children's rights to a normal education and the opportunities to be with typically developing children.
- The second is that there is a lack of evidence for the benefits of special education over inclusive education.

These views have been promoted extensively, and my experience of talking with EPiTs and many EP practitioners is that there is a high level of support for these positions. However, the basis for these positions concerns two different discourses. The first is concerned with *rights* and the second with *effectiveness* (Lindsay 2003). Each is important, but they are different. For example, it may be the case that an effective intervention is rejected because it is deemed to undermine a child's rights. However, it is also important to examine whether taking a position based on rights undermines or abuses a child's access to an effective education (Lindsay 2007).

Furthermore, there are many rights that can be attributed to a child. If inclusive education is seen as a right it is important also to examine the status of this right compared with other rights (Mithaug 1998). A further complication arises when considering also the rights of the parent and the balance with the child's rights. This is also complicated when the responsibility of the parent for decision-making compared with the child's is taken into account. When and on what basis does the right of the parent have supremacy over the child's right in decision-making about the latter's future education?

The point is that these are not only complex issues, they are also contested. Some have an empirical basis and can, in principle, and, however difficult, be open to research. Questions of rights have a legal basis, and can be changed by amending the law. But *both* are values-related. For example, the decision to carry out research into the effectiveness – or otherwise – of inclusive education is, in part, a value judgement. Some argue that there is no need for such research as inclusion is a rights not an effectiveness issue. On the other hand, evaluation of the effectiveness of inclusive education requires consideration of research design including measures such as what value is placed on cognitive compared with socio-emotional outcomes.

I have used inclusive education as an example here not only because it is a key area of policy but also because EPiTs and EPs in practice face the issue on a daily basis. There are technical questions regarding assessment and advice on how to meet a child's needs but there is also a values-laden context that influences a series of choices an EPiT or EP might make.

The ethical basis for practice

Ethical codes in psychology are, perhaps surprisingly, relatively new. That of the American Psychological Association (APA), for example, was not introduced until 1952. It took the APA a number of years of debate and development before the first version of their code was accepted. While there was much support for this initiative the case *against* a code was also presented. For example, Hall (1952) argued against a formal code as 'I think it plays into the hands of crooks on the one hand and because it makes those who are covered by the code feel smug and sanctimonious on the other hand' (p.430). He further argued that 'decent mature people do not need to be told how to conduct themselves' (p.430). This view did not prevail but it does raise an important issue. To what extent should ethical behaviour be reliant on a code that specifies actions as opposed to someone having an inherent appreciation of the ethical issues and making decisions based on those principles?

The following section examines the European Federation of Psychologists Associations Meta-code of Ethics which sets out both ethical principles and specifications of behaviour.

The EFPA Meta-code

An analysis of ethical codes across seven countries indicated a good deal of commonality but some important differences between codes (Lindsay 1992). In 1995 the European Federation of Psychologists Associations (EFPA)[1] approved a Meta-code of Ethics for all member associations. Unlike the codes of psychological associations such as the BPS and APA, the Meta-code was designed to guide associations rather than individual psychologists. This has been very successful. Those with existing codes, including the British Psychological Society, have revised those codes to comply with the Meta-code. Countries with less well-developed systems, particularly in Eastern Europe, have taken the Meta-code and used it to help devise their own codes. A ten-year review found that little needed to be changed to produce the revised Meta-code (Meta-code of Ethics (2nd edn), which was approved by the EFPA General Assembly in 2005 (www.efpa.eu, accessed 8 April 2008).

The Meta-code comprises four principles plus specific areas of content relating to each principle. Importantly for decision-making, the Meta-code stresses the interdependence of the four Principles, stating:

> It should be recognised that there will always be strong interdependence between the four main ethical principles with their specifications.
>
> This means for psychologists that resolving an ethical question or dilemma will require reflection and often dialogue with clients and colleagues, weighing different ethical principles. Making decisions and taking action are necessary even if there are still conflicting issues. (European Federation of Psychologists Associations 2005, Section 3)

Hence, fundamental to the Meta-code is the requirement on the psychologist to reflect on practice and the ethical challenges that arise.

---

1 At this time the organisation was known as the European Federation of Professional Psychologists Associations (EFPPA)

Ethical principles in the Meta-code

The four ethical principles set out in Section 2 of the Meta-code bear a strong resemblance to those in the APA code (American Psychology Association 2002) and that of the Canadian Psychological Association (CPA) (2000). Each will be considered and its relevance related to frameworks of practice.

RESPECT FOR A PERSON'S RIGHTS AND DIGNITY

> Psychologists accord appropriate respect to and promote the development of the fundamental rights, dignity and worth of all people. They respect the rights of individuals to privacy, confidentiality, self-determination and autonomy, consistent with the psychologist's other professional obligations and with the law.

This Principle helps psychologists to orientate their practice in relation to the client. It recognises the reality of the legal framework in which we work. It also acknowledges other obligations. The primary focus, however, is on the psychologist's approach to working with the client. In EP practice the client may be one, or more, of a number of persons, including the child, parent, teacher, school and community.

The first construct is that of 'appropriate respect': that is, there is no absolute blanket specification that the same level of respect be given to all those concerned. The EP or EPiT must consider this as a *relative* concept. However, the Principle is also fundamentally about growth, promoting development of fundamental rights, dignity and worth. There is no suggestion of inhibiting these for some of those concerned. This distinction has gained salience with the concerns, particularly in the US, about the role of psychologists working for the military in advising on effective interrogation methods, including alleged torture techniques (American Psychological Association Presidential Task Force on Psychological Ethics and National Security (2005), www.apa.org/releases/PENSTaskForceReportFinal.pdf, accessed 1 June 2008, but for a critical discusion also see Lindsay (in press) and www.democracynow.org/article.pl?sid=07/08/20/1628234, accessed 1 June 2008).

These issues are generally less acute in EP/EPiT practice but, for example, consider the dilemma of being told by a young client that he intends to carry out an act that has serious consequences for one or more other people. This raises the question of the balance between maintaining confidentiality and the responsibility to be paid to a person at risk. The case often quoted in the literature is that of *Tarasoff* v. *Regents of the University of California* (see Bersoff 2003 for a review) where a student informed a psychologist that he intended to kill his girlfriend. This Principle identifies confidentiality and self-determination, for example, but its relativity implies the need for the EP/EPiT to reflect on responsibilities to all pertinent persons.

COMPETENCE

> Psychologists strive to ensure and maintain high standards of competence in their work. They recognise the boundaries of their particular competencies and the limitations of their expertise. They provide only those services and use only those techniques for which they are qualified by education, training or experience.

There is a developmental process that starts from the day an EPiT starts on a postgraduate programme of initial training and which continues throughout their professional life as an EP. In practice the growth curve of competence will largely be steeper in the training period and the first year or two of practice. The BPS in its requirements for chartered status specifies three years postgraduate training and experience. With a three-year doctorate this criterion will be met at the end of the programme but I believe there is a case for a period of induction postqualification.

'High standards' are specified here as an aspiration. This takes account of the different point of development for each psychologist. Even so, there is a need to exhibit *appropriate* competence. For example, early work as an EPiT may include assessments using skills that are still being mastered. This is a necessary phase but an assessment in which important decisions on a child are being made requires mastery level as a minimum. Hence, recognition of boundaries of competence is fundamental.

This is not simply an EPiT matter. As new techniques are developed or introduced to a psychologist's repertoire the same developmental process from acquisition of skill to fluency and mastery must be carried out. Decision-making regarding practice must therefore take account of level of competence and the purpose of the task and its import.

These requirements may be seen as likely to inhibit the development of new practice but this need not necessarily follow. Educational psychology practice in the UK has developed substantially since the late 1960s and the time of the Summerfield Report (Department for Education and Science 1968). During the 1970s and 1980s, in particular, many new ways of working were developed – in some cases with EPiTs working with tutors to explore new practice (Burden 1978). In those days of under-staffed services (by current standards) and a substantial influx of newly trained EPs there was much innovative practice. Today's EPiTs entering the profession have a potentially much stronger system to support the development of competence, with EPs in greater number and having higher collective levels of experience.

RESPONSIBILITY

> Psychologists are aware of their professional and scientific responsibilities to their clients, to the community, and to the society in which they work and live. Psychologists avoid doing harm and are responsible for their own actions, and assure themselves, as far as possible, that their services are not misused.

This Principle requires that, when presented with a request to intervene – whether by advice to others or direct intervention themselves – EPs must consider a range of responsibilities. Note that this Principle specifies both professional and scientific responsibilities, reflecting the status of educational psychology as an applied, science-based profession.

Scientific responsibility includes the avoidance of misuse of psychological knowledge. This is an area that poses particular challenges to a branch of applied psychology that operates within a political or policy-related domain, as exemplified by inclusive education. As noted above, this has been a dominant policy for many years. It could be argued that it has a clear foundation in England in the 1928 recommendations of the Wood Committee[2] (see Lindsay 2003 and Cole 1989 for a fuller discussion). Certainly, New Labour promoted inclusion in both education and broader social policy. Also, inclusion became defined not only with respect to SEN but also with reference to social inclusion.

With respect to this Principle the EP has a duty to avoid the misuse of psychological knowledge. So, what is the scientific knowledge base that supports inclusive education? As I have argued before, this is not straightforward as, on the contrary, there is *no* clear evidence for the superiority of inclusive education (Lindsay 2007). In some respects there are encouraging results to support inclusive education, but overall the evidence is close to equivocal. Equally, there is no clear evidence for the superiority of segregated special education. Rather, the situation is far more complex. This is not surprising given that inclusive education is not an intervention comparable to, for example, a programme to help a child overcome a specific phobia, or even a programme to aid reading development. Each of these, to differing degrees, is concerned with a relatively limited number of variables that could influence success. Compare this situation with inclusive education where there are factors at all levels from government policy down to the specifics of classroom practice.

In the case of the child with a phobia the scientific basis for actions is relatively straightforward. The research literature will be very helpful and, in the case of many such problems, there will be a good basis for guiding action and estimating the probability of success. In the case of a reading difficulty the situation is

---

2   Board of Education (1929) *Report of Mental Deficiency Committee* (The Wood Report). London: HMSO.

more complex. Research shows that a number of different child-based factors are relevant to appropriate interventions and the probability of success including:

- the relative contribution of visual or auditory perception
- language (and within this domain phonemic, morphemic, sentence or paragraph levels)
- memory, and the relationship of memory with context
- motivation, etc.

In addition, there are school factors including:

- resources
- teacher skill and the availability of support staff and their skill levels
- absolute time, and the ability to distribute practice optimally.

Parental factors including support are also important.

With respect to inclusive education, however, the situation is far more complex. Possible relevant factors include child, teacher, parent, and school factors but there is no specific *intervention* that is comparable to a programme for a phobia or even reading difficulties. Rather, 'inclusive education' is a fuzzy construct. It is far more complex and also much more contested. Consequently, even attempting a scientific analysis with the aim of determining whether it is appropriate or the probability of being appropriate in any particular case is far more problematic.

The implications of this analysis are that an ethical approach to scientific responsibility requires the EP to be very circumspect in ensuring not only up-to-date knowledge of research findings but also a recognition of the differential limitations of research knowledge for different types of intervention. Furthermore, it is necessary to recognise that in some cases a decision on intervention may be based less on scientific knowledge and more on socio-political policy. The case of inclusive education falls firmly in the latter. Interestingly, however, it is not alone even among these three examples. For example, in the early 1990s the concern about reading standards led to a major scientific but also socio-political debate (Cato and Whetton 1991). Politicians and policy-makers also joined in. This was often referred to as the 'phonics versus real books' debate. There was evidence but it had limitations. Reviews such as that by Adams (1990) strengthened the research base. More recent research has further improved our understanding of the relative importance of different approaches, although it could be argued that we need to develop more knowledge about the interaction between approaches and individual children: even very successful programmes have children who fail to make expected progress.

So, to return to the ethical question, the Principle implies that EPs must recognise the quality of the scientific basis for their opinions, judgements, advice and actions. Furthermore, it is necessary to relate the science to the policy framework in which practice takes place.

This Principle has a wide range of coverage. Educational psychologists are required to be aware of their responsibilities to the community and wider society as well as to specific clients. Take the example of an adolescent referred to an EP for challenging behaviour. Long-standing debates within the profession have centred on the question: 'Who is the client?' In the example of a Head Teacher seeking the involvement of an EP there is typically the question: 'Am I being asked to help the young person or the school?' However, this Principle poses a different question. Rather than ask who is the client, the EP would now need to ask: 'To whom do I owe a responsibility? And what is its nature?' The EP may decide that responsibility is owed to several persons and the wide-community, as indicated in the Principle. This could well conflict with the answer to the question, 'Who is the client?' Even using the concept of primary and secondary clients does not obviate this problem, although invoking primary and secondary responsibility can be argued.

The limitation with an approach that focuses solely on the identification of the client is that the basis of demarcation may differ. The concept of 'primary client' may be articulated in terms of the needs and focus of intervention. In the preceding example the young person with behavioural difficulties could be considered to be the primary client whereas the Head Teacher may be considered the secondary client (as agent to bring the young person to the attention of the EP). It should also be acknowledged that the Head Teacher may disagree and consider that he or she is the primary client, acting on behalf of the young person and, perhaps, the school. From the perspective of this Principle it is necessary to examine the basis of the pattern of responsibilities, not to take these for granted. A common issue that arises under this principle is the need to balance responsibility with risk. The maintenance of confidentiality with clients is typically the most common type of ethical dilemma revealed by research studies (Lindsay and Clarkson 1999; Lindsay and Colley 1995). Balancing the obligations to the primary, or first-order, client against risk to others – whether a specific person or persons or a general risk to members of society – is a common dilemma among therapists.

The second element of this Principle adds a further dimension. Not only must EPs take responsibility for their own actions, they must also endeavour to ensure that their services are not misused. The challenges resulting from working within an organisation compared with independent practice are pertinent here. Most EPs are employed in public service. The employer base is changing from the hegemony of local authorities (LA) to a mix that includes organisations effectively running the LA functions. Each has the potential to seek to influence EP practice. External pressures on the employer can lead to pressures on EPs that might clash with professional judgements, particularly with respect to service and individual EP priorities. Some EPs have also claimed in responses to workshops I have run, and in complaints to the British Psychological Society, that they have felt 'leaned on' to produce recommendations that are more palatable to the employer.

The fundamental issue here also arose in the enquiry of the House of Commons Select Committee on Education. In 2007 they sought comments to questions that concerned them following the publication of their earlier report (House of Commons Education and Skills Select Committee 2006). Implicit in this enquiry was the suggestion that *because* the EP was employed by the LA and *because* the LA had responsibility for making provision for children with SEN, the LA could *not* reasonably be given the responsibility for assessing those needs. Given the role of EPs in this process, this concern would apply to them also.

However, it is reasonable to assume that an EP (or education officer) who is acting ethically will take this into account. Furthermore, this model of dual duty is not unique to education. Other services, including the NHS, also assess and then make provision to meet needs. Nevertheless, the issue is serious. Implicit is a sense of distrust, that LAs (or EPs) cannot – or will not – make judgements based on an ethical sense of responsibility as set out in this Principle. This fear is not new. I recently re-read Bernard Coard's 1971 pamphlet *How the West Indian Child is Made Educationally Sub-normal in the British School System*. In his chapter on assessment, Coard poses now all too familiar concerns about the assessment process but he also states with reference to the validity of a particular assessment:

> Now some of the *less honest* Educational Psychologists will say that they take account of these factors by stating in their report on the test that the child seemed upset, or disturbed etc. (Coard 1971, p.16, emphasis added).

Coard's argument is that it is not possible to use such observations made during the assessment process to recalibrate the results and hence make a more rounded 'clinical' judgement rather than simply reporting test results. The implication is that this behaviour is not good assessment practice but rather is imputed to be an indicator of a 'less honest' EP.

The Principle of Responsibility poses challenges to the *totality* of an EP's approach to problem-solving. Its scope goes beyond issues such as competence to perform particular professional actions. It locates EP practice firmly in the interface between the EP, individual client, second-order client (e.g. LA or other employer) and national policy-makers. The Principle also identifies the need to think through actions nor only in terms of the need of the primary client but also with respect to the *responsibilities* to others.

INTEGRITY

> Psychologists seek to promote integrity in the science, teaching and practice of psychology. In these activities psychologists are honest, fair and respectful of others. They attempt to clarify for relevant parties the roles they are performing and to function appropriately in accordance with those roles.

Integrity starts with the EP, with a requirement to be self-reflective and open about personal and professional limitations. This is particularly salient as part of normal practice for the EPiT and early-career EP. At these stages of development it is not reasonable to expect the psychologist to be master of all knowledge and techniques that might be called upon: the scope of educational psychology is so vast. What is necessary is, first, to be aware of one's limitations and, then, to be open about them. Well-organised programmes of initial training take this into account by carefully increasing the range and complexity of tasks for the EPiT. However, even the most well-organised programme cannot prevent the unexpected. Building in strategies to address these events is therefore required.

A related issue concerns EPs and EPiTs who may be undergoing difficult experiences. Over the professional life-span of a typical EP it may be predicted that most will have to deal with major life events including deaths, accidents and mental-health challenges among close family and friends and/or themselves. There will also, typically, be times of great joy – for example, the development of positive relationships, the birth of a child and the success of partners, friends and children. There may be a tendency to consider only the former experiences as they pose essentially negative challenges but in fact all of these life events have the potential for disorientating an EP, to varying degrees. Hence the RPs' emotional status, and its transitory or persistent nature, is a relevant factor when determining a plan of action for dealing with requests for a psychological intervention.

Integrity also covers the need to be open and straightforward. Presenting assessments and opinions, whether orally or in written form, demands both accuracy and the intention to communicate to the relevant other(s). A number of studies over the years have suggested that EPs' reports are not always characterised by high readability and salience (e.g. Cranwell and Miller 1987). Of course, there is a technical factor concerning particular concepts and terms but the responsibility is on the EP *to communicate* not on the recipient to interpret.

Frameworks for problem-solving can include the formulation of hypotheses to be tested. The Principle of Integrity requires also that possible alternative hypotheses are not suppressed. Some frameworks encourage a wide range of possible hypotheses and so are less likely to fall foul of this requirement, although they may be less efficient than a *sequential* strategy for action. In either case, there is a benefit in reviewing the decision-making process to explore whether alternatives have not been properly considered. As indicated here, the process is not only an element in a feedback and review model to formulate a plan and explore the data, it is also an ethical necessity to avoid suppression (even if unwittingly) of possible data or formulation.

When EPs were almost universally public servants employed by an LA there were relatively few types of potential conflicts of interest. The most common was possibly that discussed above where the LA set priorities or had expectations at variance with those of the EP. The broadening of the profession and the development of a market in public services has changed this. Finance is now an issue. Services need to earn income to support their activities; the amount and proportion will vary but this requirement does increase the possibility of conflicts of interest. For example, services may be sold to another LA, possibly reducing resources available to the home LA. A more challenging situation concerns the EP who is employed by an organisation that may have a differential benefit from particular results, e.g. where one assessment outcome indicates that a child or young person has needs that, for a price, the organisation is set up to meet.

In such circumstances there is an obligation on the EP to be honest and accurate with regard to the financial implications of the professional relationship with the child and parent. Note that this is more subtle than the more obvious situation where a psychologist explicitly sells a service or when a programme of theory is agreed with a competent adult. In the example above the EP would need, explicitly, to build into the framework of analysis and intervention at least two elements:

- a sensitivity to the potential conflict of interest and the need to be explicit about this; and
- a careful analysis which seeks to ensure that the assessment and recommendations for action are ethically sound.

EPs are also required under this Principle to ensure that in writing their reports and statements, or in expressing a professional opinion in any form, they have carefully evaluated such documents' accuracy as well as any limitations these may have. A simple example concerns the use of score ranges rather than specific scores to take account of the reliability of the measure. But the requirement is more pervasive. The use of any framework should include a series of judgements of the accuracy of both the data and the hypotheses formulated or tested on the basis of these data. There should also be a summative judgement of the impact of the sum of these estimates.

An ethical problem-solving framework

Other chapters have set out a number of different problem-solving frameworks. The ethical framework presented here is potentially relevant to each of these.

Consequently, in this section I shall present a framework that can be generalised rather than tied to a particular problem-solving framework.

The guidance presented here is based upon the 3rd edition of the Canadian Psychological Association Code of Ethics (CPA 2000) revised to be appropriate for EPs. These ten steps set out the processes that need to be integrated with the problem-solving framework.

1. Identify not only the primary client but all the individuals and groups that might reasonably be expected to be affected by the decision.

2. Identify all the ethically relevant issues and practices that apply to the primary client, other individuals and groups involved, and those that apply to the systems (e.g. school) or family in which the presenting problem arose. In doing so, consider the appropriate interests, rights and other characteristics of these persons and systems relevant to ethical decision-making.

3. Consider how personal bias, self-interest, ideological preference or stress being experienced, whether your own or those of others, might influence your decision-making and advice and their receptivity by relevant others.

4. Consider a range of options for your advice and action, taking into account your competence.

5. Conduct a risk assessment, taking into account likely short-term, continuing and long-term risks and benefits of each option on the primary client and others affected (e.g. family, other children and young people, teachers). Also take into account the impact on the wider system (e.g. the school, local authority) and society in general.

6. Select your choice of action after this option appraisal using ethical principles supported by ethical standards and specifications (e.g. BPS Code or EFPA Meta-code)

7. Take appropriate action with a willingness to assume responsibility for the consequences of your action (EP) or by shared responsibility with your supervisor (EPiT).

8. Evaluate the results of your actions from an ethical point of view.

9. Extend your responsibility by being prepared to alter your actions/advice if consequences are negative: this will require re-engagement with the ethical decision-making process.

10. Reflect on the process and use this to guide future approaches to problem-solving.

Conclusions

In this chapter I have argued that any problem-solving framework used by EPs should be informed by an awareness of ethical issues. I have used the EFPA Meta-code as a framework to exemplify actions as this has European currency; it is also the template for the British Psychological Society's *Code of Ethics and Conduct* (British Psychological Society 2006). Codes are helpful tools but I have also argued for the need to think carefully about the ethical principles as well as any specific standards. Furthermore, I have argued that EPs also need to consider their own values and how these, or the values of others, need to be examined as part of the framework for problem-solving that is adopted. Finally, I have proposed a model of ethical decision-making that should be integrated with the particular problem-solving framework adopted by EPs, examples of which are set out in other chapters.

This integration should start at the beginning of initial training. EPs need to develop functional problem-solving frameworks fit for the purpose of addressing the wide range of issues with which they are faced. For this process to be ethically sound, consideration of values and ethics is necessary from an early stage, arguably from day one of an EPiT's training.

References

Adams, M.J. (1990) *Beginning to Read.* London: MIT Press.

American Psychological Association (2002) *Ethical Principles of Psychologists and Code of Conduct.* Washington, DC: American Psychological Association. Accessed 1 June 2008 at www.apa.org/ethics/code2002.pdf

American Psychological Association Presidential Task Force on Psychological Ethics and National Security (2005) *Report of the American Psychological Association Presidential Task Force on Ethics and National Security.* Washington, DC: American Psychological Association.

Bersoff D.N. (2003) *Ethical Conflicts in Psychology* (3rd edn). Washington, DC: American Psychological Association.

British Psychological Society (2006) *Code of Ethics and Conduct.* Leicester: BPS.

Burden, R. (1978) 'Schools Systems Analysis: A Project-centered Approach.' In B. Gillham, (ed.) *Reconstructing Educational Psychology.* Beckenham: Croom Helm.

Canadian Psychological Association (2000) *Canadian Code of Ethics for Psychologists* (3rd edn). Ottawa: CPA. Accessed 8 April 2008 at www.cpa.ca/aboutcpa/boardofdirectors/committeess/ethics

Cato, V. and Whetton, C. (1991) *An Enquiry into LEA Evidence on Standards of Reading of Seven-year-old Children.* Windsor: NFER.

Coard, B. (1971) *How the West Indian Child is Made Educationally Sub-normal in the British School System.* London: New Beacon Books.

Cole, T. (1989) *Apart or Apart? Integration and the Growth of British Special Education.* Milton Keynes: Open University Press.

Cranwell, D. and Miller, A. (1987) 'Do parents understand the terminology used by professionals in their children's statements of special needs?' *Educational Psychology in Practice 3*, 7–32.

Department for Education and Science (1968) *Psychologists in Education Services* (The Summerfield Report). London: HMSO.

European Federation of Psychologists Associations (2005) Meta-code of Ethics (2nd edn) Brussels: EFPA. Accessed 8 April 2008 at www.efpa.eu

Hall, C.S. (1952) 'Crooks, codes and cant.' *American Psychologist 7*, 430–431.

House of Commons Education and Skills Select Committee (2006) *Special Educational Needs. Third Report of Session 2006–6 Vol. 1*. London: The Stationery Office.

Lindsay, G. (1992) 'Educational Psychologists and Europe.' In S. Wolfendale, T. Bryans, M. Fox, A. Labram and A. Sigston (eds) *The Profession and Practice of Educational Psychology*. London: Cassell.

Lindsay, G. (1995) 'Values, ethics and psychology.' *The Psychologist: Bulletin of the British Psychological Society 8*, 448–451.

Lindsay, G. (1996) 'Children with special educational needs: some ethical issues for practitioners in the United Kingdom.' *International Journal of Practical Approaches to Disability 20*, 12–18.

Lindsay, G. (2003) 'Inclusive education: A critical perspective.' *British Journal of Special Education 30*, 3–12.

Lindsay, G. (2007) 'Educational psychology and the effectiveness of inclusive education/mainstreaming.' *British Journal of Educational Psychology 77*, 1–24.

Lindsay, G. (in press) 'Ethical Challenges for the Future.' In G. Lindsay, C. Koene, H. Øvreeide and F. Lang (eds) *Ethics for European Psychologists*. Göttingen, Germany: Hogrefe & Huber.

Lindsay, G. and Clarkson, P. (1999) 'Ethical dilemmas of psychotherapists.' *The Psychologist: Bulletin of the British Psychological Society 12*, 4, 182–185.

Lindsay, G. and Colley, A. (1995) 'Ethical dilemmas of members of the Society.' *The Psychologist: Bulletin of the British Psychological Society 8*, 214–217.

Mithaug, D.E. (1998) 'The Alternative to Ideological Inclusion.' In S.J. Vitello and D.E. Mithaug (eds) *Inclusive Schooling: National and International Perspectives*. Mahwah, NJ: Lawrence Erlbaum Associates.

PART THREE
Executive Frameworks for Trainees and Practitioners

CHAPTER 4

The Monsen *et al.* Problem-Solving Model Ten Years On

Jeremy J. Monsen and Norah Frederickson

A decade ago Monsen, Graham, Frederickson and Cameron (1998) presented their formulation of the Problem-Analysis Framework as a work in progress. We aimed not only to disseminate an accountable model to guide professional decision-making, problem-solving and practice, but also to stimulate debate about such issues within the community of educational (and applied) psychologists, training providers and trainees. The 1998 Problem-Analysis Framework had initially been developed to assist trainee educational psychologists better integrate the knowledge acquired through training and experience in order to guide their decision-making, problem-solving and action within the complex and ill-structured real-life applied problems with which they were expected to work

The importance of utilising systematic problem-solving approaches within applied psychology practice – and educational psychology in particular – has had a long history. By definition, applied psychologists largely work with complex and ill-structured problems, and need robust problem-solving approaches that are conceptually broad, as well as being parsimonious. The 1998 Problem-Analysis Framework offered one way of understanding and managing this complexity.

It is now ten years since the original article appeared and, given its increasing use in the United Kingdom and beyond, it is timely to further delineate some of the key theoretical and conceptual influences that were used in its formulation and to present some of the developments that have occurred in response to both experience and feedback (Annan 2005; Kelly 2006; Woolfson *et al.* 2003). These have resulted in the current re-worked, six-phased Problem-Analysis cycle for use with trainee educational and child psychologists.

Introduction

The British Psychological Society's core curriculum for the newly instigated applied doctorates in Educational and Child Psychology continues to view problem-solving as being central to effective practice (British Psychological Society 2006). Applied psychology is at its core a problem-solving profession, where solving problems is seen as the joint generation of a range of possible solutions to an issue, a concern or a dilemma within real-world applied settings for the explicit purpose of making a positive difference (Eisenhauer and Gendrop 1990; Pearson and Howarth 1982). It is argued that the cognitive, interpersonal and technical skills required in gathering information about a client's problem situation and in implementing and evaluating solutions are similar in all branches of applied psychology. Initial training provides psychologists with a set of core skills (including domain-specific content knowledge, decision-making and problem-solving skills), which can be used to respond to a wide range of client requests and concerns.

The BPS guidance to training providers can be seen as being more prescriptive than descriptive (Argyris 1993a, 1993b). So although the importance of obtaining an accurate understanding of a client's problem situation is emphasised, there is little guidance or, indeed, published literature on exactly *how* such an understanding is achieved, *how* it develops, and *what* factors support or hinder its development (Argyris 1999; Robinson and Halliday 1987, 1988). Many of those involved with the initial training of Educational and Child Psychologists (ECPs) in the United Kingdom have sought to bridge this gap – writing about the central place that problem-solving has as a core competency, and proposing frameworks or models to guide the problem-solving process and the development of expertise in its application (Cameron and Stratford 1987; Frederickson, Webster and Wright 1991; Gameson *et al.* 2003a, 2003b; Miller and Leyden 1999; Miller *et al.* 1992; Monsen *et al.* 1998; Sigston 1992; Woolfson *et al.* 2003).

This chapter describes the conceptual basis and operational processes of one such approach, the current re-worked, six-phased Problem-Analysis Framework which is presented in the appendix to this chapter for ease of cross-referencing throughout the chapter. The six-phased version streamlines the procedural processes and makes its conceptual basis more explicit than was presented in the 1998 version (Annan 2005; Kelly 2006; Woolfson *et al.* 2003).

Located firmly within the modern scientist-practitioner movement in applied psychology (Lane and Corrie 2006), one of the main assumptions underpinning the current version of the Problem-Analysis Framework[1] is that the complex and

---

1   Unless stated otherwise all reference to the Problem-Analysis Framework refers to the current re-worked six-phased version.

ill-structured problems of practice with which applied psychologists (and trainees) are routinely involved can be seen to represent a complex set of interactions between the psychologist (trainee) and others, involving the explicit management of a range of information-processing and problem-understanding strategies and tasks. This position sees the psychologist and client(s) as both being involved in an active inquiry-based process, as 'meaning-seekers' and 'problem-solvers'. This view is informed by theoretical models of how experts and novices go about solving complex and ill-structured real-life problems and related research into the constraints of human working memory, cognition and information processing. These theoretical and conceptual influences are explored further in the following sections, where it is argued that the effectiveness of any assistance provided to clients by psychologists will be dependent upon their competence and skilfulness in two inter-related cognitive processes: first, skills in *analysing* and second, skills in *reasoning* in relation to the often large amounts of information generated when investigating complex real-life dilemmas.

Key theoretical and conceptual influences

In the following sections we discuss the major theoretical and conceptual influences that have guided the development of the Problem-Analysis Framework, both the 1998 and current version. The first is Dewey's 'progression-by-steps' approach to applied problem-solving, and the second is insights derived from 'information-processing theory'.

The progression-by-steps approach to applied problem-solving

Within the context of applied psychology training successful problem-solving can be seen as being characterised by a progression through a set of clearly defined steps. Most of the published problem-solving and related consultative frameworks (see Figure 4.1) can be seen to have built upon the five steps of reflective thinking proposed by Dewey (1933):

1. Suggestions, in which the mind leaps forward to a possible solution (*i.e. the identification of the problem*).

2. An intellectualisation of the difficulty or perplexity that has been felt (i.e. directly experienced) into a problem to be solved (*i.e. the clarification of the problem*).

3. The use of one suggestion after another as a leading idea, or hypothesis, to initiate and guide observation and other operations in collection of factual material (*i.e. the use of hypotheses*).

4. The mental elaboration of the idea, or supposition as an idea or supposition (reasoning, in the sense in which reasoning is a part, not the whole, of inference) (*i.e. reasoning about the possible results of acting on one or another hypothesis, and choosing one*).

5. Testing the hypothesis by overt, or imaginative action.

(See Dewey 1933, pp.199–209, italic script added by chapter authors.)

Operations involved in effective problem-solving

1. General orientation.
2. Problems definition and formulation.
3. Generation of alternatives.
4. Decision-making.
5. Verification.

Source: D'Zurilla and Goldfield (1971)

Teaching children interpersonal problem-solving skills

1. Problem-solving orientation.
2. Problem identification and goal setting.
3. Generation of alternative solutions.
4. Consideration of consequence and decision making.
5. Making plans and checking for success.
6. Integration of problem-solving behaviour.

Source: Thacker (1982)

A problem-centred approach to the delivery of applied psychological services

1. a) List assets.
   b) List problems, complaints, difficulties.
2. Select a priority problem.
3. Specify the priority problem operationally.
4. Collect data relevant to the problem.
5. Identify probable factors contributing to the problem.
6. Specify a desired outcome.
7. Plan possible interventions. Select the best alternative.
8. Implement intervention plan.
9. Record and monitor the effects of the agreed intervention.
10. If outcome is successful, select the next priority from list (item 1) or agree that no further intervention is necessary. If outcome is unsuccessful, repeat steps 4-9.

Source: Cameron and Stratford (1987)

A basic sequence for problem-solving

1. Identifying the problem.
2. Analysing the problem.
3. Generating multiple solutions.
4. Designing plans for actions.
5. Forecasting consequences of intended actions.
6. Taking action.
7. Evaluating the actions.

A procedure for helping a team of educators to solve organisational problems in schools.

Source: Schmuck et al (1972)

Problem-solving sequence

1. Define and clarify the problem.
2. Analyse the forces impinging on the problem.
3. Brainstorm alternative strategies.
4. Evaluate and choose among alternatives.
5. Specify consultee and consultant responsibilities.
6. Implement the chosen strategy.
7. Evaluate the effectiveness of the action and recycle if necessary.

A problem-solving model of school-based consultation.

Source: Gutkin and Curtis (1982)

---

1. Problem identification.
2. Problem analysis.
3. Plan formulation.
4. Plan implementation.
5. Plan evaluation.

Source: Bergan and Kratochwill (1990)

Figure 4.1: Problem-solving frameworks

Dewey's model is based upon applying the scientific method to real-life experience, so that 'transformation of scientific findings into rules of action' can result (Dewey 1929, p.19). His description of reflective thought was developed from his observations of how ordinary people went about processing information when confronted with conceptually complex real-life problems. Dewey saw many advantages of applying the scientific method to real-life problems in that it provided a functional means of control, allowed for public testing of formulations (in the form of hypotheses), and offered the possibility of generating evidence for change. However, Dewey acknowledged that the sequence was not fixed, with some steps being passed through quickly, whilst others needed more time and/or a number of re-runs. When things went wrong with the process Dewey suggested that it was helpful to go back and review the problem-solving steps so far undertaken to see where an error of logic or judgement may have occurred.

A number of limitations in Dewey's original formulation can also be identified, for our purposes the most important being the conception of reflection on action as an individual activity. His work was grounded in the view that people (student teachers in Dewey's case) learnt to reflect upon their practice (i.e. their action in the real world) individually. There is a lack of explicit emphasis given to the ways in which people develop and extend their depth of understanding within dialogues with others. By contrast, Argyris and Schön (1974) and other writers have advocated that the efficacy of problem understanding and reasoning is greatly enhanced by active critical dialogues with suitable mentors or supervisors, developing accordingly the Critical/Accessible Dialogue framework that has been applied in Educational and Child Psychology (ECP) practice (Cameron and Monsen 1998; Robinson 1993).

Information-processing theory
The development of the Problem-Analysis Framework was also greatly influenced by insights derived from information-processing theory. This approach is concerned with the identification of the component skills involved in effective problem-solving, rather than in describing the progression-by-steps that might underlie such a process (Dawson 1998). Information-processing theory seeks to explain how people can solve a variety of problems despite the constraints placed upon them by the limitations of working memory and cognitive processing (Ranyard, Crozier and Svenson 1997; Rose 1999; Wenger and Carlson 1995). Working memory is defined as the 'conscious ability to process information on-line while performing cognitive tasks' (Rose 1999, p.44). It is working memory that is of central importance to on-line problem-solving, and current thinking indicates that the average person, at best, can process between five and nine separate new pieces of information at any one time (Anderson, Reder and Lebiere 1996; Rose 1999).

A further user constraint to successful problem-solving is the amount of domain-specific knowledge that is available to the problem-solver. This issue is often omitted or given much less emphasis in discussions on problem-solving. The assumption appears to be that process skills are more important than content knowledge. However, content knowledge appears to be as essential to effective problem-solving as are interpersonal and cognitive skills and strategies (Schraagen 1993; Shin, Jonassen and McGee 2003).

Effective real-life problem-solving is very dependent upon the problem-solver's skill in using a range of cognitive strategies that help make connections between the large amounts of information available to him or her (both from the client and from existing content knowledge), notwithstanding his or her limited working short-term memory capacity. Early work by Robinson (1987) in delineating strategies of relevance to developing trainee educational psychologist thinking drew on Newell and Simon's (1972) problem–space theory, which still remains a seminal influence in contemporary information-processing theory and research (Dawson 1998).

A central tenet of problem–space theory is that when people move from an initial problem state towards a solution state they form a mental representation of the problem, which in this chapter is called a 'problem map'. The problem map undergoes a series of transformations as the problem-solver tries to move from the initial problem state to a solution state. These transitions are achieved by the problem-solver employing a series of cognitive operations, or strategies, such as means–ends analysis. Means–ends analysis is a particularly important heuristic principle which consists of three main steps:

- first, the person notes the difference between the initial state and the goal state
- second, he or she creates sub-goals to reduce this observed difference, and
- third, he or she selects an operator that will solve this sub-goal.

Research on expert problem-solvers shows that they acquire through experience mechanisms for internally representing the problem space. This internal model acts as a pre-condition for planning, reasoning, anticipating and controlling subsequent cognitive behaviour (Ericsson and Lehmann 1996).

There are a number of questions about the applicability of problem–space theory to applied psychology practice:

- The theory was developed on the basis of laboratory research undertaken with people (mostly undergraduates) solving highly structured problems like the Tower of Hanoi, maths, chess or logical reasoning tasks. There is a concern about the ecological validity and generalisability of the results of puzzle-based problems.

- The puzzle problems used in Newell and Simon's research were usually unfamiliar to the participants, who had very little prior knowledge about such problems. In contrast many of the problems encountered by ECP require considerable amounts of prior specialist knowledge in order to work effectively with them (Schraagen 1993). This is needed to define what is and is not part of the initial problem state, to develop and experiment with a range of operators, and to define what the goal state may be.

- The knowledge required to solve puzzle problems is usually present in the statement of the problem itself. In real-life, ill-defined problem situations much of the information required to solve the problem is not initially present. Much of the difficulty faced by an ECP is trying to sort out what information derived from the teacher, parent/care-giver, pupil, the environment and from his or her own content guides is relevant in solving the problem.

Problem–space theory provides a useful account of the problem-solving processes involved when people go about solving well-defined problems. With more ill-structured real-life problems the theory has to be extended. The value of the theory is that it highlights that two processes are involved:

- an *understanding* process that generates a problem map from the initial problem state, and
- a *solving* process that searches this problem map to reach the goal state.

It recognises the central role that understanding plays, as Simon (1978) suggests: 'The relative ease of solving a problem will depend on how successful the solver has been in representing critical features of the tasks in his problem space' (p.276). The task facing an ECP in this regard is considered in the next section.

The characteristics of the problems with which ECPs work

Most of the problem situations that require the involvement of an ECP can be seen to be ill-structured in nature. Compared with well-structured problems, ill-structured problems are more complex, have fewer definite criteria for deciding if a solution has been reached and lack complete information. Many ECPs begin work on a formal request by interviewing, usually, the teacher and/or parent/care-giver (i.e. the main problem-owners). The starting point in this kind of scenario will often be an incomplete and possibly inaccurate statement from, for example, a teacher about concerns she is experiencing with a boy (Tim) in her class. What actually is the teacher's problem? Is she unable to manage Tim's behaviour because the behaviour is so extreme that no reasonable person would expect her to cope with it? Does Tim have some unrecognised physical, learning and/or emotional problem that is not being dealt with? Are there family-based factors contributing to Tim's behaviour? Is Tim's behaviour actually that extreme and problematic? Are the teacher's curriculum and general management and organisation skills inadequate? Or is it necessary to consider a complex inter-relationship of these and other, as yet unknown, factors, and, if so, which ones, and how do you know and ascertain their relevance? However, the criteria as to what counts as relevant information is not clear. Both the purpose of the ECP involvement and, in Newell and Simon's terms, the 'goal state' of problem-solving with the teacher may not be known – or may at best be unclear, broad and abstracted.

As described above, information-processing theory highlights some useful ways of working with the types of ill-structured problems that face ECP. Part of the task for the psychologist is to reduce the complexity of the problem situation by actively and collaboratively processing and sorting problem details into some form of problem map. This means that if an ECP is to facilitate a joint understanding of a given situation it will not be helpful to begin by finding out everything about the problem. Given the constraints of human working memory the practitioner must find strategies that make it possible to work with teacher information sequentially and purposefully rather than all at once in a haphazard manner (Glaser 1984; Greeno, Collins and Resnick 1996; Robinson and Halliday 1987, 1988; Rose 1999).

Information-processing theory also suggests that problem-solvers develop a series of 'moves' to make connections between the initial problem state and the goal state. These moves would be evaluated regularly to check that they were in fact leading to changes in the desired direction. In the example of the teacher mentioned earlier, this process would require the psychologist to test out that what he or she was doing was actually helping to achieve a goal (jointly formulated between the psychologist and the client in the form of a set of clear statements that outlined the desired end-solution states). In the example given this might be 'By the end of the summer term Tim will be on-task for 70% of the time during structured periods...'. The solution state would be achieved by a series of deliberate operations, which were regularly checked against the psychologist's and client's developing constructions of the problem (via their problem map which would be consistent with the information available to both of them at the time).

SUMMARY

The overall strategy for working effectively with ill-structured problems appears to involve the psychologist (and client) transforming the initial problem into a series of better structured sub-problems, which have goals which can be specified and evaluated. This is the purpose of Phase 1 of the current re-worked Problem Analysis Framework (see appendix). The lack of clarity and definition of purpose that made the problem ill-structured in the first place does not go away. However, at any one point in time the psychologist and the problem-owner(s) will be working jointly on a relatively well-structured sub-problem, which is part of the larger problem space. This larger problem space is represented by a problem map designed to identify the key aspects of the problem (problem dimensions within problem-analysis), and their inter-relationships, in a way that is accurate, complete and helpful to the process of facilitating change (Ericsson and Lehmann 1996; Glaser 1984; Robinson 1987). Identification of sub-problems cannot be achieved by simply using means–ends analysis since the goal in such problems is not defined. Hypothesis-testing as a deliberate and orchestrated cognitive strategy appears to overcome this inherent constraint.

Hypothesis-testing as an aid to the problem-understanding task
When an ECP first begins work with a teacher in exploring the problem situation there is often very little information available to the ECP. Yet despite this lack of detailed information the psychologist is able to generate a range of 'initial guiding hypotheses'. Hypothesis-testing as a cognitive strategy provides a means for the practitioner to transform the initial problem state into a series of structured sub-propositions leading towards a solution state. It also provides the psychologist with a conceptual framework within which to integrate and manage the potentially large amount of information provided by the client and derived from wider investigations. If a given hypothesis is relevant, then certain details and further questions will follow. Each hypothesis-set guides the collection of information that is then used to either support or disconfirm its relevance to understanding the current problem situation.

So in Phase 2 of the current re-worked Problem-Analysis Framework (see appendix) initial guiding hypotheses are developed by the psychologist drawing both on the facts of the case and on stores of knowledge and experience held in long-term memory, which are referred to in this chapter as 'content-guides', but are more commonly called 'schemata' (Anderson, Spiro and Anderson 1978; Wilden and La Gro 1998). A schema is a metaphor for an internal 'organising framework of knowledge about a specific domain which both influences the use of information and also filters out irrelevancies that structure the "sense making" cognitions of the person' (Wilden and La Gro 1998, p.177). Schemata provide a means by which incoming information can be organised, matched and checked. Schemata evolve with experience, becoming more elaborate, organised and easily accessed. Such content-guides consist of the body of knowledge in psychology (and other domain-specific information) available to the psychologist, experience with similar or related problems (sometimes referred to as 'case-based scripts' (Shin *et al.* 2003), and other knowledge (e.g. legislation, policy, practice guidance, professional Codes of Conduct/Ethics and so on). The content-guides assist the practitioner to construct questions and to identify relationships, patterns and interconnections between what initially may seem to be unrelated 'chunks' of information (Glaser 1984).

In our earlier example of the teacher with the challenging pupil, the psychologist might start the problem-solving process with at least two initial guiding hypotheses:

- 'It could be that the difficulties the teacher is experiencing with managing the boy's behaviour might be due to the fact that the boy's behaviour is extreme and disturbed,' and
- 'It could be that the teacher, who is in her second year of teaching, might not be very skilful in managing the boy's behaviour.'

Such hypotheses immediately reduce the initial problem state to a search for information around the behaviour of the boy and the teacher's responses to it. The hypotheses generated will determine what questions are asked, and the information obtained will be matched to each hypothesis to test its relevance (Elstein and Schwartz 2002). One of the key contributions to the development of both the 1998 and the current re-worked version of the Problem-Analysis Framework was the explicit rather than implicit role that hypotheses play as conceptual movers (in Newell and Simon's terms) in bridging the gap between the initial problem state and the goal state (Frederickson *et al.* 1991).

Developing expertise in applied psychological problem-solving

Educational psychology appears unique amongst the applied professions in having connoted 'expertise' as a derogatory term over the past three decades. Recently, there has been an apparent reversal in this trend as it has proved difficult to identify the 'added-value' or 'unique contribution' of the profession without laying claim to some form of expertise or specialism in order to justify roles and salaries. Lichtenberg (1997) defines expertise as the ability to perform 'qualitatively well in a particular task domain' (p.189). Within this chapter such a definition is helpful in three important ways:

- First, it views expertise as being linked with practice and experience.
- Second, the quality of performance is seen as a defining characteristic. Although speed and quality have been found to be related (Chi, Glaser and Farr 1988), quality, rather than speed, would seem to be a more relevant critical feature for expertness. Experts are

seen as being 'expert' because of the quality of their reasoning skills. This reasoning is qualitatively superior to that of non-experts.
- Finally, experts usually excel in their own specific domain area. There is little evidence that a person expert in one area can successfully transfer his or her skills to another domain (Ericsson and Charness 1994; Ericsson and Lehmann 1996; Lichtenberg 1997; Wiley 1998).

Research consistently demonstrates that it is the quality of a problem-solver's domain-specific knowledge and experience (content-guides, or 'case specific scripts') held in long-term memory and his or her ability to retrieve and utilise these to solve problems that differentiates experts from novices (Schraagen 1993; Wiley 1998). These content-guides serve as reservoirs for hypotheses (and other domain-specific knowledge and experience) that can be called upon during the hypothesis-testing process (Elstein, Shulman and Sprafka 1990; Glaser 1984).

Elstein and Schwartz (2002) noted in their review of problem-solving by medical practitioners that both experienced and inexperienced diagnosticians employed a systematic process of generating and testing diagnostic hypotheses. However, experienced diagnosticians did not actually generate significantly more hypotheses, nor did they hold more of them in their working memory, nor were they any more thorough in their data collection than inexperienced diagnosticians. What experienced diagnosticians *did do* was to make more accurate interpretations of the patient's data to test their hypotheses, suggesting that they had more domain-specific knowledge than their less experienced counterparts. Elstein and Schwartz (2002) found that problem-solving competence 'varied greatly across cases and was highly dependent on the clinician's mastery of the particular domain' (p.730).

The other best predictor of problem-solving success within ill-structured problem domains is the propositional reasoning competence of the problem-solver – that is, his or her skilfulness in being able to reason with the information available to him or her, and in being able to formulate and articulate clear unambiguous arguments based on such an understanding (Shin *et al.* 2003).

In terms of training applied psychologists, learning about reading or behaviour difficulties (even if supported with illustrated case examples) is very different from being able to recognise such issues when faced with an ill-structured problem that may or may not involve reading or behaviour. By suggesting that a particular example illustrates a specific type of problem, the tutor, and not the trainee, has transformed the ill-structured task into a well-organised problem. The challenge for tutors is to enable trainees to undertake these transformations themselves. The literature on learning and skills acquisition would indicate that such learning would involve a range of graded experiential opportunities in solving a range of 'real problems' that required trainees to discriminate which knowledge is relevant and how to progressively test its appropriateness to a given issue (Eruat 1994; Halpern 1998). Training programmes may well see placement experiences providing such a rigorous apprenticeship, although there is limited evidence to confirm this assumption.

Increasingly, however, these issues are being addressed directly as many educational psychology training programmes are adopting problem-based learning (PBL) as a major mode of curriculum delivery (Dewey 2006; Kerr and Smith 2005). Having developed in medical education, problem-based learning is defined as 'an approach to professional education that makes use of real life problems as a stimulus for learning' (Van Berkel and Schmidt 2000, p.231). With emphasis on team working and self-directed learning at different stages of the process, it has rapidly become the method of choice in many areas of professional training (Schwartz, Mennin and Webb 2001). For example, a recent symposium for educational psychology trainers in 2007 received reports on PBL developments from 9 of the 13 training programmes in England, Wales and Northern Ireland.

The following section describes the current re-worked Problem-Analysis Framework used in working with trainee educational and child psychologists (and beginning practitioners).

What is problem-analysis?

Problem-analysis can be viewed as a conceptual meta-cognitive framework that can be used to guide and integrate the problem-understanding and reasoning tasks key to effective applied problem-solving. The 1998 and the current re-worked Problem-Analysis Framework were initially formulated to assist Trainee Educational and Child Psychologists (TECP) to guide and structure their thinking when working with complex professional problems (Monsen et al. 1998; Robinson 1987). However, there is no reason why the core principles around thinking and reasoning cannot be usefully employed by practising ECPs as well, although the procedural processes and structures might be different in form, though not function (see Kelly 2006; Woolfson et al. 2003).

The current re-worked Problem-Analysis Framework is based upon the various theoretical, conceptual and practical considerations detailed in previous sections of this chapter. Trainees are helped to conceptualise 'the facts of the situation' derived from these real-world problems in ways that facilitate understanding by themselves, their clients, other practitioners, their peers and their tutors. The assumption is that subsequent action and unique intervention will be more successful because they are based upon a more accurate analysis of presenting difficulties.

The problem situations with which trainees (and applied ECPs) work can initially appear overwhelming to both the practitioner and the client. It is not surprising then that trainees initially lose sight of the problem situation as a whole in an attempt to 'contain the situation' by focusing too early on what seems to be the most relevant aspects of the request, the 'priority problem' (Robinson 1987). On the other hand, clearing order does need to be established from the mass of information received before a clear path of action can be negotiated, and implemented. The role of the trainee is to reduce the complexity of the problem situation and report back in such a way that is helpful to those the trainee has been invited to assist.

The Problem-Analysis Framework demands that the trainee does more than record actions taken, the data obtained and agreed outcomes: information needs to be organised *conceptually*. Based upon the arguments presented earlier, one way to manage such a complex task is for the trainee (and practitioner) to use their content knowledge of the discipline of psychology (and their own experiences) to formulate initial guiding hypotheses (see appendix, Phase Two) to focus their thinking and action. The trainee then systematically investigates the efficacy of these various lines of initial inquiry, culminating in the development of a model that transforms the details of the situation into a 'problem map' (see appendix, Phase Three) and an argued conceptualisation/formulation (i.e. see appendix, Phase Four: integrated conceptualisation. These describe the key problem dimensions (aspects of the situation found to be problematic) and their interconnections and leads to a clear plan for focused action (i.e. the unique intervention, Phase Five). Embedded throughout the cycle is critical evaluation not only of the intervention itself but also of the trainee's own actions in the form of a reflective commentary (see appendix, Phase Six).

Subsequent developments to the nine-step Problem-Analysis Framework

Following its publication in 1998 a number of areas for development were subsequently identified in relation to aspects of the nine-step Problem-Analysis process (Kelly 2006; Woolfson *et al.* 2003). Some of these changes have been conceptual, the others have been structural (i.e. combining and streamlining the nine steps into six phases that make more explicit the dynamic conceptual process and stresses the need for supervision and 'accessible dialogues' in developing trainee thinking: see Figure 4.2).

It was acknowledged by the authors when working with trainees and beginning practitioners that trainees actually impose their own subjective interpretation on the information collected. Although this may be based upon logic as well as evidence, ultimately only one possible integration of the problem dimensions is selected by the trainee and client at any one time. It is this subjective interpretation that forms the basis for the selection of the appropriate

```
                                          ┌─────────────────────────┐
┌─────────────────────────┐              │ Phase 2 – Initial guiding│
│ Phase 1 – Background    │              │ hypothesis              │
│ information, role and   │              └─────────────────────────┘
│ expectations            │
└─────────────────────────┘
                            'PROBLEM-
                            ANALYSIS'
┌─────────────────────────┐                ┌─────────────────────────┐
│ Phase 6 – Monitoring and│  Clear conceptualisation, │ Phase 3 – Identified    │
│ evaluation of actions   │  and clarity leading to   │ problem dimensions      │
│ and outcomes            │  focused interventions    │                         │
└─────────────────────────┘                └─────────────────────────┘

┌─────────────────────────┐              ┌─────────────────────────┐
│ Phase 5 – Intervention  │              │ Phase 4 – Integrated    │
│ plan and implementation │              │ conceptualisation       │
└─────────────────────────┘              └─────────────────────────┘
```

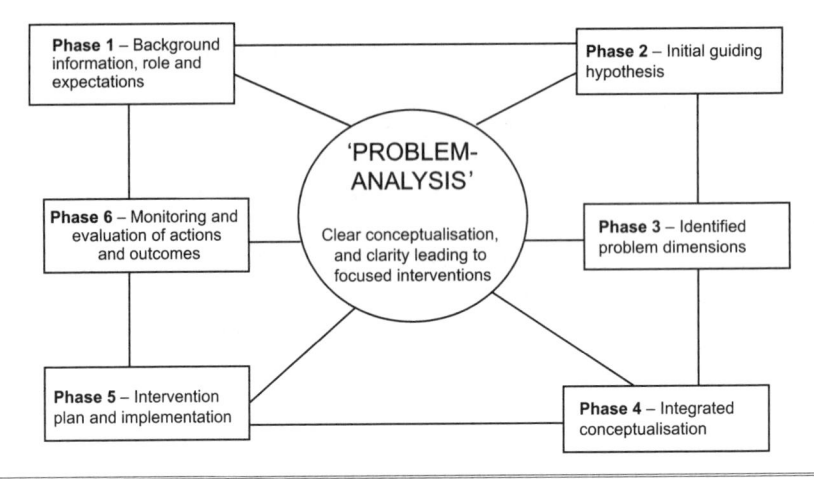

The Problem-Analysis Framework (Monsen et al. 1998)	
Step 1: Clarify the request and check out the need for psychologist's involvement.	**Step 5**: Integration of problem dimensions.
Step 2: Negotiate and contract role.	**Step 6**: Feedback, agree problem analysis and devise intervention plan.
Step 3: Guiding hypotheses and information-gathering.	**Step 7**: Agree action plan implementation.
Step 4: Identify the dimensions of the problem.	**Step 8**: Evaluation of action.
	Step 9: Self-reflection and critical evaluation.

Figure 4.2: The 2008 and 1998 problem-analysis frameworks

intervention. It was therefore seen as particularly important to have much clearer guidance, not only for the identification of initial guiding hypotheses but also for integrating resultant problem dimensions in a more systematic manner. Initially the nine-step Problem-Analysis Framework used the Causal Modelling Approach developed by Morton and Frith (1995) to conceptualise the 'problem map'. However, after further refinements a modified Interactive Factors Framework (IFF) (Frederickson and Cline 2002; see also appendix, Figure 4.3) was developed and integrated within the Problem-Analysis process.

The IFF requires trainees to actively consider different levels of analysis and their interactions when formulating initial guiding hypotheses, problem dimensions and subsequent integrating problem formulations and intervention approaches. Trainees are encouraged to critically explore hypotheses at the levels of Biology, Cognition (including Affect), Behaviour and Environment (or Eco-Systemic, see Bronfenbrenner 1979). The appendix presents the current six-phase cycle that is now being used instead of the nine-step version as the conceptual framework to guide trainee understanding and reasoning within their applied work and the criteria used to judge relative quality.

Concluding comments

Both the 1998 and the current re-worked Problem-Analysis Framework were devised to promote the development of high-quality, robust, applied problem-solving skills by trainee ECPs. This chapter has presented some of the key theoretical and conceptual elements that were used to inform this process. The work of Dewey, Newell and Simon and the unique constraints implicit in the role of the applied psychologist were considered in relation to the question 'How does an applied psychologist go about working with the complexities inherent in the types of cases with which he or she is presented?' It was argued that this task involves understanding and reasoning processes. As such, Problem-Analysis represents a meta-conceptual framework which trainees (and ECP) can use to guide their thinking and action, if that is the task they intend to undertake. By viewing Problem-Analysis as a meta-framework other theories and approaches can be easily accommodated so long as they are consistent with the propositional reasoning tasks implicit in Problem-Analysis.

The challenge for any such framework is to support the trainee in working with others in the problem situation to make sense of it in a way that leads to positively evaluated outcomes. Some reductionism is involved – otherwise the complexity and confusion that characterise complex practice problems are simply replicated or, worse still, compounded. A lack of actionable guidance is often raised as an issue with approaches derived from Social Constructionism – for example, by Efran and Clarfield (1992) who question how it might help a psychologist 'deal more effectively with a quarrelling couple, a cocaine-addicted teenager, a suicidal husband, a house-bound agoraphobic, an obsessive hand-washer, or a high-school drop-out' (p.215). On the other hand, the naïve realism of a 'traditional' scientific approach runs the risk of over-simplification in which small practitioner-defined successes are not considered by the client to have addressed the 'real problem', which then takes on new manifestations. The modern scientist-practitioner approach (Lane and Corrie 2006) is grounded in 'Critical Realism', which acknowledges both the central role that social processes, discourse and narratives play in shaping individual perceptions and the existence of a social reality independent of individual constructions. All perceptions are not equally valid or approaches equally appropriate and systematic means can be employed for testing and selecting between these.

Within an increasingly accountable professional working context a particular advantage to employing the current re-worked six-phased Problem-Analysis Framework is the explicit checks and balances incorporated as part of the process (e.g. there is an explicit and coherent rationale for all action, and a clear basis for contracting the services to be delivered and providing a means of considering the extent to which the contract had been fulfilled). Monitoring, review and evaluation are embedded within the Problem-Analysis cycle and performance criteria, against which the quality of the Problem-Analysis can be judged, are made explicit (see appendix, Phase 6: Monitoring and evaluation of outcomes and reflective commentary). Such criteria encourage critical self- and guided reflection and support the development of practice through helping trainees (and psychologists) evaluate their contribution in achieving improved outcomes for children and young people in partnership with others. Ultimately, we would argue that the value of training psychologists to use any of the sophisticated practice frameworks described in this book must be judged in relation to whether such frameworks have brought, or can bring, positive change in schools, families and community settings.

References

Anderson, J.R., Reder, L.M. and Lebiere, C. (1996) 'Working memory: activation limitations on retrieval.' *Cognitive Psychology 30*, 221–256.

Anderson, R.C., Spiro, R.J. and Anderson, M.C. (1978) 'Schemata as scaffolding for the representation of information in connected discourse.' *American Educational Research Journal 15*, 433–439.

Annan, J. (2005) 'Situational analysis: A framework for evidence-based practice.' *School Psychology International 26*, 2, 131–146.

Argyris, C. (1993a) *Knowledge for Action: A Guide to Overcoming Barriers to Organisational Change.* San Francisco, CA: Jossey-Bass.

Argyris, C. (1993b) 'On the nature of actionable knowledge.' *The Psychologist 16*, 29–32.

Argyris, C. (1999) *On Organisational Learning* (2nd edn). Oxford and Massachusetts: Blackwell.

Argyris, C. and Schön, D.A. (1974) *Theory in Practice.* San Francisco, CA: Jossey-Bass.

Bergan, J.R. and Kratochwill, T.R. (1990) *Behavioral Consultation and Therapy.* NY: Plenum Press.

British Psychological Society (2006) *Core Curriculum for Initial Training Courses in Educational Psychology.* Leicester: British Psychological Society, Division of Educational and Child Psychology Training Committee.

Bronfenbrenner, U. (1979) *The Ecology of Human Development.* Cambridge: MA: Harvard University Press.

Cameron, R.J. and Monsen, J.J. (1998) 'Coaching and critical dialogue in educational psychology practice.' *Educational and Child Psychology 15*, 4, 112–126.

Cameron, R.J. and Stratford, R.J. (1987) 'Educational Psychology: A problem-centred approach to service delivery.' *Educational Psychology in Practice 2*, 4, 10–20.

Chi, M.T.H., Glaser, R. and Farr, M.J. (1988) (eds) *The Nature of Expertise.* Hillsdale, NY: Erlbaum.

Dawson, M.R.W. (1998) *Understanding Cognitive Science.* Oxford: Blackwell.

Dewey, J. (1929) *The Sources of a Science of Education.* The Kappa Delta Pi Lecture Series. New York: Horace Liveright.

Dewey, J. (1933) *How We Think: A Restatement of the Relation of Reflective Thinking to the Educative Process.* Boston, MA: D.C. Heath and Co. (Originally published 1910).

Dewey, J. (2006) *Problem Based Learning: The Panacea for Professional Training and Transformation of Tutor Role?* University College London DEdPsy Thesis, Part 2. Available at http://webct.man.ac.uk/extepvle/problem%20based%20learning%2018.pdf, accessed 5 August 2007.

D'Zurilla, T. and Goldfield, M. (1971) 'Problem solving and behavioral modification.' *Journal of Abnormal Psychology 78*, 1, 107–126.

Efran, J.S. and Clarfield, L.E. (1992) 'Constructionist Therapy: Sense and Nonsense.' In S. McNamee and K.J. Gergen (eds) *Therapy as Social Construction.* London: Sage.

Eisenhauer, L.A. and Gendrop, S. (1990) *Review of Research in Nursing Education, 3.* NJ: National League for Nursing.

Elstein, A.S. and Schwartz, A.S. (2002) 'Clinical problem solving and diagnostic decision making: Selective review of the cognitive literature.' *British Medical Journal 324*, 729–732.

Elstein, A.S., Shulman, L.S. and Sprafka, S.A. (1990) 'Medical problem solving: a ten-year retrospective.' *Evaluation and the Health Professionals 13*, 1, 5–36.

Eraut, M. (1994) *Developing Professional Knowledge and Competence.* London: The Falmer Press.

Ericsson, K.A. and Charness, N. (1994) 'Expert performance: Its structure and acquisition.' *American Psychologist 49*, 8, 725–747.

Ericsson, K.A. and Lehmann, A.C. (1996) 'Expert and exceptional performance: Evidence of maximal adaptation to task constraints.' *Annual Review of Psychology 47*, 273–305.

Frederickson, N. and Cline, T. (2002) *Special Educational Needs, Inclusion and Diversity: A Textbook.* Buckingham: Open University Press.

Frederickson, N., Webster, A. and Wright, A. (1991) 'Psychological assessment: A change of emphasis.' *Educational Psychology in Practice 7*, 1, 20–29.

Gameson, J., Rhydderch, G., Ellis, D. and Carroll, T. (2003a) 'Constructing a flexible model to integrate professional practice – Part 1: Conceptual and theoretical issues.' *Educational and Child Psychology 20*, 4, 96–108.

Gameson, J., Rhydderch, G., Ellis, D. and Carroll, T. (2003b) 'Constructing a flexible model to integrate professional practice – Part 2: Process and practice issues.' *Educational and Child Psychology 22*, 4, 41–55.

Glaser, R. (1984) 'Education and thinking: The role of knowledge.' *American Psychologist 39*, 2, 93–104.

Greeno, J.G., Collins, A.M. and Resnick, L.B. (1996) 'Cognition and Learning.' In D.C. Berliner and R.C. Calfee (eds) *Handbook of Educational Psychology.* MacMillan Library Reference. New York: Simon and Schuster MacMillan, Prentice Hall International.

Gutkin, T.B. and Curtis, M. (1982) 'School-based Consultation: Theory and Techniques.' In C.R. Reynolds and T. Gutkin (eds) *The Handbook of School Psychology.* New York: Wiley.

Halpern, D.F. (1998) 'Teaching critical thinking for transfer across domains.' *American Psychologist 53*, 4, 449–455.

Kelly, B. (2006) 'Exploring the usefulness of the Monsen problem-solving framework for applied practitioners.' *Educational Psychology in Practice 22*, 1, 1–17.

Kerr, C. and Smith, E. (2005) *An Evaluation of the Perceived Effectiveness of Problem Based Learning on the Dundee MSc Educational Psychology Training Programme.* Available at www.bps.org.uk/downloadfile.cfm?file_uuid=C49B7248-1143-DFD0-7E4D-280341529F54&text=pdf, accessed 4 July 2008.

Lane, D.A. and Corrie, S. (2006) *The Modern Scientist-Practitioner. A Guide to Practice in Psychology.* London: Routledge.

Lichtenberg, J.W. (1997) 'Expertise in counselling psychology: A concept in search of support.' *Educational Psychology Review 9*, 3, 221–238.

Miller, A. and Leyden, G. (1999) 'A coherent framework for the application of psychology in schools.' *British Educational Research Journal 25*, 3, 389–400.

Miller, A., Leyden, G., Steward-Evans, C. and Gammage, S. (1992) 'Applied psychologists as problem solvers: Devising a personal model.' *Educational Psychology in Practice 7*, 4, 227–236.

Monsen, J.J., Graham, B., Frederickson, N. and Cameron, S. (1998) 'Problem analysis and professional training in educational psychology: An accountable model of practice.' *Educational Psychology in Practice 13*, 4, 234–249.

Morton, J. and Frith, U. (1995) 'Causal Modelling: A Structural Approach to Developmental Psychopathology.' In D. Cilchette and D.J. Cohen (eds) *Developmental Psychopathology.* New York: Wiley..

Newell, A. and Simon, H.A. (1972) *Human Problem Solving.* Englewood Cliffs, NJ: Prentice-Hall.

Pearson, L. and Howarth, I.C. (1982) 'Training professional psychologists.' *Bulletin of the British Psychological Society 35*, 375–376.

Ranyard, R., Crozier, W.R. and Svenson, O. (1997) (eds) *Decision Making: Cognitive Models and Explanations.* London and New York: Routledge.

Robinson, V. (1987) 'A problem-analysis approach to decision-making and reporting for complex cases.' *Journal of the New Zealand Psychological Service Association 8*, 35–48.

Robinson, V. (1993) *Problem-Based Methodology: Research for the Improvement of Practice.* Oxford: Pergamon Press.

Robinson, V. and Halliday, J. (1987) 'A critique of the micro-skills approach to problem understanding.' *British Journal of Guidance and Counselling 15*, 2, 113–124.

Robinson, V.M.J. and Halliday, J. (1988) 'Relationship of counsellor reasoning and data collection to problem-analysis quality.' *British Journal of Guidance and Counselling 16*, 1, 50–62.

Rose, S. (1999) (ed.) *From Brains to Consciousness? Essays on the New Sciences of the Mind.* Harmondsworth: Penguin Books.

Schmuck, R.A., Runkel, P.J., Saturen, S.L., Martel, R.T. and Derr, C.B. (1972) *Handbook of Organisational Development in Schools.* Palo Alto, CA: National Press Books.

Schraagen, J.M. (1993) 'How experts solve a novel problem in experimental design.' *Cognitive Science 17*, 285–309.

Schwartz, P., Mennin, S. and Webb, G. (eds) (2001) *Problem Based Learning: Case Studies, Experience and Practice.* London: Kogan Page.

Shin, N., Jonassen, D.H., and McGee, S. (2003) 'Predictors of well-structured and ill-structured problem solving in an astronomy simulation.' *Journal of Research in Science Teaching 40*, 1, 6–33.

Sigston, A. (1992) 'Making a Difference for Children: The Educational Psychologist as Empowerer of Problem-solving Alliances.' In S. Wolfendale, T. Bryans, M. Fox, A. Labram and A. Sigston (eds) *The Profession and Practice of Educational Psychology.* London: Cassell Education.

Simon, H.A. (1978) *The Sciences of the Artificial* (2nd edn). Cambridge, MA: MIT Press.

Thacker, J. (1982) *Steps to Success: An Interpersonal Problem Solving Approach for Children.* Windsor: NFER-Nelson.

Van Berkel, J.M. and Schmidt, H.G. (2000) 'Motivation to commit oneself as a determinant of achievement in problem-based learning.' *Higher Education 40*, 231–242.

Wenger, J.L. and Carlson, A. (1995) 'Learning and the coordination of sequential information.' *Journal of Experimental Psychology 21*, 1, 170–182.

Wilden, S. and La Gro, N. (1998) 'New frameworks for careers guidance: Developing a conceptual model of the interview.' *British Journal of Guidance and Counselling 26*, 2, 175–193.

Wiley, J. (1998) 'Expertise as mental set: The effects of domain knowledge in creative problem solving.' *Memory and Cognition 26*, 4, 716–730.

Woolfson, L., Whaling, R., Stewart, A. and Monsen, J.J. (2003) 'An integrated framework to guide educational psychologist practice.' *Educational Psychology in Practice 19*, 4, 283–302.

Appendix to Chapter 4

The New, Re-worked, Six-phased 'Problem-Analysis' Cycle

Phase One: Background information, role and expectations

The first phase involves clarifying the request and checking out the need for a trainee's[2] involvement. Clarification is generally sought from the person(s) who identified the problem in the first place (the 'problem-owner'/client). The trainee will be seeking to discover what the issues are and what the problem-owner hopes to achieve by consulting with him or her (and his or her supervising psychologist). Part of this initial discussion will involve ascertaining whether a referral to, or the involvement of other agencies/practitioners is required, given the nature of the initial concerns expressed.

If a psychological perspective *is* warranted it is important for the trainee to negotiate a clear understanding with the client about what the scope of his or her involvement will be (e.g. what his or her role, brief and purpose are – *negotiate and contract a clear starting role*). Such a tacit contract details those aspects of the problem situation that will initially be focused on, along with tentative working performance targets. In each case explicit rationales are provided. The trainee needs to give a clear indication of the scope and parameters of the investigative process, including how the problem-owner (and others) will be included, their role and how information will reported back to them and intervention plans negotiated, monitored and reviewed.

The request is usually negotiated with the problem-owner, who, in most situations, will be the person(s) with a vested interest in solving the problem (e.g. a class teacher, a year tutor or a parent/care-giver). A common mistake during this phase is to negotiate a brief solely with a person who is strategically distant from the problem situation (e.g. Head Teacher, departmental head or SENCo). After discussions with the problem-owner, the request is either accepted in the same (or modified) form, or referred back. This then becomes the joint working brief.

---

[2] The term 'trainee' has been used in this secton, however the material is equally applicable to practising psychologists.

Phase Two: Initial guiding hypotheses
Part 1: Initial guiding hypotheses
On the basis of the information so far collected via an initial client interview, the trainee begins to generate tentative initial guiding hypotheses that will help focus and direct subsequent investigations and collection of information. Initial guiding hypotheses are formulated with direct reference to the unique details of the presenting problem situation – to the theoretical, research and applied knowledge base within the discipline of psychology. Initial guiding hypotheses are framed as 'If so, then what' propositions.

While the initial guiding hypotheses define manageable sub-problems that are likely to be relevant, a holistic overview of the problem situation is maintained through the development of a 'problem map' in the form of an Interactive Factors Framework (IFF) (see Figure 4.3). All the initial guiding hypotheses are represented with arrows linking hypothesised cognitive and affective influencing factors with tentatively recorded behavioural-level specific descriptions of pupil behaviour and with information about biological, school and home-based factors (e.g. obtained from the initial teacher and parent/care-giver interviews, records and other professionals). Over the course of the Problem-Analysis cycle the IFF will be altered many times as new information is identified and processed conceptually. It is useful to represent 'strengths' (both within individuals and their environments) on the IFF as this information can assist in ruling out some hypotheses, generating new ones and providing any insights into what interventions might be effective in later phases.

Part 2: Active investigation (data collection and assessment)
Having formulated a range of within child and broader eco-systemic initial guiding hypotheses about what could be going on to perpetuate difficulties and how improvements might be effected, the trainee is now in a position to systematically investigate these various lines of inquiry (i.e. to collect information that may support or dis-confirm these initial guiding hypotheses). The trainee can draw on the full range of direct and indirect assessment techniques at his or her disposal. In seeking to 'triangulate' key conclusions it is important that confirmatory information is sampled from more than one source and that a sound (reliable, valid, culturally appropriate) range of investigatory approaches has been drawn upon.[3]

---

3   The Strategy of *triangulation* is used within Problem-Anasysis as a form of cross-checking. For example, once an initial guiding hypothesis has been confirmed by two or more independent investigatory proccess its likely 'validity' is greatly increased. The triangulations approach used within Problem-Analysis has been criticised as evidence of naïve realism. It is acknowledged that the method produces just one of the many possible constructions of the problem situation, and assumes that data collected from different sources using different methods can be regarded as equivalent in terms of teir ability to address hypotheses in the form of propositions. Nonetheless triangulation makes possible a richer and more complex investigation of complex real-world problem situations.

APPENDIX TO CHAPTER 4

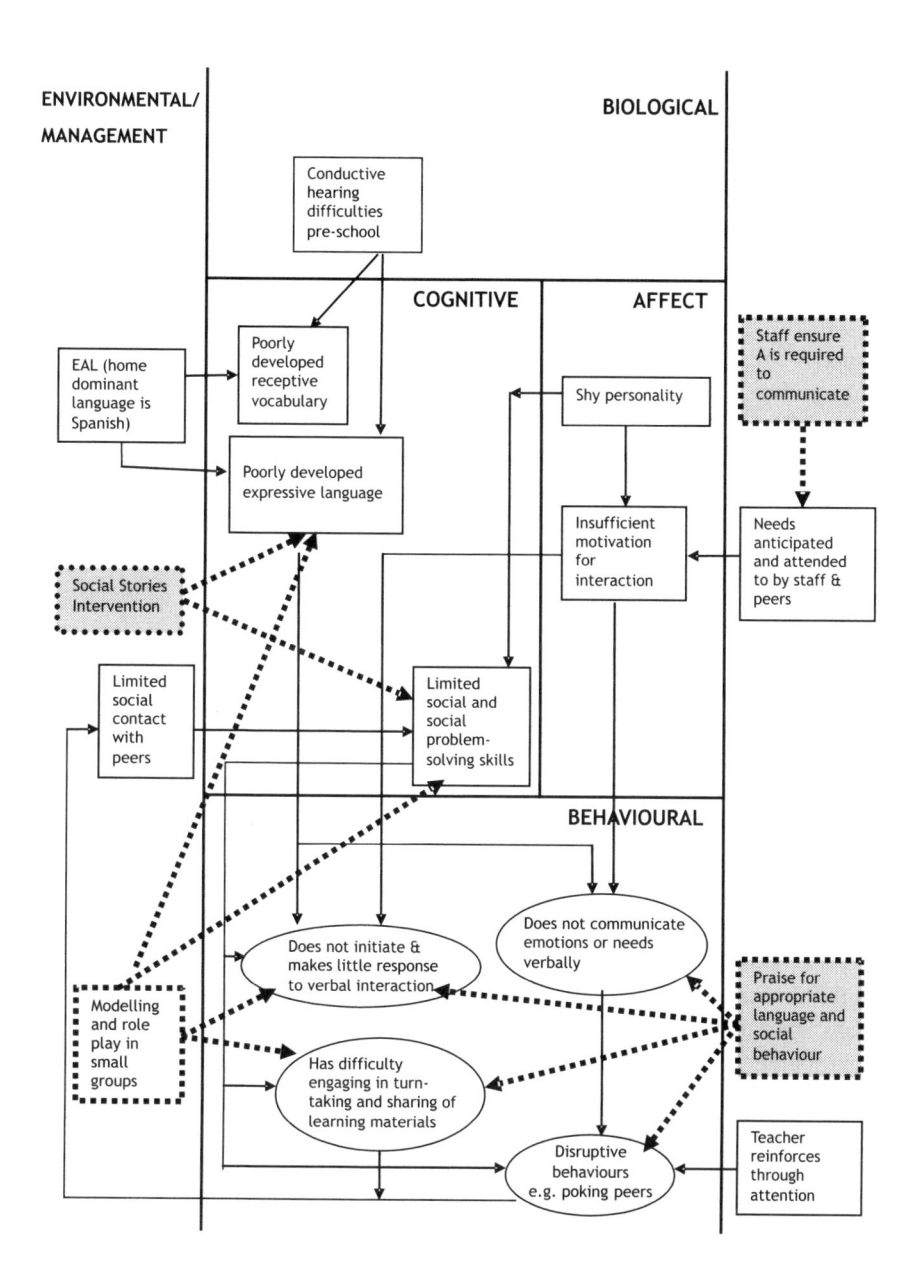

Figure 4.3: Interactive Factors Framework diagram for A, aged six years, whose teacher consulted an EP on account of 'Difficulty initiating and sustaining verbal interaction with adults and peers in a range of social situations'

Phase Three: Identified problem dimensions

On the basis of the investigations undertaken as part of Phase Two the trainee sorts and combines the information obtained to identify at a conceptual level what aspects in the problem situation are currently problematic. These conceptual categories are called 'problem dimensions'. Each problem dimension is given a clear and unambiguous title or label. The main dimensions isolated need to cover the key conceptual areas of the problem situation for which there is triangulated evidence and be linked (e.g. same titles or labels are used) throughout the written or oral presentation.

A critical task here for the trainee is to make sure that all relevant problem dimensions are covered and that supporting information is presented for all dimensions (i.e. a mini integration is provided that clearly argues why a given area is 'problematic'). Specific supporting information, such as test results and interviews, can be located in the Appendices in the form of tables or summaries. It is important to note that dimensions are presented in terms of *behaviours* (e.g. limited self-correction skills) and/or relevant *constructs* (e.g. limited impulse control) not by the assessment devices used (e.g. Neale Analysis of Reading Ability) or by un-integrated data (e.g. child's views or parent's/care-giver's views).

Phase Four: Integrated conceptualisation
Part 1: Integrating statement

The main task during this phase is to formulate an over-arching integrating statement that argues for possible interconnections, influences and 'causal relationships' between problem dimensions and priorities for action that will inform intervention planning. The integrating hypothesis(ses) chosen are based on logic and sound research and must help make sense of the information collected and lead to a clear rationale for subsequent intervention recommendations and actions.

The second task is for the trainee to give reasons for the selection of one or more of the dimensions as being a priority for intervention rather than targeting all dimensions. Some dimensions may be selected as priorities because they are hypothesised as contributing to others or it may be predicted that by focusing on x dimension(s) changes in the other problem areas are likely. Dimensions may also be prioritised because they require immediate intervention (e.g. child abuse, teacher or child socio-emotional issues), or because they are the only accessible dimensions.

In undertaking this conceptual task the trainee must be mindful that the integrating or linking hypothesis(ses) are consistent with the evidence presented in previous phases and that his or her reasoning is clear and coherent (e.g. why have selected dimensions been chosen as priorities or, equally, why have all dimensions been selected?). Whilst constructing his or her statement other plausible alternative conceptualisations need to be evaluated for 'goodness of fit' and, if discounted, reasons given. It is important also that arguments are supported with reference to sound contemporary research.

Part 2: Interactive Factors Framework diagram
In this phase a coherent working version of the IFF is completed. The IFF displays all of the problem dimensions identified, together with other relevant aspects of the problem situation for which there is evidence. The integrating hypothesis(ses) will be shown via arrows indicating the connections between the Behavioural, Cognitive, Affective, Environmental and Biological level variables as argued in the integrating statement. As can be seen from the dotted lines in Figure 4.3, the IFF diagram also presents the recommended intervention(s) – again using arrows to clearly indicate *how* intervention strategies are predicted to impact upon the priority problem dimensions.

Influences between problem dimensions (and other elements) in the IFF diagram are sometimes mutual, leading to vicious or virtuous cycles. Where this is thought to be happening the factors concerned can be connected by double-headed arrows representing bi-directional interactions. In these cases, a decision may be taken at Phase Five to change whichever of the two factors is easiest to alter. However, in most cases one of the factors will be conceptualised as exerting a stronger influence on the other and a uni-directional arrow should be used for conceptual clarity.

Phase Five: Intervention plan and implementation
Agreed action plan, feedback and agree problem-analysis and devise intervention plan
During this phase the trainee uses his or her 'working' conceptualisation of the problem situation (Phase Four) and the reasons for the intervention approach(es) being considered in the form of a menu with which to negotiate and agree a 'final' action plan with the problem-owner(s). An important skill for the trainee is to be able to detach from his or her working conceptualisation so that he or she can actively listen to the problem-owner in order that valid new perspectives and insights can be integrated into plans. One of the trainee's roles is to act as a 'critical friend' to the problem-owner in carefully critiquing arguments for or against particular courses of action and locating them firmly back in the agreed logic of the working conceptualisation. Such a process encourages ownership and increases the likelihood of implementation of any intervention. During this 'critical dialogue' it is vital that the problem-owner considers the manageability of any proposed plan, as well as the detail of monitoring arrangements (both internal and external).

An outcome of Phase Five is that the integrating statement and IFF are reviewed and revised as necessary, with the final intervention plan being developed in active consultation with those directly involved in the situation: teachers, care-givers and children/young people. This said, interventions must also be consistent with the agreed core principles outlined in the integration statement, efficacy evidence, psychological theory and research, logic and/or best practice guidance, with the rationale for the intervention being made explicit to all parties. Once an intervention has been agreed, the trainee guides the discussion towards the details of implementation: the who, what, when, where, and procedures for recording, monitoring and evaluating. It is important to check out, rather than assume, that those involved have the skills and key resources needed to implement the intervention successfully, and that they are realistic about the commitment of time and effort involved. Periodic contact with the trainee – for example, by telephone, text, or email – can provide access to advice and support and increase the likelihood of intervention implementation.

Phase Six: Monitoring and evaluation of outcomes

This phase involves a joint evaluation with all those who have been involved in trying to improve the problem situation. The participants evaluate the status of the problem following their efforts. (This may involve consideration of the on-going records being kept by teachers/care-givers and/or pupils themselves or it may involve further data collection, such as a post-intervention reading test or behaviour-monitoring checklists to allow pre- and post-intervention comparisons.) The participants decide whether satisfactory progress is apparent in relation to the evaluation criteria set in Phase Five and consider further actions that may be needed (from further investigations to regular reviews of progress). If progress is judged to be satisfactory, maintenance procedures may be identified to ensure that the problem situation does not recur and systemic implications of what has been learnt that may be relevant to other similar problems in the future discussed.

Reflective commentary

Trainees are asked to critically reflect on their involvement in considering how effective they were at each of the phases in the Problem-Analysis cycle. Specific performance criteria for each phase have been developed, based upon earlier work by Robinson (1987) to guide this process. For example, trainees are asked to consider the following when judging Problem-Analysis quality:

- At Phase Three – Were the problem dimensions accurate, complete and clear?

- At Phase Four – Did the integrating statement make clear the relative importance of the problem dimensions, and the 'causes' of the priority problem?

- At Phase Five – Were the intervention plans specific, appropriate and complete?

- At Phase Six – Did the criteria for evaluation enable clear pre- and post-intervention comparison and make use of both qualitative and quantitative information?

Trainees are also encouraged to identify factors across phases that supported or constrained their functioning (e.g. 'I did not listen carefully enough at Phase One but pursued my own agenda and ended up negotiating a brief and subsequent actions that were vague, ill-focused and which were not judged at Phase Five to have actually assisted the problem-owner'). Emphasis is also placed on tutor and/or peer consultation to provide a 'critical friend' perspective, not only on the efficacy of the actual intervention negotiated and implemented, but also on trainee performance and quality of analysis (e.g. from listening to or viewing interview tapes, reviewing the logic and clarity of written and oral work and from feedback from the problem-owner, parents/care-givers, pupils, supervisor, tutor, other trainees and so on).

CHAPTER 5

The Constructionist Model of Informed and Reasoned Action (COMOIRA)

John Gameson and Gillian Rhydderch

Introduction

In this chapter we will be:

- introducing and describing the structure and basic processes underpinning the Constructionist Model of Informed and Reasoned Action (COMOIRA)
- explaining some background and contextual issues relating to the construction of COMOIRA
- summarising the core principles, concepts and theories that underpin all aspects of COMOIRA and describing the main functions, processes and practice issues relating to its core
- describing the main functions, processes and practice issues relating to the eight key decision points
- providing a brief overview of the variety of ways in which COMOIRA has been used; and
- exploring some of the perceived strengths, potential benefits, potential weaknesses and challenges of COMOIRA for trainees, educational psychologists (EPs) working in the field, training programmes for EPs and other practitioners who choose to use the model in practice or in training.

Within the context of this relatively short chapter, it will not be possible to cover all of the issues listed above in depth or to provide a comprehensive 'user guide'. Readers who are interested in a more detailed exploration of COMOIRA and the issues associated with it might wish to read this chapter in conjunction with three other publications (Gameson *et al.* 2003; Gameson *et al.* 2005; Rhydderch and Gameson in preparation). Those publications address, in more depth, some conceptual and theoretical issues underpinning the model, some process and practice issues relating to the model, and some illustrations of the model in use.

The structure and basic processes underpinning COMOIRA

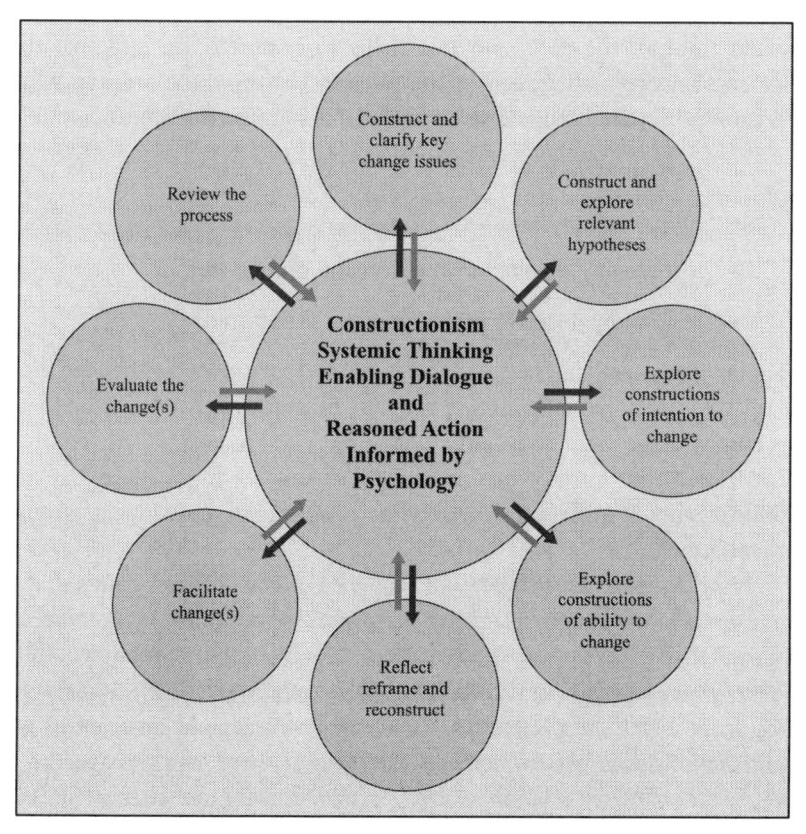

Figure 5.1: Visual representation of COMOIRA (first published in Gameson et al. 2003)

In Figure 5.1 you will see in visual form the main structure of COMOIRA, which comprises a 'core' set of principles, concepts and theories and eight key decision points – each of which has a specific set of functions that the authors consider to be helpful when working with people to promote change. The core and all the key decision points are supported by a series of reflective and reflexive questions (Gameson *et al.* 2003), which are designed to help all relevant people think carefully about complex process issues associated with change. Those questions encourage practitioners to be reflective and reflexive by using psychology explicitly to 'make sense of' and guide:

- their own behaviours, as well as the behaviours of other people involved in the process (e.g. service users or other practitioners)
- their own practice; and
- the process of change itself.

The arrows in Figure 5.1 indicate that movement between key decision points is always through the core, and this helps to reinforce the idea that the core elements underpin all aspects of the process. However, the order in which key decision points are used is essentially flexible because the sequence can:

- start anywhere
- follow any path
- include any number of key decision points; and/or
- repeat key decision points as often as required.

Flexibility is essential because it enables people to choose how they use the model in relation to a potentially infinite diversity of issues and needs within their local, specific, unique and constantly changing circumstances. The flexibility of COMOIRA also ensures that the model is suitable for work across different contexts and at different levels with a variety of individuals, groups and organisations.

It follows that the number and sequence of key decision points that people choose to use will vary in relation to their specific needs and circumstances. It also follows that there are no prescribed or absolute right/wrong, good/bad or better/worse ways to use COMOIRA. The extent to which the model is considered to be helpful and effective at any time will depend on relevant people's constructions of how far it helped them make sense of, and manage, the chosen process of change in relation to their particular needs and circumstances.

At one level, the model is intended to provide individuals, groups and organisations with a coherent structure and a clear set of inter-related functions and processes to guide what people think about 'issues' and what they choose to do to promote change(s). However, COMOIRA is in fact more than a set of procedures, signposts or decision points as the 'core' aims to ensure that people remain alert to the many different theories, as well as the rationale and/or 'evidence', underpinning the process at any given time. In addition, the model promotes iterative or recursive processes similar to those underpinning action research (Forward 1989) except that COMOIRA is more flexible because its processes are not necessarily linear or directional – although they can be, if required.

Furthermore, COMOIRA focuses explicitly on the process and language of change and, within this context, attempts to integrate concepts such as 'identification' and 'treatment' (Wedell 1970), 'assessment' and 'intervention' (DECP 1998 and 1999) plus 'problem definition', 'problem clarification' and 'solutions' (Miller *et al.* 1992), which are all re-framed and reconstructed within COMOIRA as aspects of the change process. This idea of focusing directly on the process and language of change is consistent with approaches developed by Burden (1997), Carr (2004), O'Hanlon (2006) and Prochaska (1999, cited in Carr 2004). It makes sense to focus directly and explicitly on the language and concepts of change because there are likely to be reciprocal influences between the ways in which people choose to construct and talk about issues and what they assume and/or expect should be done about those issues.

It is helpful to think of COMOIRA as a heuristic, rather than an algorithmic set of procedures for solving problems. The term 'heuristic' is associated with encouraging and enabling people to discover solutions to problems for themselves. This is consistent with the idea of using and adapting a flexible, iterative process of trial and error rather than a set of rules. The Oxford Reference Online defines the term 'heuristic' as:

> A rough-and-ready procedure or rule of thumb for making a decision, forming a judgement, or solving a problem without the application of an algorithm or an exhaustive comparison of all available options, and hence without any guarantee of obtaining a correct or optimal result. (Oxford Reference Online 2007)

By contrast, an algorithm usually involves a sequential, routine, prescriptive and often repetitive set of instructions or basic operations, sometimes with branching pathways and a finite number of steps for solving problems (Oxford Reference Online 2007). Unlike algorithms, heuristics cannot have proven procedures that promise success because they are flexible, open-ended and responsive to unpredictable and changing situations. Heuristic approaches are, therefore, likely to be more helpful than prescribed algorithmic procedures when working with people in their local, specific, unique and unpredictable social contexts and psychological territory (Gillham 1999).

Background and contextual issues

The foundations for COMOIRA were laid in the late 1990s within the context of the MSc Professional Training Programme for educational psychologists at Cardiff University. At that time, members of the programme team were becoming increasingly interested in encouraging trainees to understand and explore the complex and important conceptual, theoretical and process issues associated with professional practice, particularly those associated with promoting and managing change. Until that time, trainees at Cardiff (and previously at Swansea) were expected to use 'The Iterative Model of Fieldwork Enquiry' to inform their fieldwork. That model had been adopted as a consequence of the British Psychological Society's (BPS's) expectation that training programmes for EPs should encourage trainees to use sequential problem-solving models and systematic, hypothesis-testing approaches to inform and guide their professional practice. Trainees were also expected to write process accounts on selected pieces of work which demonstrated that they had:

- engaged in on-going, in-depth work over time
- used the sequential stages of the model to inform the process in which they had engaged
- explored relevant problems and facilitated appropriate solutions
- monitored and evaluated outcomes
- applied psychological and other relevant theories to the work they had done
- reflected on the process and their role within it and had considered the critical/salient aspects of learning which had emerged for them; and
- identified what they might have done differently with hindsight.

The Iterative Model of Fieldwork Enquiry was fundamentally a sequential, problem-solving model and was influenced by the approach to training educational psychologists used at Exeter University (Phillips 1987) and also by Herbert (1987) and other problem-solving approaches that emerged during the late 1980s and early 1990s (Miller *et al.* 1992).

Also at that time, the programme team at Cardiff was interested in numerous tensions relating to the ways in which trainees seemed to be constructing their own roles and needs, the roles and needs of EPs in local authority settings, the role of the profession, and the role of the training programme. These gave rise to the following observations.

- Trainees often seemed to experience a mismatch between what they were expected to do in order to meet the requirements of the university-based training programme and what they thought their fieldwork supervisors expected of them in their placement locations.

- As the amount of time spent on fieldwork placements increased, some trainees seemed to develop the view that university-based expectations and requirements appeared to become less relevant to their needs within the context of their fieldwork placements, and increasingly irrelevant to the everyday work of EPs in the 'real world'.

- Some trainees appeared to expect the training programme to provide them with a collection of discrete practical techniques that they could use in the field. During their fieldwork activities, they frequently used specific approaches or interventions (e.g. Social Skills Training, Anger Management or Circle Time) that were predetermined at the start of those pieces of fieldwork without careful exploration of needs and contextual issues.

- On the whole, fieldwork supervisors seemed keen to enable trainees to engage in on-going, in-depth work that focused on the explicit application of psychology to promoting, monitoring and evaluating change. Many fieldwork supervisors reported that they wanted to work in such ways themselves but they often felt constrained by established procedures (e.g. the statutory assessment process) and the expectations of their service users (e.g. local authorities, schools and parents). Consequently, they generally engaged 'reluctantly' in short-term, expedient work, which appeared to be driven by pragmatic and/or administrative processes and which seemed to have little to do with the explicit application of psychology or with engaging people in change. However, this work was often valued by local authorities, schools and parents and was partly maintained in some services by evaluation criteria that emphasised the need for EPs to cover a large number of 'cases'. Some fieldwork supervisors considered that such approaches did little to reinforce the unique contributions that EPs could make as applied psychologists because much of that work could probably be carried out by other professionals (e.g. advisory teachers, classroom assistants and administrators).

- The Iterative Model of Fieldwork Enquiry and other problem-solving models seemed to be limited by their linear, algorithmic, sequential 'procedures', which did not promote the explicit application of psychology and were not themselves informed explicitly by psychological theories.

- During recent decades, the practice of EPs in local-authority contexts appears to have been dominated by fashionable, sometimes polarised or competing approaches and techniques. For example, during the 1980s behavioural psychology seemed to be most popular as a means of understanding and managing behaviour. More recently, numerous other specific trends have emerged: for example,

  - Models of Consultation (Wagner 2000; Watkins 2000)
  - Solution-Focused/Oriented Approaches (Lines 2002; Rhodes and Ajmal 1995)
  - Circle Time (Lown 2002)
  - Circle of Friends (Frederickson, Warren and Turner 2005)
  - Social Skills Training (Denham *et al.* 2006), and
  - Cognitive Behaviour Therapy (Westbrook, Kennerley and Kirk 2007).

The authors came to believe that encouraging trainees to use COMOIRA would help to address some of the tensions outlined above, and would prepare them for entry into the profession in ways that challenge the status quo, promote innovative and creative approaches to professional practice, and consolidate and expand the unique role of the EP as an applied psychologist.

Ideas from the core of COMOIRA: Theories, functions, processes and practice issues

Social Constructionism, Systemic Thinking, Enabling Dialogue and Informed and Reasoned Action are placed at the core of COMOIRA because they underpin and influence all aspects of the process, including what and how people think about issues and what they choose to do at each of the key decision points. It is extremely unlikely that practitioners can engage in any activities that are not influenced by one or more of the core principles, concepts and theories. These are therefore fundamental to COMOIRA because they cannot be avoided. Gameson *et al.* (2003, 2005) have addressed these issues in more detail but some selective aspects are discussed briefly below.

Social Constructionism

This is an essential feature of COMOIRA because it has major implications for all aspects of professional practice. As described earlier in this book, this theoretical approach holds that all knowledge and views of the world are socially constructed through language within cultural and historical contexts (Burr 2003). This 'view of events' asserts that it is simply not possible to identify objective facts, truths and realities because all knowledge and views of the world are subjective and phenomenological. 'All knowledge is derived from looking at the world from some perspective or other, and is in the service of some interests rather than others' (Burr 2003, p.6). It follows that individuals, groups, organisations and societies are likely to construct many different, sometimes conflicting, but equally convincing 'truths' and 'realities' – all of which might be accepted as appropriate, relevant and valid within their own cultural contexts. However, some might acquire a privileged status and come to be accepted as the best, correct or most appropriate versions of events, sometimes to the extent that they devalue others. For example, positivist, empiricist discourses have tended to dominate constructions of evidence-based practice (Nieboer, Moss and Partridge 2000).

Social Constructionism emphasises that different theoretical approaches simply provide different frames of reference or conceptual frameworks that lead to different constructions of practice, all of which are supported and validated by their own 'persuasive' or 'convincing' discourses. Consequently, all knowledge, evidence and models of practice (including COMOIRA), no matter how convincing, rigorous and scientific they appear, are socially constructed and supported by powerful discourses and rhetorical devices (Gergen 1999). These ideas clearly have significant implications for the 'privileged' concept of 'evidence-based' practice that espouses universal and generalisable facts, truths and realities. They imply that outcomes should be carefully monitored and rigorously evaluated in relation to the local, specific, unique and changing contexts in which people work together to facilitate change(s). In order to avoid the danger of charlatanism, practitioners obviously do need to substantiate and verify their approaches to professional practice. However, the concept of 'evidence' clearly needs to be treated with considerable caution and it might be helpful to reconstruct 'evidence-based' practice as 'informed and reasoned' practice. The latter seems to be a more inclusive concept.

Some selected implications of Social Constructionism for professional practice are considered below.

- Different practitioners and service users are likely to construct their own 'convincing' and 'powerful' versions of events, which they might consider to be more accurate and more appropriate than those of other people.

- When people convince themselves that their versions of events are the most appropriate, they are likely to find it difficult to accept that other people might have constructed different truths and realities which, to them, are equally powerful and convincing.
- The powerful and convincing truths and realities that people construct will have implications for the process of change and might become strong obstacles to change.
- Social Constructionism implies that practitioners need to focus on engaging with individuals, groups and organisations in ways that help all relevant people to accept, validate, explore and make sense of one another's unique constructions of events.
- Change issues, ways of working together at the different decision points and the effectiveness or relative value of outcomes will all need to be constructed jointly between practitioners and service users within their unique, phenomenological contexts.
- 'Evidence' might mean different things within different discourses or constructions and relevant people will need to work closely together to construct and jointly agree what worked for them, at that time and in that context.
- The extent of knowledge and the nature of evidence used to promote certain approaches (for example, Cognitive Behaviour Therapy) are what happen to be available at any given time. Both are subject to a dynamic process of change.

Systemic Thinking

This is informed by Systems Theory and is included within the core of COMOIRA for the following main reasons.

- People are themselves complex organisms/systems who live and work within complex systemic contexts (e.g. families, schools and psychology services).
- Systemic Thinking asserts that it is unhelpful and artificial to adopt reductionist approaches because there are unavoidable, complex and reciprocal interactions between systems and subsystems relating to individuals, groups and organisations.
- It is helpful to maintain a holistic frame of reference and a systemic approach that takes account of complex systems and subsystems:

- intrapersonal (e.g. people's theories, beliefs, mindsets and psycho-biological factors)
- interpersonal (e.g. roles, positions, relationships and methods of communication); and/or
- contextual/organisational (e.g. policies, procedures, methods of service delivery, politics and codes of conduct).

- There are circular patterns of relationships or influences between different aspects of systems and subsystems. For example, the way in which an EP decides to respond to a request for help from a service user is likely to influence how that service user behaves, and vice versa. Practitioners need to remain alert to these interactionist principles in order to monitor and manage the unavoidable impact that they have on others, and also to avoid deluding themselves into believing that they can be 'objective' or 'detached'.

- Systemic approaches and Systemic Thinking should not be confused with approaches that focus only on systematic work with groups and organisations. Systemic approaches need to be informed and guided by ideas and key concepts from Systems Theory (Frederickson 1990a). These might include, for example:

  - hard and soft systems
  - open and closed systems
  - boundaries and levels of engagement
  - punctuation, or the ways in which people choose to frame issues and information
  - equifinality, or the idea of getting to the same point by different routes
  - circular relationships and feedback loops
  - homeostasis or equilibrium; and
  - symptomatic and fundamental solutions.

  Further information about these and other aspects of systems theory are described by Campbell, Coldicott and Kinsella (1994) and Dowling and Osborne (1994).

- Systemic Thinking aims to promote lasting strategic change(s) as opposed to reactive, symptomatic change(s) or 'quick fixes'.

Enabling Dialogue

This is a term devised by Gameson *et al.* (2003). It is included as an important core concept because all professional practice takes place within interactive social contexts, and the impact of professional practice depends to a large extent on the nature and quality of relationships between key people. The fundamental importance of this idea is illustrated by the following assumptions/assertions.

- The nature and quality of outcomes will be influenced by the nature and quality of relationships between the practitioner, the service user(s) and other key people (Green 1996, 2006).

- Positive partnerships and collaborative or joint working will have a beneficial influence on the process and the outcomes.

- It is important to ensure that all relevant people give informed consent to engage voluntarily in positive partnerships, and, in order to do so, they will need to know as much as possible about other relevant people's roles and the process to be followed.

- Positive outcomes and long-term changes are more likely to occur when relevant people feel engaged, empowered and enabled to make sense of and to manage their own change issues.

- Positive partnerships, engagement and empowerment aim to promote self-efficacy, confidence and independence, as opposed to dependence.

- It is important for all relevant people to maintain appropriate relationships and boundaries so that each can decide what to take from the collaborative work and can retain full ownership of what to do next.

These ideas are not original and many practitioners will recognise the influence of Glasser (1999), Miller and Rollnick (2002) and Rogers (1957) – all of whom emphasise the central importance of 'people factors', especially people's perceptions of the nature and quality of relationships between practitioners and service users. However, few models or frameworks for practice seem to make explicit reference to these essential factors.

Informed and Reasoned Action

This is included as an essential aspect of the core for the following reasons.

- All practice-based decisions are influenced by theoretical and philosophical assumptions or perspectives, even when these are not made explicit and may not even be consciously considered by the person(s) making the decisions. It is simply not possible to avoid the influence of theoretical and philosophical assumptions (Bigge and Shermis 1992).

- It follows that all practice-based decisions are likely to vary in relation to the particular theoretical and philosophical positions that have been chosen, intentionally or otherwise, at any given time. For example, Attachment Theory (Bowlby 1988), Choice Theory (Glasser 1999) and Systems Theory (Campbell *et al.* 1994) are each likely to generate different responses and choices of action.

- As applied psychologists, EPs have a duty to choose very carefully and to make explicit the theories and the rationale (including 'evidence') they are using to make sense of issues and to promote and manage change. This is particularly important when EPs are being challenged to demonstrate that they have unique and valuable psychological contributions to make across the education community.

- Within the context of COMOIRA it would not be helpful to judge different theories, philosophies and rationales as being good/bad, right/wrong or better/worse in any absolute sense. Rather, it would be important to accept that they might all be valid and helpful but that their relative value will depend on how people perceive or construct them within their unique phenomenological circumstances or contexts.

- This aspect of COMOIRA is intended to maintain people's awareness of the complexity of choices, the importance of choosing carefully and the need to make the application of psychology explicit.

The authors take the view that trainee EPs, other professionals and service users cannot escape the impact of core concepts and theories. Gameson *et al.* (2005) have discussed some practical implications of the many different theories, models and belief systems that might influence people's practice decisions.

Main functions of the core

The core principles, concepts and theories have two main sets of functions. First, they can be used to make sense of what is going on and the ways in which people are choosing to think, feel and act within their local, specific and unique contexts. Second, they can be used to guide how people choose to engage with one another; how they think about issues; what they choose to do at any given time; and what process they choose to follow to address their 'issues'. The two sets of functions are inter-related and clearly have major implications for practice decisions. Some examples of relevant questions and issues are suggested below, all of which apply to the EP/practitioner as well as to service users.

- How are relevant people choosing to construct their views of events and what are the implications of their constructed truths and realities for the role of the EP or other practitioner, and for engaging relevant people in the process of change? What discourses are they choosing to use and what impact do these appear to have? Are they empowering or disempowering people? For example, models associated with identifying conditions such as Attention Deficit Hyperactivity Disorder and Oppositional Defiant Disorder might cause teachers, parents and pupils to feel disabled and disempowered if they believe that change will not be possible or that specialist expertise is required to understand and manage these 'disorders'.

- What other constructions of the same issues might be possible or relevant and what would be the likely implications of these? What other discourses might be more helpful and empowering? What can the EP/practitioner do to construct jointly with relevant people some alternative discourses (shared ways of thinking and talking) that might set the scene for appropriate change(s)? People are more likely to work together to change, and to maintain those changes, when their actions are based on shared views of events.

- What systems, subsystems and contextual issues (these might include intrapersonal, interpersonal and organisational systems or subsystems) seem to be particularly relevant to these people in this specific and unique situation? What concepts and processes from Systems Theory will be helpful in making sense of the current situation/context and in deciding how to proceed? This aspect of COMOIRA reflects the principles underpinning the Interactive Factors Framework (see Frederickson and Cline 2002).

- Which individual people and/or groups are engaged at this stage in the process? At what level are they engaged? What is the nature of the relationships between relevant people and between relevant people and the EP/practitioner? Which other people (individuals or groups) would it be helpful for the EP/practitioner to engage with at this stage in the process and at what level? What does the EP/practitioner need to do in order to facilitate collaborative relationships, engagement and Enabling Dialogue that will promote empowerment and set the scene for relevant people to make appropriate change(s)? Miller and Rollnick (2002) emphasise that real and lasting change often depends on the quality of relationships between practitioners and service users, which need to be harmonious or concordant rather than discordant or adversarial. Facilitating engagement might include, for example, using some of the fundamental relationship skills described by Rogers (1957). Effective collaboration might be enhanced if the EP/practitioner explains the model to all relevant people and negotiates/agrees how to use it in relation to their local, specific and unique circumstances/needs.

- What psychological and/or other theories or other rationale/evidence seem to be implied in the ways that relevant people are constructing their versions of events and the discourses they are choosing to use? What psychological and/or other theories or other rationale/evidence might the EP/practitioner use or find out about to help make sense of the current situation? What psychological and/or other theories or other rationale/evidence might the EP/practitioner share with relevant people in order to inform decisions about what to do next?

Main functions, processes and practice issues relating to the eight key decision points

COMOIRA is based on the idea that some or all of the key decision points are likely to be relevant and helpful when working with people to facilitate desired change(s). They are designed to complement one another and to be used in conjunction with the core because they are all informed by the core. Movement between the decision points is always through the core, for reasons described above. Like the core, the eight key decision points also have two main inter-related sets of functions: namely, to help people make sense of what is going on; and to guide how people choose to work together to promote desired changes.

The main functions of each decision point are identified in text contained in relevant parts of the model shown in Figure 5.1 and these have been explored in more detail by Gameson et al. (2005). However, some selected functions of each point are considered briefly below. Although the decision points are presented, inevitably, in a sequential manner within this chapter, the order has been randomised to reinforce the idea that the model is flexible and the process can:

- start anywhere
- follow any path
- include any number of key decision points; and/or

- repeat key decision points as often as required.

Furthermore, although each key decision point is presented as a discrete stage in the model, the points are not mutually exclusive and there is likely to be some overlap between them. For example, a change issue may also be constructed as a hypothesis, and vice versa. The reflective/reflexive questions presented by Gameson *et al.* (2003) provide further insights into the functions of each point. Like the issues relating to the core, those relating to the key decision points apply to the EP/practitioner as well as to other people. Also, there are clearly many different practical approaches that people might choose to adapt and use in order to carry out the functions at each key decision point and at the core.

Reflect, re-frame and reconstruct
This prompts all relevant people to stop and think in order to:

- reflect carefully together on issues emerging from the four main aspects of the core as well as those emerging from the request for help and from other key decision points
- consider and explore jointly some possible alternative ways to re-frame and/or reconstruct these issues in order to promote the process of change; and
- consider together what needs to be done next and which part of the model might help to promote and maintain relevant and appropriate change(s).

Issues that emerge might include:

- people's constructions and discourses relating to the request for help
- assumptions and expectations about the positions and roles of all relevant people involved, especially in relation to ownership, empowerment and dependency
- relevant people's belief systems and hypotheses in relation to what is causing and maintaining the issues, as well as what action needs to be taken, when, how and by whom
- the construction of change issues
- theories and concepts underpinning what seems to be happening
- systems and subsystems considered to be relevant at the time

- what people think about the quality of relationships and levels of engagement
- what people think about the process so far
- who should implement the desired changes
- how those changes should be monitored and evaluated; and
- who should monitor and evaluate the changes.

These issues are likely to be relevant at every key decision point.

Review the process
This helps all relevant people to stop and think in order to:

- consider together what has happened and how the process has gone so far
- consider, and if necessary reconsider, relevant people's roles in the process so far
- take account of how COMOIRA has been used so far
- check what other options might be relevant at this point; and
- decide what needs to be done next and by whom in order to maintain the change process (for example, to decide whether to continue with the process by moving to another key decision point or to disengage – and if so, how).

Construct and explore relevant hypotheses
This enables all relevant people to explore together the belief systems, assumptions and expectations that are likely to impact on the process. These might include people's chosen constructions of factors believed to be causing and maintaining the issues of concern, as well as their beliefs about desired changes or outcomes. These are important because people's hypotheses about causes are likely to be related to what they believe needs to be done to bring about the desired change(s). If key people in the system have different, potentially competing, hypotheses it might be difficult to engage them in collaborative work to facilitate the desired change(s). COMOIRA is based on the assumption that it will be helpful to share and explore the implications of people's different hypotheses in order to jointly reconstruct and choose which ones to explore.

Evaluate the change(s)

This enables all relevant people to monitor and evaluate together the outcomes in relation to the desired or intended change(s). At this point, people need to consider:

- how to jointly construct and establish the criteria for success
- how to evaluate relevant people's constructions of success in relation to the desired or intended changes within their local, specific and unique contexts and in relation to the original request for help
- who will do what to monitor and evaluate the desired changes
- how far all relevant people have engaged in the process and changed what they agreed to change; and
- whether relevant people feel empowered to maintain and manage the desired or intended changes without over-dependence on the practitioner.

Explore constructions of intention to change

This helps all relevant people to explore together how far each:

- maintains ownership of relevant issues and processes
- intends to do something different in order to promote the chosen changes
- is ready and willing to change; and
- is committed to investing time and energy in making the desired or intended change(s).

The Theory of Planned Behaviour (Armitage and Connor 2001) suggests that intention to change is a strong predictor of actual behavioural change but, of course, this will need to be explored in relation to the specific people concerned and the context in which they find themselves.

Facilitate change(s)

This prompts all relevant people to decide together who will make the desired or intended changes. The main function of activities at this point is to facilitate changes in ways that empower and enable people to maintain and manage those changes independently. Clearly, a wide range of approaches might be relevant at the point, including, for example: Motivational Interviewing (Miller and Rollnick 2002), Cognitive Therapy (Leahy 2003), Solution-Oriented Work

(Selekman 1997) and Soft Systems methodology (Frederickson 1990b). These approaches may focus on facilitating change(s) with individuals, groups and/or organisations and might include considering, for example:

- aspects of school/classroom ethos
- approaches used to motivate/engage pupils and staff
- the school/classroom behaviour-management plan
- school/classroom rules/expectations
- procedures for communicating about and dealing with problems
- procedures for communicating with parents
- the use of support services
- teaching methods and the delivery of the curriculum
- adults' and other children's perceptions of the issue and the language/discourses they choose to use to think/talk about it
- the knowledge and skills of the adults and other children and the ways in which these are used
- the child's own perceptions of the issue and the language/discourses s/he chooses to use to think/talk about it; and
- the knowledge and skills of the child concerned and the ways s/he uses these.

Explore constructions of ability to change
This enables all relevant people to explore together how far they and others:

- consider they have the skills required to make the desired or intended changes
- feel they have the right to make those changes; and
- feel confident in their ability to make and maintain those changes.

Construct and clarify key change issues
This helps all relevant people to explore together how people are choosing to construct:

- exactly what they would like to be different;
- who they think should make those changes; and

- when, where and how they should make the change(s).

One important aim is to share and explore together the different change issues that key people have constructed. If, for example, key people have constructed conflicting or competing change issues it is likely that they will have different, potentially conflicting ideas about the desired or intended changes – as well as about who should do what to make the changes. Unless key people can jointly construct, clarify and agree relevant change issues, they will probably continue to pull in different directions, with little understanding of one another's perspectives. In such a situation it may be difficult to facilitate appropriate changes (Gameson *et al.* 2005). Reaching consensus and /or enabling people to clarify or modify their views will probably constitute important aspects of the change process.

Ways in which COMOIRA has been used

Many trainees at Cardiff have used COMOIRA very effectively to guide a wide range of collaborative fieldwork activities in relation to work with individuals and groups. These activities have covered a variety of issues, including concerns about learning as well as concerns about social, emotional and behavioural issues. The authors of this chapter also use COMOIRA to guide their own generic fieldwork activities with individuals, groups and organisations within their respective psychology services.

Although COMOIRA was first developed as a learning model for trainee EPs, the authors originally considered that it would also be relevant to qualified and experienced EPs – as well as to a much wider range of practitioners in other professions – in order to help them understand and manage the work they do with service users, especially in relation to the process of change. More recently, however, the authors have realised that the original construction of COMOIRA as a model of professional practice was too narrow and that the model can be relevant and useful within much wider contexts. It can be used, for example, with individuals, groups and organisations to guide flexible approaches to case studies and action research. It has already been used to:

- plan and deliver personal and professional development or training sessions
- elicit and evaluate structured feedback on training or development sessions
- understand, facilitate and manage change within the context of professional supervision
- structure university-based sessions; and

- enhance structured reflection and professional development within teams and organisations.

It has also been used by individuals alone who wish to engage in personal reflection to promote their own personal and professional development and change.

Because there is potentially an infinite range of possible ways in which COMOIRA might be used to engage people in the process of change, it clearly isn't possible within the context of this chapter to provide a helpful range of worked examples of the model in use. We, the authors, consider that it would be unhelpful and inappropriate to select just one such example, which might be misinterpreted as an example of 'best' practice and might in turn undermine the essential open-ended, flexible and creative aspects of COMOIRA. When introducing COMOIRA to trainees and colleagues, the authors aim to empower and enable people to come to terms with the model and to use it in ways that meet their own personal and professional needs. Although this is a challenging process, especially in the early stages, it seems important to emphasise that worked examples of the model in use might be interesting but they are not necessary, and may even be disempowering and counter-productive, if they lead people to emulate those examples. The authors are very keen to encourage people to experiment with innovative ways of using COMOIRA. Some illustrations of the general ways in which COMOIRA has been used, and the complex issues associated with the idea of providing worked examples, are discussed in more detail by Rhydderch and Gameson (in preparation).

Strengths, potential benefits, potential weaknesses and challenges of COMOIRA

COMOIRA was initially constructed as a learning model to help trainee educational psychologists make sense of and manage their own professional practice, particularly in relation to understanding and managing the dynamic process of change. In this sense, it provides a flexible, adaptable but coherent framework, within which trainees can learn about, explore and use a very wide range of theories, models and psychological approaches, all of which might be relevant throughout different stages of the change process. The authors consider that these flexible, inclusive and integrated aspects of COMOIRA are major strengths because they help to avoid the danger of introducing trainees to an *ad hoc*, out of context, disconnected or fashionable collection of theories and approaches. Within COMOIRA, all theories and approaches are linked explicitly to the process of engaging people in change.

Previous sections of this chapter have already highlighted some other strengths of COMOIRA – for example:

- it enables trainees and practitioners to maintain an interactive, collaborative approach
- it emphasises the need to enable and empower service users
- it is a meta-model because it can integrate and accommodate an infinite variety of theories and approaches within the same structure and process
- it focuses directly on promoting, monitoring and evaluating change
- it encourages the skilful application of many complex and sophisticated psychological theories at many different levels
- it encourages those who use it to be reflective and reflexive
- it promotes rigorous, accountable, ethical and reasoned action
- it helps to promote and reinforce the unique contributions that EPs can make across the education community
- it is suitable for collaborative work at many different levels with individuals, groups and organisations
- it encourages EPs to work as informed but creative psychological practitioners, not purely scientific practitioners; and
- it encourages people to make explicit the theories and rationale underpinning their practice.

Some people think of COMOIRA as a model of the Consultation approach, and it is certainly true that it includes some of the theories, attributes and processes outlined by Wagner (2000) and Watkins (2000). However, the authors consider that COMOIRA is inclusive, flexible and adaptable enough to accommodate many of the ideas, components and processes underpinning a wide range of other models and frameworks, including, for example:

- the Interpersonal Problem-Solving Approach (Thacker 1983)
- a range of sequential problem-solving approaches (Miller *et al.* 1992)
- the SPARE Wheel Model (Burden 1997)
- the Problem Analysis Process (Monsen *et al.* 1998)
- the Framework for Psychological Assessment (DECP 1998, 1999)
- the Interactive Factors Framework (Frederickson and Cline 2002)
- the Integrated Framework to Guide Educational Psychologist Practice (Woolfson *et al.* 2003)

- frameworks associated with Activity Theory (Leadbetter 2005)
- Appreciative Inquiry (Passmore and Hain 2005); and
- Research and Development in Organisations: RADIO (Timmins *et al.* 2006).

Although COMOIRA is clearly a flexible, inclusive and integrated model of professional practice, it can also be used in many other ways, some of which have been described earlier. Within the context of the professional training programme at Cardiff, the model has helped to address (and has certainly had a positive impact upon) many of the tensions outlined briefly above. Furthermore, although the model is clearly suitable for addressing complex issues and concerns, it can also be used with relatively 'uncomplicated' issues and, whilst it is not intended to be prescriptive or directional, it can be used directionally (i.e. in a clockwise sequence starting with 'Construct and clarify key change issues'), if desired. Finally, in addition to the reflective and reflexive questions associated with the model (Gameson *et al.* 2003), COMOIRA is supported by a comprehensive set of forms, which serve as *aide mémoires* and provide opportunities for recording information and ideas relevant to the core and to each key decision point. Copies of these can be obtained from the authors (School of Psychology, Cardiff University, Tower Building, Park Place, Cardiff, CF10 3AT; email dedpsyadmin@cardiff.ac.uk).

At the time of writing, COMOIRA is included as a fundamental and central aspect of the D.Ed.Psy. professional training programme at Cardiff University. For example, trainees are expected to use the model to inform and guide selected fieldwork experiences, as well as the process accounts they write. Trainees, fieldwork supervisors and university-based practical work tutors are encouraged to use the model to structure their formal supervision meetings. Tutors also use COMOIRA to structure and inform some university-based sessions. However, because the model is flexible, inclusive and integrated, it encourages and allows trainees to use an eclectic range of theories, models and approaches with the aspiration that they will be empowered and enabled to choose for themselves how they want to work in future and what sort of applied psychologists they want to be. Although COMOIRA is structured and detailed, it is not prescriptive.

Within the spirit of COMOIRA, however, every strength or potential benefit might also be construed as a weakness, a limitation or a challenge, depending on how people choose to construct and/or reconstruct these. For example, when introduced to COMOIRA, some people tend to construe its integrated, flexible, adaptable and creative attributes as weaknesses or threats. People sometimes report that they feel overwhelmed and confused initially because the model, together with its reflective and reflexive questions, and its forms, appears complex, confusing and time-consuming to understand and to use. These kinds of responses might be expected because new and unfamiliar ideas often feel very challenging, especially when they cause people to reflect on the possibility of changing their own well-established and often very comfortable practices.

Getting to grips with new ideas, skills and competencies often involves an uncomfortable personal journey through the stages of unconscious incompetence, conscious incompetence, conscious competence and unconscious competence, where the conscious incompetence stage can feel particularly threatening (Businessballs.com 2007). It is interesting that some people construe this challenging journey as a positive, exciting and liberating process, which might open the door to new ways of working. As expected, however, others construe the journey as an uncomfortable, painful and unnecessary process.

When such strong feelings occur, some people behave in ways which might be interpreted as fight or flight responses (Neimark 2007). Fight behaviours might be apparent when people attack COMOIRA or try to chase it away, often with hostile rather than constructive criticism. Flight behaviours might be apparent when people actively avoid COMOIRA and state explicitly that they want nothing more to do with it, occasionally even before they have taken the time to make sense of it. Sometimes people actively seem to encourage others to engage in fight or flight responses to the model. Often people justify and rationalise their behaviours or responses with comments indicating that the model is too complex or irrelevant, that it is incompatible with established practices or that it does not offer anything new. Sometimes, people's views of COMOIRA and the complexities and skills associated with the psychology of change seem to suggest that they view the EP as someone who mainly engages in short-term, expedient work and who, therefore, needs only quick, pragmatic approaches.

Furthermore, it is important to bear in mind that most models are likely to appear complex and unwieldy when they are new and unfamiliar. See, for example, the flow chart produced by Wedell (1970), the sequential problem-solving flow charts presented by Miller *et al.* (1992) and the Framework for Psychological Assessment (DECP 1998 and 1999). It is interesting also to consider that flow charts showing an overview of the different components and processes underpinning Solution-Oriented work, the statutory assessment process, playing a musical instrument, swimming or driving a car would all appear very complex. However, people who are able to engage in these at a level of unconscious competence are not daunted by their relative complexities. On the contrary such people usually appreciate those complexities and understand that all aspects of the 'models' or approaches are necessary but that they are never used all at the same time. In addition, when people respond negatively to COMOIRA, they frequently seem to attribute the causes of their feelings and responses to the model itself, rather than to their own interactions with it. At those times, they do not seem to appreciate that the model is inert and has no life of its own. The impact it has on people can only ever be a product of their construction of it and the way they choose to interact with it.

Of course, the above 'views of events' have been selectively constructed on the basis of certain theories and assumptions chosen by the authors. Within the spirit of COMOIRA, it would be possible to re-frame or reconstruct all these 'views of events' in other ways. For example, they could be taken to indicate that people have not been engaged readily, willingly and actively in the process of exploring the model and reviewing their existing approaches. In this sense, it would be appropriate to use COMOIRA to explore, for example:

- how relevant people are constructing their views of the model
- who has been engaged in the process so far and how
- what hypotheses people have constructed about the model and other related issues
- what needs to change
- who needs to make those changes; and
- how the changes should be made in order to engage people more positively in the process of beginning to use COMOIRA.

Within the context of the Cardiff training programme, most trainees seem to embrace COMOIRA with enthusiasm and they use the model to apply their extensive knowledge of psychology in very skilful and creative ways. However, some trainees do appear to engage in the fight or flight responses described above, perhaps because the model highlights feelings associated with conscious incompetence when it challenges their willingness and ability to draw upon and apply their knowledge of psychology. Perhaps also this is because it challenges their preconceived views of the EP as someone who engages in pragmatic, expedient activities. Some trainees tend to be ambivalent about COMOIRA and appear to pay 'lip service' to the model because it is a 'programme requirement'. The challenge for the programme team is to explore ways of using COMOIRA to engage all trainees (as well as more practising EPs and other practitioners) actively and positively in the process of beginning to use the model.

Concluding comments

This relatively short chapter has provided an outline of the structure of COMOIRA and some contextual issues relating to the initial phases of its development. It has also considered some theoretical, conceptual, functional and process issues associated with the model; some ways in which it has been used; and some of its perceived strengths, benefits, weaknesses, disadvantages and challenging aspects.

Many trainees, qualified EPs and some colleagues associated with other EP training programmes have provided encouraging and positive feedback about COMOIRA as well as some helpful and constructive critical observations. However, there are clearly many challenges and tensions still to address and the authors are planning that the next phases of development will include:

- eliciting more structured feedback and ideas from present and past trainees, as well as from fieldwork supervisors, about the development of COMOIRA as a learning model within the professional training context
- engaging in research with past trainees and other qualified EPs to explore the relevance and usefulness of COMOIRA to EPs and other practitioners working in the field
- eliciting more structured feedback from service users about aspects of the model and its usefulness
- engaging in research to explore the relationship between COMOIRA, other models of service delivery and the wider contexts in which they are used
- using COMOIRA to engage in new ways of carrying out research: for example, exploring the extent to which other models of service delivery within local-authority services focus on the process of change and the explicit application of psychology
- encouraging the programme team, trainees and other colleagues to experiment with a wider range of new and creative uses of COMOIRA
- developing further the use of COMOIRA for consultations with teams and organisations
- developing further the use of COMOIRA to guide the process of supervision; and
- extending the use of COMOIRA to structure and inform more aspects of the Cardiff training programme within the university and in fieldwork contexts.

References

Armitage, C.J. and Connor, M. (2001) 'Efficacy of the theory of planned behaviour: A meta-analytic review.' *British Journal of Social Psychology* 40, 471–499.

Bigge, M. and Shermis, S.S. (1992) *Learning Theories for Teachers*. New York: Harper Collins.

Bowlby, J. (1988) *A Secure Base: Clinical Applications of Attachment Theory*. London: Routledge.

Burden, R.L. (1997) 'Research in the real world: An evaluation model for use by applied educational psychologists.' *Educational Psychology in Practice 13*, 1, 13–20.

Burr, V. (2003) *Social Constructionism.* London and New York: Routledge.

Businessballs.com (2007) *The Conscious Competence Learning Model.* Accessed 16 July 2007 at www.businessballs.com/consciouscompetencelearningmodel.htm

Campbell, D., Coldicott, T. and Kinsella, K. (1994) *Systemic Work with Organisations: A New Model for Managers and Change Agents.* London: Karnac Books.

Carr, A. (2004) *Positive Psychology: The Science of Happiness and Human Strengths.* Hove: Brunner-Routledge.

Denham, A., Hatfield, S., Smethurst, N., Tan, E. and Tribe, C. (2006) 'The effect of social skills interventions in the primary school.' *Educational Psychology in Practice 22*, 1, 33–51.

Division of Educational and Child Psychology (DECP) (1998) *A Framework for Psychological Assessment and Intervention: Draft 1.* Leicester: British Psychological Society.

Division of Educational and Child Psychology (DECP) (1999) 'A framework for psychological assessment and intervention.' *DECP Newsletter 89*, 6–9.

Dowling, E. and Osborne, E. (1994) *The Family and the School: A Joint Systems Approach to Problems with Children.* London: Routledge.

Forward, D. (1989) 'A Guide to Action Research.' In P. Lomax (ed.) *The Management of Change: Increasing School Effectiveness and Facilitating Staff Development through Action Research.* BERA Dialogues 1. Clevedon: Multilingual Matters Ltd.

Frederickson, N. (1990a) 'Systems Approaches in EP Practice: A Re-evaluation.' In N. Jones and N. Frederickson (eds) *Refocusing Educational Psychology.* London: Palmer Press.

Frederickson, N. (1990b) *Soft Systems Methodology: Practical Implications in Work with Schools.* London: University College.

Frederickson, N. and Cline, T. (2002) *Special Educational Needs, Inclusion and Diversity: A Textbook.* Buckingham: Open University Press.

Frederickson, N., Warren, L. and Turner, J. (2005) '"Circle of Friends": An exploration of impact over time.' *Educational Psychology in Practice 21*, 3, 197–217.

Gameson, J., Rhydderch, G., Ellis, D. and Carroll, H.C.M. (2003) 'Constructing a flexible model of integrated professional practice: Part 1, Conceptual and theoretical issues.' *Educational and Child Psychology 20*, 4, 96–115.

Gameson, J., Rhydderch, G., Ellis, D. and Carroll, H.C.M. (2005) 'Constructing a flexible model of integrated professional practice: Part 2, Process and practice issues.' *Educational and Child Psychology 22*, 4, 41–55.

Gergen, K.J. (1999) *An Invitation to Social Constructionism.* London: Sage.

Gillham, B. (1999) 'The writing of *Reconstructing Educational Psychology*.' *Educational Psychology in Practice 14*, 4, 220–221.

Glasser, W. (1999) *Choice Theory: A New Psychology for Personal Freedom.* New York: HarperPerennial.

Green, J.M. (1996) 'Engagement and empathy: A pilot study of the therapeutic alliance in outpatient child psychiatry.' *Child Psychology and Psychiatry Review 1*, 4, 130–138.

Green, J.M. (2006) 'Annotation: The therapeutic alliance – a significant but neglected variable in child mental health treatment studies.' *Journal of Child Psychology and Psychiatry 47*, 5, 425–435.

Herbert, M. (1987) *Behavioural Treatment of Children with Problems: A Practice Manual.* London: Academic Press.

Leadbetter, J. (2005) 'Activity theory as a conceptual framework and analytical tool within the practice of educational psychology.' *Educational and Child Psychology 22*, 1, 18–28.

Leahy, R.L. (2003) *Cognitive Therapy Techniques: A Practitioner's Guide.* New York: Guilford Press.

Lines, D. (2002) *Brief Counselling in Schools: Working with Young People from 11 to 18.* London: Sage.

Lown, J. (2002) 'Circle Time: The perceptions of teachers and pupils.' *Educational Psychology in Practice 18*, 2, 93–102.

Miller, A., Leyden, G., Stewart-Evans, C. and Gammage, S. (1992) 'Applied psychologists as problems solvers: Devising a personal model.' *Educational Psychology in Practice 7*, 4, 227–236.

Miller, W.R. and Rollnick, S. (2002) *Motivational Interviewing: Preparing People for Change.* New York and London: The Guilford Press.

Monsen, J., Graham, B., Frederickson, N. and Cameron, R.J. (1998) 'Problem analysis and professional training in educational psychology: An accountable model of practice.' *Educational Psychology in Practice 13*, 4, 234–249.

Neimark, N.F. (2007) *Mind/Body Education Centre: The Fight or Flight Response.* Accessed 16 July 2007 at www.thebodysoulconnection.com/EducationCenter/fight.html

Nieboer, R., Moss, D. and Partridge, K. (2000) 'A great servant but a poor master: A critical look at the rhetoric of evidence-based practice.' *Clinical Psychology Forum 136*, 17–19.

O'Hanlon, B. (2006) *Change 101: A Practical Guide to Creating Change in Life or Therapy.* New York: W.W. Norton and Company.

Oxford Reference Online (2007) Search for *Heuristic* and *Algorithm*. Accessed 15 May 2007 at www.oxfordreference.com/views/GLOBAL.html?authstatuscode=202

Passmore, J. and Hain, D. (2005) 'Appreciative inquiry: Positive psychology for organizational change.' *Selection Development Review 21*, 5, 13–16.

Phillips, P. (1987) *The Fieldwork Model of Enquiry.* Document produced for the M.Ed. Educational Psychology Training Course. Exeter University.

Prochaska, J. (1999) 'How Do People Change and How Can We Change to Help Many More People?' In M. Hubble, B. Duncan and S. Miller (eds) *The Heart and Soul of Change.* Washington, DC: American Psychological Association.

Rhodes, J. and Ajmal, Y. (1995) *Solution Focused Thinking in Schools.* London: BT Press.

Rhydderch, G. and Gameson, J. (in preparation) 'Constructing a flexible model of integrated professional practice: Part 3, The model in practice.'

Rogers, C.R. (1957) 'The necessary and sufficient conditions of therapeutic personality change.' *Journal of Consulting Psychology 21*, 2, 95–103.

Selekman, M.D. (1997) *Solution-Focused Therapy with Children.* New York and London: The Guilford Press.

Thacker, J. (1983) *Steps to Success: An Interpersonal Problem-Solving Approach for Children.* London: NFER-Nelson.

Timmins, P., Mohammed, B., McFadyen, J. and Ward, J. (2006) 'Teachers and consultation: Applying research and development in organisations (RADIO).' *Educational Psychology in Practice 22*, 4, 305–319.

Wagner, P. (2000) 'Consultation: Developing a comprehensive approach to service delivery.' *Educational Psychology in Practice 16*, 1, 9–18.

Watkins, C. (2000) 'Introduction to the articles on consultation.' *Educational Psychology in Practice 16*, 1, 5–8.

Wedell, K. (1970) 'Diagnosing learning difficulties: A sequential strategy.' *Journal and Newsletter of the Association of Educational Psychologists 4*, 7, 23–29.

Westbrook, D., Kennerley, H. and Kirk, J. (2007) *An Introduction to Cognitive Behaviour Therapy: Skills and Applications.* London: Sage.

Woolfson, L., Whaling, R., Stewart, A. and Monsen, J. (2003) 'An integrated framework to guide educational psychologist practice.' *Educational Psychology in Practice 19*, 4, 283–302.

CHAPTER 6

The Woolfson *et al.* Integrated Framework: An Executive Framework for Service-Wide Delivery

Lisa Woolfson

Introduction
Why did we develop the Integrated Framework?[1]
Our first experience of using a framework was with the 1999 to 2001 cohort on the University of Strathclyde two-year M.Sc., the professional training programme for educational psychologists in Scotland. The Monsen *et al.* Problem-Analysis Framework (Monsen *et al.* 1998) was suggested by the programme team simply as a training tool to help these trainee educational psychologists plan and evaluate their work. At that time those of us who were to become the first three authors of the Woolfson *et al.* Integrated Framework (Woolfson, Whaling, Stewart and Monsen 2003) were respectively a tutor and two trainees on this programme. We observed that both the quality of trainee input and their analysis and justification of their professional approach to practice benefited from the use of the Monsen *et al.* framework because it:

- provided a systematic structure to aid trainee thinking about the complex, messy problems that are presented by schools, families and young people for EP/trainee involvement
- encouraged trainee EPs to reflect on and to be explicit about what assessments they were undertaking, and why

---

[1] The first version of the Integrated Framework appeared in Woolfson *et al.* (2003). All tables and figures have been reproduced from the original paper with the kind permission of Angela Stewart, Ruth Whaling and Jeremy Monsen and of Taylor and Francis (UK) Journals www.informaworld.com. Figure 6.1 is a revised version of a list of steps presented in the original paper.

- helped them consider how the outcome of the assessment would impact on decisions about intervention plans; and
- made links between assessment and intervention more explicit, justifiable and transparent.

These were clearly important benefits that trainees would want to carry over into their work as educational psychologists – and they viewed them as just as essential to systematic, effective and accountable practice once training was over. The Integrated Framework authors then sought to develop a structure that could similarly promote accountability and transparency for both individual psychologists as well as for psychological services, within an ever-more litigious climate where practitioners and services need to be able to justify their assessment and intervention input.

While the nine steps of the Monsen *et al.* framework were excellent for breaking down the task for training purposes, it seemed less user-friendly for the more experienced practitioner who would be able to merge steps together with an overview. Indeed, even by the second year of their training programme, trainee EPs were already able to internalise some of these steps and were ready to utilise a more simplified framework. They no longer felt there was value for them in working their way through nine separate steps. This pointed to the need for a new, more user-friendly framework that could be used by experienced practitioners.

Key influences

Furthermore, Woolfson *et al.* also wanted to make explicit and integrate within this new framework two additional conceptual influences that they viewed as highly significant for effective EP work: namely an ecological systems approach and interdisciplinary collaboration. Although Frederickson (1990) had earlier noted EP interest in applying Systems Theory as developed by von Bertalanffy (1968) to their work in schools, much of EP work still continued to be at an individual level (e.g. Stobie 2002). Moreover, it may be argued that this recognition of, and addressing problems at, different levels may indeed be a significant and unique aspect of the EP's input (Cameron 2006).

We therefore embedded a structure based on Bronfenbrenner's (1979) social ecology model inside the Integrated Framework to ensure that a holistic understanding of the child's problems within the contexts in which they present would be central to all EP assessment and intervention plans. Bronfenbrenner viewed the family system as nested within an extended family system, which is nested within the local community system, within the larger society, just like a set of Russian dolls. The family and the classroom, then, are examples of micro-systems in which EPs commonly target their assessment and intervention work.

Meso-systems are the relationships between these micro-systems. Behaviour, thus, is viewed not as linear cause and effect but interactional, with the child's behaviour both influencing and being influenced by, for example, the teacher's. Rather than adopting a 'main effects' model that focuses on within-child deficits, or disadvantaged family environment, as the main contributory causal factor to problems presenting in school, Bronfebrenner's ecological systems approach within the Integrated Framework was intended to help EPs to address the complexity of the problems with which they deal – by encouraging them always to examine the next social system to find solutions to problems that present within nested systems (Garbarino 1992). It enables problem analyses and intervention solutions to be identified at the levels of child, class, school, family and community in order to help EPs take account in assessment and intervention phases of the different micro- and meso-systems that may influence the presenting problem.

Additionally, the Integrated Framework is a transparent structure in that its intention is that the EP is not the only person to be aware of what framework is being used and how the process of involvement and collaboration will continue. Central to the Integrated Framework is the crucial recognition that EPs, parents, teachers and young people all bring a valuable perspective to the problem-solving situation and that all stakeholders' views and behaviours have meaning and make sense within the social situation in which they find themselves. Embedded in the principle of collaboration with stakeholders is an awareness that some stakeholders – for example, teachers, speech and language therapists (SALTs) – are also fellow professionals with a particular, perhaps different, world-view of the problem that emerges from their professional training. The Integrated Framework is designed to be shared with the other stakeholders to promote joint understanding of the nature of the problem and how to progress in dealing with it. This collaborative perspective sits comfortably with Dunst, Trivette and Deal's (1988) principles of good intervention practice for professionals, and also with Wagner's (2000) consultation model as applied to EP practice in schools in the UK. Both build on Systems Thinking as discussed earlier – Dunst *et al.* on social systems, while Wagner's focus is more on Systems Thinking from family therapy work.

In recognising that all stakeholders have an important perspective to contribute, it is made explicit within the Integrated Framework that this should include the child where appropriate. Current thinking and legislation now advocates this position, e.g. United Nations Convention on the Rights of the Child 1989 (UN 1989), the Children Act 1989 (HMSO 1989) and the Code of Practice accompanying the 1993 Education Act, Children (Scotland) Act 1995 (HMSO 1995).

The Integrated Framework advocates an approach in which there is *interdisciplinary* or *transdisciplinary* collaboration to negotiate and agree joint goals. These forms of collaboration are next to each other at one end of a continuum of collaboration, according to Bailey's (1984) triaxial model – ranging from *unidisciplinary* at the other end of the continuum (where each professional deals individually with the client and there is in effect no team at all), through *multidisciplinary* where each professional works individually and then meets within a multi-professional group to report their individual goals, through the development of joint goals in an *interdisciplinary* team, to the *transdisciplinary* team at the other end of the continuum (where stakeholders not only agree joint goals but may also train each other in areas of recognised expertise to share roles and responsibilities across professional boundaries).

The five phases of the Integrated Framework

The Integrated Framework consists of a sequence of five phases (see Figure 6.1). There are, however, feedback loops between phases to allow for new insights and new information that may necessitate a return to an earlier phase to reformulate hypotheses. For example, it may be that Phase 5 evaluation shows that some areas did not show the expected progress following intervention. Or that some new information has come to light during the intervention phase and after assessment was completed. This would mean returning to Phase 2 to examine the problem situation with the new information presented as new guiding hypotheses, and proceeding through Phases 2 and 3 again – carrying out further information-gathering to confirm new hypotheses, with likely impact on intervention plans in a new Phase 4. We will now look at each phase in more detail.

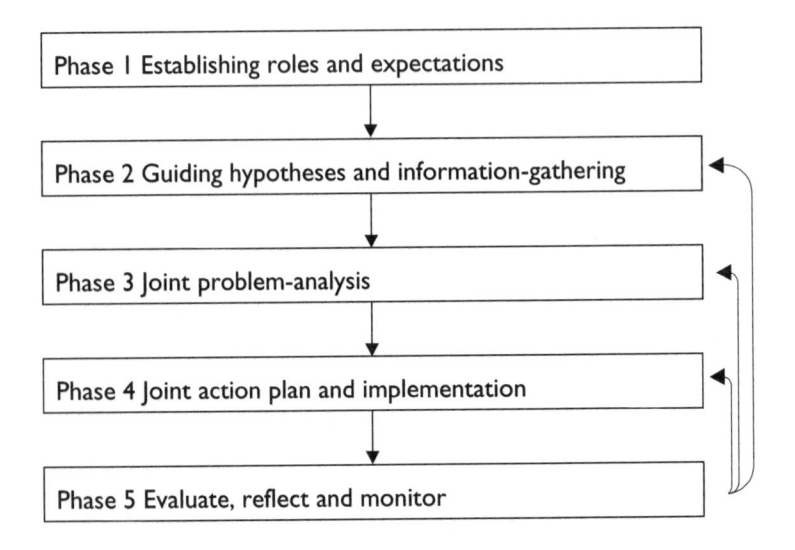

Figure 6.1: The Integrated Framework

Phase 1: Establishing roles and expectations

Phase 1 aims to lay the groundwork for effective collaboration and problem-solving. The EP needs to clarify what the referring agents/problem-owners seek to achieve with EP involvement – indeed, even to check that EP involvement is appropriate for the specific problem under discussion. Negotiation of the desired role is an important component of this phase. Once there is broad agreement on expectations, the EP and the problem-owners together should identify who the other stakeholders are, for example, the family and extended family, teachers, support assistants, social workers, playground supervisors, community medicine practitioners, therapists and, of course, the child him- or herself. The inclusion of the child, or young person, wherever appropriate reflects that the child is also seen as having a part to play in contributing to change. Although there is a move away from a within-child deficit view of the problem to one of bringing about change in the systems, beliefs and behaviours that might impact on the presenting problem, this does not mean that the child has no contribution to make to either the problem or to actions that could change the situation. A multi-causal assessment and intervention approach is therefore taken in which child factors as well as systems and contextual, interactional factors may contribute. Thus it is not simply the case that only the adults around the child are responsible for bringing about change. The child too, if old enough, can be actively involved in working towards change too.

A joint meeting involving all stakeholders should then be arranged. At this meeting the EP should explicitly share with stakeholders the five-phase process that the EP and stakeholders will be involved in. All roles, including that of the EP, should be clarified and negotiated if necessary to aid transparency and facilitate joint working. Before moving to Phase 2, either directly at that meeting or by arranging a date for a Phase 2 meeting, the team should agree who will be responsible for taking and distributing minutes of meetings, and who should be on the distribution list for these minutes. If the school is the problem-owner, then it is usually best if the school takes on this role. The aim of Phase 1 is to ensure that everyone is clear how the team will proceed jointly towards possible solutions. EPs can often identify opportunities through service-level agreements to address Phase 1 systemically in order to develop agreed principles of working that do not necessarily need to be negotiated anew for each piece of work.

Phase 2: Guiding hypotheses and information-gathering

In Phase 2 the EP uses active listening skills to facilitate stakeholders (including the child, where appropriate) to share their ideas and provide background information on their perception of the problem situation. The EP will help stakeholders to re-frame ideas and hunches as hypotheses for which supporting evidence will be gathered, and will encourage stakeholders to re-frame their view of the problem in order to consider it at different ecological levels. This is particularly important when the problem is initially presented as something intrinsic to the young person or to a problematic group of learners. In Phase 2, the EP suggests his/her own hypotheses. These will be based on psychological knowledge, background reading, theory, research and prior experience in other similar situations as well as in that specific school. Note that no particular psychological perspective is proscribed here, so that the EP is free to be as eclectic or as directed as he or she wishes to be in the psychological perspective that he or she brings. This is why the Integrated Framework is indeed an executive practice framework because any particular psychological model or theoretical approach to EP work can sit comfortably inside the overall five phase process. It is left to the practitioner to determine what psychological knowledge he or she chooses to bring to Phase 2 and to subsequent phases. Nor does the Integrated Framework specify methods of working within each phase, but instead offers an executive framework that aims to ensure the process moves along through:

- needs analysis
- formulation of key issues to be addressed
- intervention plan and
- evaluation and reflection (which may result in a feedback loop to rethinking of formulation of key issues).

The aim of Phase 2 is to provide an initial, tentative picture of the presenting problem that can be used to guide information-gathering. Table 6.1 provides an example of a completed summary proforma that records the agreed actions from a meeting, which would be sent to the distribution list identified in Phase 1. This Phase 2/3 summary proforma records hypotheses at different ecological levels, as well as who will be responsible for the required information-gathering. It also has a column for identifying the source of each hypothesis, as all stakeholders will contribute their ideas here. As well as hypotheses based on experience or prior knowledge of class and school-level factors in a particular school, the EP will also generate hypotheses using psychological knowledge and current research findings from background reading.

At the Phase 2 meeting a time-plan for information-gathering should be agreed, as well as the date of the Phase 3 meeting.

Phase 3: Joint problem-analysis
The key task of the EP in Phase 3 is to identify all the Phase 2 hypotheses that were confirmed by the information gathered by the stakeholders (see Tables 6.1

Table 6.1: Phase 2/3 summary proforma

Phase 2			Phase 3	
Level	Source	Hypotheses	Information-gathering	Confirmed?
Individual	Nursery staff, mother, SALT	Language is delayed.	Staff and mother to keep language samples, SALT assessment, EP assessment, using REELS (Bzoch and League 1991).	Yes
	EP	There are delays in other developmental areas.	Staff and mother to observe and record skills using PIP Developmental Checklist (Jeffree and McConkey 1998). EP assessment using SGS II (Bellman, Lingam and Aukett 1996).	No
	SALT, EP	Aggressive behaviour serves a function for David.	Functional behaviour analysis with ABC (antecedents, behaviour, consequences) monitoring sheet. Key worker to implement at school, mother to implement at home, EP to help analyse.	Yes
	Mother	David lacks confidence.		No

Phase 2			Phase 3	
Level	Source	Hypotheses	Information-gathering	Confirmed?
Class/School	EP	Few organised opportunities for peer interaction in nursery structure.	EP classroom observation and consultation with nursery staff.	Yes
	EP	Nursery staff would benefit from greater knowledge of positive behaviour-management strategies.		Yes
Home/ Community	Social Worker	David gets what he wants at home by having a tantrum.	SW to observe at home and consult with mother.	Yes
		David is not given sufficient opportunities to be independent at home.		Yes

Key:
SALT = Speech and language therapist
REELS = Receptive-Expressive Emergent Language Scale
EP = educational psychologist
SW = social worker

and 6.2) and then to collate them all into a preliminary problem-analysis to present for discussion at the Phase 3 feedback meeting (see Figure 6.2). The EP's analysis here should provide an explanatory overview of how different contributing psychological, behavioural, contextual and systems factors might influence the problem situation. Such a focus on explanatory variables and their possible contribution to outcomes is in fact one of the most distinctive contributions of an EP (Cameron 2006). It is important to retain the different ecological levels within this analysis as the Phase 3 problem-analysis will serve as the springboard for intervention planning, and this helps stakeholders to see within which systems intervention should be targeted.

Table 6.2: Summary of Phase 3 problem dimensions

Level	Problem dimension	Supporting evidence
Individual	Language delay.	REELS SGS II SALT assessment PIP Developmental Checklist Language samples
	Aggressive behaviour and tantrums.	Classroom observation data Nursery staff interviews
Class/School	Need for structured opportunities for social interaction.	Classroom observation data Nursery staff interviews
	Need for staff development in supporting language development and behaviour management.	
Home/Community	Management at home.	Mother interview SW observation ABC analysis Nursery staff interviews
	Difficult morning separations.	
	Need for David to develop control and independence.	

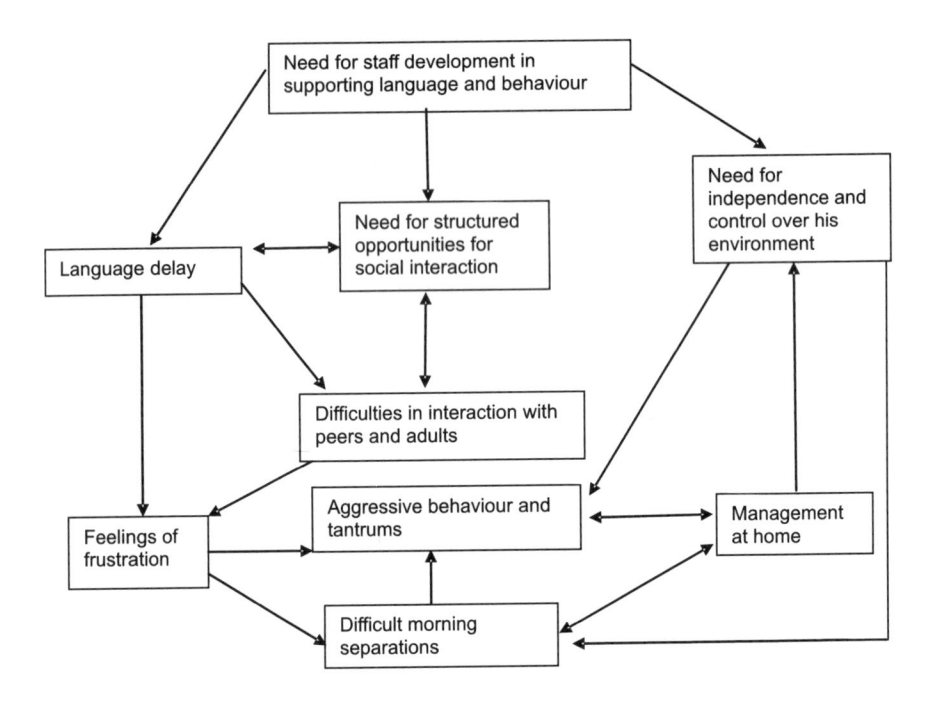

Figure 6.2: Phase 3 problem-analysis

At the Phase 3 feedback meeting, the EP presents this tentative formulation of the different contributing factors and the priority areas for intervention that these imply. Hypotheses that were not confirmed will also need some discussion as stakeholders who proposed these may need support in undertaking the task of re-framing their view of the problem, since this view was not supported by evidence. Bear in mind that new hypotheses may emerge that require a temporary return to Phase 2 for further information-gathering (see feedback arrow in Figure 6.1). A new, shared view of problem dimensions will be agreed at this meeting, which will enable moving on to Phase 4 to establish a joint action plan composed of interventions pointed up by the problem dimensions identified.

Phase 4: Joint action plan for implementation

Intervention plans emerging from Phase 3 should not only take account of the problem dimensions but also consider carefully where systems' strengths lie and which of the identified factors are more or less amenable to change. During this phase, the EP brings to the stakeholder team his or her specialist psychological knowledge of possible effective interventions deriving from a sound evidence-base. Plans for evaluation are thoroughly embedded in Phase 4, and the team arranges who is responsible for gathering this data at the end of the intervention period. Table 6.3 provides an example of an agreed Phase 4 action plan with details of stakeholders' roles in intervention and evaluation. This can be used as a minute of the meeting and shared with the distribution list. The final task of Phase 4 is to arrange the date of the Phase 5 feedback meeting.

Phase 5: Evaluate, reflect and monitor
In this final stage the stakeholders reflect on the evaluation findings to analyse both process and outcomes in Phase 4, compared with what was planned (see Table 6.4). The aim is for the team to engage in a critical reflection to determine what worked, what didn't and how this experience might inform future working, e.g. as in Frederickson and Cameron (1999). If outcomes were not successful, this may inform a return to an earlier phase to gather more assessment data or to repeat the intervention or carry out a more suitably tailored version of the intervention. Where the intervention plans *have* resulted in the intended outcomes, then the focus is likely to be on developing a maintenance plan and on what individual stakeholders' responsibilities are for monitoring this in the future. A further important part of Phase 5 is the EP's personal reflection on his/her involvement in order to identify strengths and weaknesses and to address continuing professional development needs. This personal reflection is best carried out at the psychological service base with a colleague as mentor.

Why use this framework?
The Integrated Framework can be used to inform work at any ecological level within the class, school, family or wider community. It applies equally well to EP casework with an individual child or work with problems that centre on a group, a class, a school, a family, as it does to an authority-wide problem such as school non-attendance for which EP intervention may be a contribution to policy development. It does not specify methods of assessment and intervention, or theoretical orientation; nor is it tied to any particular psychological approach beyond the broad psychological framework that it provides as scaffolding to accommodate EPs' individual areas of psychological expertise. For example, Solution-Focused working – currently a preferred approach for many EPs in the UK (Stobie, Boyle and Woolfson 2005) – sits perfectly within the Integrated Framework as it provides a generic infrastructure within which Solution-Focused expertise may be applied. Thus, the Integrated Framework offers EPs an executive framework that ensures the assessment and intervention process is carried out collbratively, at different ecological levels, and that it moves along through needs analysis, formulation of key issues to be addressed, intervention

Table 6.3: Phase 4 action plan proforma

Target area	Action	Who, when, where	Evaluation
Promoting language development	SALT advice to nursery and mother on David's specific needs. INSET.	Meeting between SALT, key worker and mother arranged for two weeks' time. SALT to deliver INSET on language development in the pre-school years during the current school session.	SALT and nursery to monitor progress and evaluate outcomes. Staff feedback questionnaire evaluation of INSET.
Improving opportunities for social interaction in the nursery	Structured group-work to be planned in the nursery for all children. David to be encouraged to interact with peers also in free choice time in nursery.	Set times for group-work to be formalised by the nursery staff at their planning meeting next week. EP to advise on whole-class strategies for enhancing social interaction for all children. Date arranged for this. Nursery staff to direct David towards activities with peers, beginning today.	School staff to record and evaluate timetabled group activities in existing school files for review at Phase 5 meeting. Separate monitoring of David's progress to be kept by staff.

Target area	Action	Who, when, where	Evaluation
Discouraging aggressive behaviour and encouraging positive behaviour	Introduction of a more structured day for all children.	Nursery staff to set times for structured group-work as above.	As above.
	Introduction of a reward system for David.	EP to help key worker devise reward system to encourage David towards more positive behaviour. Date arranged as above.	As above.
	INSET.	EP to introduce principles of positive behaviour, including ABC behaviour analysis to whole staff group at staff-development session this term.	Staff self-evaluation of practice. Staff feedback questionnaire evaluation of INSET.
	Behaviour-management advice for mother to implement at home to avoid David having tantrums.	EP to train SW who will attend staff-development session above and will then support mother at home on this.	SW and mother to monitor management of tantrums at home.
Separation between David and mother in morning	Routine with mother and nursery to be established for leaving David in the morning.	EP to discuss what works well with mother (on the basis of observations) and encourage more of this behaviour. Key worker and mother to finalise plan.	Continual monitoring by key worker and mother.

Table 6.4: Phase 5 summary proforma

Target area	Outcome	Evidence
Promoting language development	Increased staff confidence and understanding of pre-school language difficulties and David's specific problems. David's increased initiation of interaction with peers (see above).	SALT observation EP observation Staff verbal reports INSET evaluation questionnaire
Improving social interaction in nursery	Formal group-work sessions set up as part of morning and afternoon programme, now with focused group activities. David making more attempts at initiation with peers and showing greater perseverance in interaction with adults (e.g. repeating, trying again, if not understood).	Staff reports School forward plans and teacher evaluation of group activities Key worker records of David's progress EP classroom observation
Separation in morning	Still difficult.	Key worker and mother verbal reports and records

plan, evaluation and reflection. It does not impose a psychological methodology or viewpoint beyond this.

The Integrated Framework's emphasis on interdisciplinary and collaborative problem-solving work is undeniably its particular strength. This is now a commonly used and well-accepted way of working for EPs (Woods and Farrell 2006), yet there are relatively few practice models of interdisciplinary working currently being used for us to draw on. Within the Integrated Framework, the client also has a significant part in the decision-making process and the Framework assists all stakeholders, including the child and family, to take on key roles. The openness of the Framework – the emphasis on negotiation, collaboration and the centrality of valuing and respecting all perspectives – is intended to promote the demystification of professional roles and enhance effective team working. It also helps promote accountability as it provides an audit trail of actions and their underlying rationale, including those rejected hypotheses that were not supported by assessment data collected. Recording these in the respective summary proformae will make it clear that there was not sufficient data to confirm these hypotheses, rather than their appearing not to have been considered at all. The Framework thus provides evidence of the thoroughness of the investigation, showing how it went beyond the ultimately agreed actions.

So far the advantages of implementing such an executive framework have largely been expressed in terms of the benefits to the work of the individual EP. However, this executive framework can be equally useful to psychological services if applied service-wide. Some psychological services seem to be moving in the direction of developing service guidelines for practice, and the whole service has moved to a model of, for example, consultation or Solution-Focused working. These service-wide frameworks, however, may be too directive for the EPs in a psychological service who do not wish to work within the identified theoretical perspectives. The Integrated Framework gets round this by providing an executive framework that enables consistency across a service, but is neither too prescriptive nor constraining for individual EPs. It leaves the EP with plenty of latitude to implement his/her own theoretical orientation, to apply a specific knowledge base, or to follow individual interests.

As discussed above, the Integrated Framework offers a system that supports accountability by providing a recorded audit trail of evidence agreed by a team of key stakeholders. This aids services as much, and in the same ways, as it does individual EPs. Furthermore, the application of the Integrated Framework across a whole service contributes to consistency of practice between individual EPs working in that service, enabling schools to then know what to expect of the psychologist. Phase 1 works more smoothly when the EP's role and way of working is familiar to schools. The process of EP involvement is thus less a function of individual quirks, preferences and idiosyncrasies and more coherent and consistent with school's prior experiences, regardless of which member of the educational psychology service they work with. This should lead to more effective and fruitful collaborative work with schools as there will be a shared understanding of how the collaboration works, and how the EP's involvement with the school will proceed, built on previous experience that the school has had with that psychological service.

References
Bailey, D. (1984) 'A triaxial model of the interdisciplinary team and group-process.' *Exceptional Children 51*, 1, 17–25.

Bellman, M., Lingam, S. and Aukett, A. (1996) *Schedule of Growing Skills II.* Windsor: NFER-Nelson.

Bronfenbrenner, U. (1979) *The Ecology of Human Development.* Cambridge, MA: Harvard University Press.

Bzoch, K. and League, R. (1991) *Receptive-Expressive Emergent Language Scales* (2nd edn). Windsor: NFER-Nelson.

Cameron, R. (2006) 'Educational psychology: The distinctive contribution.' *Educational Psychology in Practice 22,* 4, 289–304.

Dunst, C., Trivette, C. and Deal, A. (1988) *Enabling and Empowering Families: Principles and Guidelines for Practice.* Cambridge, MA: Brookline Books.

Frederickson, N. (1990) 'Systems Approaches in EP Practice: A Re-evaluation.' In N. Jones and N. Frederickson (eds) *Refocusing Educational Psychology.* London: Falmer Press.

Frederickson, N. and Cameron, R. (1999) 'Encouraging Reflection in Teaching and Educational Psychology Practice: Questions for Reflection.' In N. Frederickson and R. Cameron (eds) *Psychology in Education Portfolio.* Windsor: NFER-Nelson.

Garbarino, J. (1992) *Children and Families in the Social Environment* (2nd edn). Hawthorne, NY: Aldine.

HMSO (1989) *Children Act.* London: HMSO.

HMSO (1995) *Children (Scotland) Act.* London: HMSO.

Jeffree, D. and McConkey, R. (1998) *Parental Involvement Project Developmental Charts* (2nd edn). London: Hodder and Stoughton.

Monsen, J., Graham, B., Frederickson, N. and Cameron, R. (1998) 'Problem analysis and professional training in educational psychology.' *Educational Psychology in Practice 13,* 4, 234–249.

Stobie, I. (2002) 'Processes of "change" and "continuity" in educational psychology – part II.' *Educational Psychology in Practice 18,* 213–237.

Stobie, I., Boyle, J. and Woolfson, L. (2005) 'Solution-focused approaches in the practice of UK educational psychologists: A study of the nature of their application and evidence of their effectiveness.' *School Psychology International 26,* 1, 5–28.

UN (1989) *Convention on the Rights of the Child.* UNGA Document A/RES/44/25. New York: United Nations.

von Bertalanffy, L. (1968) *General Systems Theory.* New York: Braziller.

Wagner, P. (2000) 'Consultation: Developing a comprehensive approach to service delivery.' *Educational Psychology in Practice 16,* 1, 9–18.

Woods, K. and Farrell, P. (2006) 'Approaches to psychological assessment by educational psychologists in England and Wales.' *School Psychology International 27,* 4, 387–404.

Woolfson, L., Whaling, R., Stewart, A. and Monsen, J. (2003) 'An integrated framework to guide educational psychologist practice.' *Educational Psychology in Practice 19,* 4, 283–302.

PART FOUR

Frameworks for Practice with Therapeutic Roots

CHAPTER 7

Consultation as a Framework for Practice

Patsy Wagner

Introduction

This chapter aims to describe Consultation in terms of its use as a comprehensive model of service delivery for a local-authority education psychology service, working with others to make a difference in the context of integrated children's services and multi-agency working. The inter-related theory and practice of Consultation, its evaluation, the benefits, and its usefulness in the initial training and the continuing professional development of EPs will be addressed, as will some key difficulties.

The model described here has developed in the author's practice as an educational psychologist in the state system in local education authority settings over the past 26 years and is still in the process of development. I have also been privileged to work on Consultation development with a large number of varied EPSs in England, Scotland and Wales over that period. The challenges in such a wide range of settings have contributed enormously to identifying the essentials of Consultation and have tested the robustness of this model. An essential feature of this model of Consultation is the interactionist, systemic and constructionist psychology that gives it meaning and relevance and that informs the practice. Such psychology reflects the complexity of the context in which we work, i.e. inter-relating systems of schools, families, local-authority systems, professionals systems, agencies, and so on. The aim of Consultation is to find the 'the difference that makes a difference' (Bateson 1972, p.271) within a collaborative and respectful practice. As Gergen states, 'A psychology that simply contributes to the status quo has little to offer the culture' (1997, p.34).

The term 'Consultation'

Consultation may not be the best term for what we do since it could symbolise going to see the doctor, with implications of an expert who makes things better by diagnosing problems and prescribing cures, as long as someone is prepared to take on the role of patient (the word's origins lie in the Latin present participle of *pati*, meaning 'suffer'). However, the term has been used for some while (Meyers 1973) to indicate a collaborative way for EPs to work with schools. So we continue to use it, and aim to ensure that the people with whom we work understand that we mean 'working together' – that we do not consider ourselves as the experts in their lives and their situations. Rather, we take the view that everyone involved in Consultation has unique expertise that contributes to the richness of the Consultation and in turn to the search for solutions. We see ourselves as having expertise in promoting this process. We avoid the use of the terms 'consultant' (with its implication of power and expert status) and 'consultee'. Concerns about the language we use inform our facilitation of meetings, where we aim to address imbalances of power and destructive distortions of meaning created through the language of deficit.

Development of Consultation: The wider context

Nearly 40 years ago Caplan (1970) described a way of working in which two professionals worked together instead of relying on one referring a child to another. This was explained as 'a voluntary, non-supervisory relationship between professionals from different fields established to aid one in his or her professional functioning... The rationale for a mental health professional spending time with a teacher... instead of a child...is based on the efficiency, impact and prevention aspects of the intervention.'

The desired effects of indirect work were described by Conoley and Conoley (1982):

> The consultant hopes that the consultee will generalize the insights and skills learned in the discussion of a single client case to the other clients (now or ever) under the care of the consultee. The benefits of consulting about a single case while the benefits spread is the efficiency of consultation. The impact rationale is the consultant's belief that clients are best treated by those who have high duration or intensity of contact with them... the regular caregivers in a client's life should be helped to be facilitative of treatment goals because they spend the most time with the clients. (p.1)

Consultation was therefore preventative: 'it follows that if generalisation and transfer of skills occur because of consultation, there is the potential for the primary prevention of…problems' (p.2). Conoley and Conoley also go on to describe what consultation is not:

> For example, consultants are different from supervisors, program developers, teachers and psychotherapists. While it is true that consultants are none of these exactly, it is also true that they do some of what each job title suggests. (p.2)

Consultation aimed to facilitate the skill development and expertise of others, rather than to replace them or provide a more 'expert' version of them. In this way it contrasted with 'referral', which encouraged the notion of more expert and knowledgeable systems. This notion of the pre-existing expertise in the system was emphasised in early literature. Gallessich (1972) put it this way:

> the primary assumption is that the system, whether it is a small unit such as a team of 2 or 3 teachers, [or one teacher in this author's view] or a larger unit, for example, a school district, contains the basic resources for effective problem-solving. (p.14)

Conoley, Apter and Conoley (1981) clarify the role:

> Consultation should not be seen, therefore, as the more knowledgeable consultant giving answers to a puzzled consultee. Rather, it must be viewed as a collaborative problem solving process during which the consultant facilitates the creative, coping skills of the consultee and learns from the consultee about the unique aspects of the problem and the consultee's situation. (p.113)

All the ideas given above are, I believe, still fundamental to what Consultation is or should be.

In the UK moves towards Consultation as a framework for EP practice have been in evidence for decades, and partly relate to calls to 'reconstruct educational psychology' (Gillham 1978). This standpoint reflected a widespread wish for change in the profession away from referral systems, psychometric assessment and reactive rather than preventative work. Many teachers at the time held the view that EPs were inaccessible and detached from the life of classrooms and schools and had little impact. It seemed that the stage was set for a sea-change in the work of EPs, and Consultation was an obvious way forward. Both EPs and teachers wanted that change, we just needed to create a service accessible to teachers, children and young people and their families as well as to the other professionals with whom EPs worked.

Consultation developed in the next few decades in EP service practice in various parts of the country, but was rarely a smooth process. Various forces had distorting effects and in some cases there was regression to more traditional models. The 1981 Education Act led to a focus on individual assessment, despite its preceding report (DES 1978) emphasising that special educational needs are relative to context. The 1988 Education Reform Act raised fears of the delegation of non-statutory EP services to schools. In order to protect services and seek resources in school the statementing rate surged, with increased psychometric assessment. Through the 1990s, and subsequently, legislation around SEN and disability has continued to re-focus on individual needs. There have also been supportive forces, for example the development of more rational methods for devolving funding to schools for children with very special needs. Some services made the shift and in some services Consultation has thrived and developed. Referring to England, DfEE (2000) concluded:

> Consultation and Solution-Focused approaches are seen as an important aspect of educational psychology services' work. A number of the services in the case studies had recently adopted the consultation approach to service delivery and saw this as key in helping to achieve a shift in the nature and balance of their work. (p.43)

Many services developing Consultation are in Wales and Scotland, and they may benefit from their distance from London and from the dominating compliance culture that government has promoted for so long and which has so often been a brake on imaginative development.

Principles for practice

A constructive principle

'The EP you create co-creates in turn the social world we all come to live in' (Jacobsen 1985). In choosing psychology that contributes to a better social world, an emphasis on Constructionist, Interactionist and Systemic psychology follows. This contrasts with those psychologies that have contributed to the exponential increase in the language of deficit in the past couple of decades. 'Furnish the population with the hammers of mental deficit and the social world is full of nails' (Gergen 1994, p.118).

A transparency principle

How we explain what we do to those with whom we are working is crucial. Similarly we aim to be open about helping others to access and develop their own expertise. In creating non-traditional practice, we can develop our repertoire in an open-handed way through flexible 'scripts' (described below).

A self-reflexive principle

Our practice is not to be found in a manual, and responds to changing contexts, so reflection on practice is essential and needs to be routine in all that we do. In addition, we would not want to apply to others any psychology that we would not be happy to apply to ourselves.

A comprehensive principle
We take the view that everything we do is Consultation – all aspects of our work as EPs are integrated into a conceptual and relational framework of Consultation (Wagner 2000). This contrasts with a model of service delivery, in which Consultation is cast as one discrete item in 'a menu' of service activities.

How do the psychologies informing Consultation translate into practice?
The psychologies of Consultation come predominantly from social psychology and are the basis of the practice. We are guided by the notion summed up as $B = f (P \times S)$, i.e. behaviour is a function of the person and the situation (Lewin 1946). This helps us to assist schools and other settings in acknowledging the power of the situation and how they can act to improve the situation for children, irrespective of what is happening in their lives outside the school. This does not mean that we underestimate the family as the primary socialising context for children, but, rather, it links to the vision we all have of schools as places that can make a difference in children's lives.

Personal Construct Psychology (Kelly 1955) informs our conversations, eliciting and exploring constructs, so as to understand and address the views that pupils develop of themselves as learners, as well as the views they have of significant others in their lives. We are interested to understand how such views might be affecting a child's progress in, for example, learning to read, and how those views can be influenced (Ravenette 1968). Symbolic Interactionism (Blumer 1969; Hargreaves 1972) emphasises that a pupil's view of him- or herself is a major cohering force and so we are interested in how such a view is built, enhanced and maintained. Consequently, we are interested in analysing how reputations are created and maintained, and in using the notion of deviance as a social construction (Hargreaves, Hestor and Mellor 1975). Such as analysis and understanding leads to more constructive interventions and change.

Systems Thinking helps us notice patterns that occur over time and in wider contexts. We work at the individual, class and organisational levels and help schools to make analyses and interventions at the three levels and to make links between them (Watkins and Wagner 2000). Although a consultation may start at the individual level, the eventual strategy suggested may be for a whole class. For example, if a child is finding it hard to cope with some family difficulties around parents separating, we might work with the teacher on activities in Personal and

Social Education that will help all the students. Our assumption is that all children at some time find feelings hard to deal with and that they will *all* benefit from working together on this area. In all our work we keep a focus on exploring how to help children and young people become more effective learners and we also always aim to consider the social and affective dimensions of learning.

Ideas from Systems Thinking and Family Therapy (Burnham 1986; Hoffman 1981) help us consider the inter-relating systems around the child, and possible conflicting expectations and their effects and how these can be addressed. The call to multi-agency work has been around for a long time and has recently been re-emphasised. However, it is not easy when different professionals work with different languages and different conceptions of what constitutes the problem and the solution. For example, in the professions of Social Care and Health, there can be a tendency for the problem to be located in the child or family and for the solution to be similarly focused, which means that medical, pathologising and 'within-the-person' models can dominate the picture. Workers in educational settings can then feel overwhelmed and impotent. A solution in such a case might be to develop more of a shared language of multi-agency working, and the EP is well placed in the system to facilitate such a development. For example, in meetings in educational settings the Consultation model and Solution-Focused Thinking have made a significant contribution to helping different agencies communicate more effectively (Harker 2001).

We aim to acknowledge and address the power of language in social interaction and in the Constructionist nature of language and discourse. We take seriously the idea that language creates reality, and seek to build a constructive discourse. We explore, in detail, what works and what things would be like if they were better. Through these detailed conversations the lives that people aspire to are more likely to eventuate. We aim to avoid the language of deficit and labelling and encourage others to describe, explore and reflect on the phenomena of their experience rather than to rely on labels. If, however, a parent asks us about, for example, dyslexia, we will explain as helpfully as we can about what is known about the varied 'manifestations' and what is known about what might help.

We try to keep a focus on learning (in its broadest sense) and on helping children become more active, engaged and successful learners in school by reflecting on when they do better in their learning and how we can build on that. We will always aim to elicit what works well for a child and when things are better. Consequently, we find it helpful to use frameworks of Solution-Focused conversations (Berg 1994; de Shazer 1985) and this has now become integrated into Consultation (Wagner and Gillies 2001), developing Solution-Focused interviews at the three levels of work. In these conversations there is an important emphasis on eliciting detailed descriptions of the occasions when things go well, in order to amplify solutions.

We use scaling question (Rhodes and Ajmal 1995) a lot in Consultation interviews since children and young people seem to respond especially well to scaling questions. Scales can be applied to a range of situations. We might ask, for example, if 10 was 'as good as it could be' and 0 was 'it couldn't be worse':

- How happy are you in school (now/last week/this term/this year/last year, etc.)?
- How confident do you feel in the corridors (now, etc.)?
- How successful are you at getting to school (or lessons) on time?
- How is your learning going (now, etc.)?

Particular activities or subjects can be explored and compared. Children can be amazingly perceptive when it comes to thinking about how their teacher might rate them and how they could improve their teacher's rating. Scaling also enables us to help children see how they have made some progress, however small that might be and whenever it might have been. It gives us a way to help them recognise the skills and resources they have and currently use, which they can celebrate and build on. A Solution-Focused approach links to features of Appreciative Enquiry (Hammond 1996), another major resource to Consultation – particularly when helping teachers identify and analyse the best of their classroom experiences.

Another technique we use is that of Narrative Thinking (White 1995), which is creatively explicit in recognising, acknowledging and utilising the expertise that people bring – helping them to voice the rich stories of their lives rather than focusing on stories of deficit. We have learned how to focus on, elicit and amplify in that process stories of competence, and how we can help others begin to change the thin stories of difficulties, or even diagnostic labels that have come to dominate and often determine the course of children's lives (Wagner and Watkins 2005). Externalising the problem (White 1989) is a process that Michael White first wrote about in relation to a child who was encopretic. 'Sneaky poo' has now an international reputation as the externalisation of that child's problem. Huntley (1999) has also shown the power of externalising with children with learning difficulties.

The model of Consultation is, therefore, in essence determined by the theory and practice of the psychologies that inform it, and which have been fundamental in its evolution. The challenge for EP practice is how to adapt ideas that may have originated in a clinical context, and to apply them in the systems and contexts in which we work. As multi-agency working has moved up the agenda in local authorities, Systemic Thinking continues to be important.

AS EPs we also need to apply psychologies to ourselves, according to the self-reflexive principle, and recognise the difficulties of role-making in a non-traditional style. We find that it is useful as a team to review the scripts that we use in order to explain ourselves to our role partners, i.e. to teachers and staff as well as to children and young people and their parents and carers and the other agencies with whom we work (Kerslake and Roller 2000). We do this with the aim of working out how to communicate effectively with others in a process that is engaging and appropriately respectful. Scripts should not be rigid or prescribed, but reflect the importance that we place on transparency and communication.

Frameworks for Consultation

Although Consultation is the over-arching framework for how we perceive and explain our role, within our practice we also use other specific frameworks (Wagner 1995). A framework is a frame to work in: it provides boundaries and helps construct a view. Frameworks embody the Social Constructionist and Systemic ways of thinking that we apply to all that we do. When those ways of thinking differ from the dominant discourse, the regular use of a framework can help create novel perspectives.

Frameworks are not simply procedures to follow, but provide a supportive structure for creative, collaborative conversations that we have in our work as EPs. They help us to work respectfully, imaginatively and systematically. These frameworks are intended to be used in an open-handed way and are made as accessible as possible to the people with whom we work. These frameworks are not fixed: they have been changed to accommodate developments in our thinking. Thus the approach and questions of Solution-Focused or Narrative Therapy, or of Appreciative Enquiry have now become more evident.

The intention has always been that the frameworks be succinct; that they provide a helpful structure to a conversation and that they are informative and can be used subsequently as useful working documents. They are not considered as, or used as, forms to fill in, but rather as structures to support conversations that are imaginative and useful.

Different frameworks are designed with particular role partners in mind and with particular purposes in mind. The three examples that follow provide a flavour of such frameworks:

- with teachers and school or centre staff
- with children and young people, parents and carers in joint school-family consultations, and
- with multi-agency groups.

The framework we used in each case provided the structure for a conversation. The process and content of the conversation related to a concern or issue that had been brought to the meeting.

'Full Consultation' with teachers and staff in schools and centres

Informal Consultation is used on those occasions when we do not meet children individually, open files or provide records for a child's school file. It comprises an informal Consultation with a teacher. It is only when a school prioritises a concern and more EP time is allocated that this becomes a Full Consultation (FC), which starts with the identification of the concern and engages in a process of working out:

- what is currently successful
- what further progress would look like, and
- what might contribute towards that progress.

FC could be about an individual, a group or an organisational-level issue. When it is about an individual, it is required that parents are already fully involved and have provided their consent for the EP's involvement.

The FC framework provides key questions that should be addressed by the teacher/staff before the Consultation occurs, as follows:

- What concerns you?
- What have you tried?
- What effects have you noticed?
- How would you like things to change? (And what would that look like?)
- What do you hope to get from this Consultation?

The fact that the teacher/staff member has had time to think about these questions before the Consultation meeting means that in many cases things that are contributing towards making a difference have been noticed before the meeting. This often leads to even more change occurring before the Consultation itself takes place. The EP uses questions that help the person to explore more dimensions of the situation and more of what is working, or might work. This helps them to find a wider repertoire of ideas and possible solutions. Questions from a Solution-Focused approach and from Appreciative Enquiry are an essential part – for example, questions that explore in detail the times when the concern is less of a concern, and what is happening at those times that helps the child engage in more active and collaborative ways.

The focus in an Individual-level Consultation is, at this stage, mainly on the child or young person in the context of the classroom and school. Our main role partners in Full Consultations over individual children and young people are usually key workers, class teachers, form tutors or year team leaders and, possibly, learning mentors and other staff as well as, when appropriate, other agencies. Including such role partners emphasises the fact that we work with the people who have a responsibility to have an overview of the whole child. Systemic Thinking can contribute lines of enquiry that open up the discussion about the child in other contexts, such as the major socialising agency of the family. However, since the aim is to focus on the child in the immediate context the focus is more on the school and classroom contexts at this stage.

Consultation provides time and space for busy professionals, such as teachers etc., who have concerns about children to have reflective conversations that make a difference. It is the *process* of Consultation that is the key to the difference that Consultation makes – not the actions that are arrived at when the Consultation is ending. If the actions themselves made the difference, then they could be prescribed without the need for Consultation. The process of Consultation helps professionals in schools or centres to take a step back and examine things in a way that helps thinking to shift towards a more Interactionist understanding away from a within-the-person explanation – and from there to a wider repertoire of possibilities for change. This wider repertoire of possibilities then translates into strategies and approaches that the key person can then draw on.

The documentation of Consultation comprises:

- the notes of key points made at the time of the Consultation
- the summary of current conclusions that is made towards the end of the Consultation, and
- the strategies and actions planned.

The documentation of Consultation comprises the notes of key points made at the time of the Consultation, the summary of current (for the time being) conclusions which is made towards the end of the Consultation, and the strategies and actions planned. It is worked out collaboratively with the key staff who the EP is working with. As such, it is a joint project between the EP and staff, which clarifies the understandings that have been reached and how things could develop and improve. It might also include further questions to explore.

In some instances, letters to teachers are also used (see Bozic 2004). However, this is not a routine practice since the documentation of Consultation as described above seems to do a very good job of keeping the work tracked and everyone appropriately involved. However, there can be key points or occasions in pieces of work when a letter to staff seems especially relevant. (For more on use of letters see below.)

INVOLVING CHILDREN OR YOUNG PEOPLE IN CONSULTATION

The classroom is usually the context for a teacher's concern. Consequently, Consultation over a child or young person in school is often preceded by an EP carrying out an observation in class or wherever the concern arises in the school. We aim to consider how well a range of features of the situation are currently organised and managed so that they encourage the development of collaborative, active, engaged, independent and effective learners. The features of the classroom that we consider to be contributory to such a situation are:

- the environment and the layout
- the social climate and groupings
- the tasks and activities
- the resources available
- the teaching support and
- the routines used by adults to engage children actively in their learning and the life of the classroom.

A snapshot observation of a child in the context of a classroom can be carried out and children in that class can be asked about their learning and the social dimensions of classroom (and school) life.

Conversations with children and young people can also take place outside the classroom, and will often mirror the approach and orientation of Consultation generally, i.e. these can be based on Appreciative Enquiry and Solution-Focused and Narrative approaches. These conversations explore in more depth the social and learning context of the classroom from the child or young person's perspective, and seek to explore and celebrate the successful ways that the child or young person has for engaging with others and in active, collaborative and effective learning (Watkins, Carnell and Lodge 2007). The use of letters to children or young people following individual interviews with them is now common practice in Consultation. This practice was inspired by the work of the Narrative Therapists (White and Epston 1990) and has become a powerful addition to the repertoire of work with children.

Letters help to crystallise further the acknowledgement and celebration of what has been explored and discussed with the child or young person, which could range across a variety of social, developmental and learning themes. For example:

- a young child who is grieving for her father talks about what she might do to recall the happy times they had and how she could talk with her mother about this, or how she could talk to her toys when she feels lonely or scared at night
- an older primary boy reflects on how he is becoming more successful in making and keeping friendships
- a young man with literacy difficulties and stress headaches in secondary school who was becoming a school refuser reflects on the times when he can spot his headaches coming on and how he might stop them by relaxing, as well as how he plans to do more of spotting the onset and relaxing himself. He can also look at how all of this will help him with his literacy, and think about which staff in school might help him develop these ideas and strategies further.

The aim is always to identify the resources *in* the person and *around* the person and to help them make the connections that will assist them in overcoming the difficulties they have been experiencing.

Joint school–family Consultation involving parents or carers

Key ideas when working with parents or carers are that:

- they all want to feel proud of their children (Berg and Steiner 2003)
- they can feel daunted by the prospect of engaging with schools when there are concerns over their children and they can feel criticised or attacked by questions that are put to them about their children at home (which seem to imply that the problem is in their parenting).

In a joint school–family Consultation the aim is to address the inevitable power imbalance through a structure that is supportive to joint working. We want to both engage parents over the work that the school or setting has done to help the child to progress, and to engage the expert knowledge that the parent has of the child. In this way a collaborative partnership becomes more than mere rhetoric. As in all our Consultations, the script that we have about the EP's role (explaining our background, training and role and how we work) is an important starter in de-mystifying and creating a greater sense of equality of expertise among everyone involved. We also explain the proposed structure of the meeting so that everyone can feel clear from the start that they have a unique and valued contribution and feel confident about how they can participate and contribute effectively.

A framework for the meeting is provided, as shown below in Figure 7.1, and is checked with everyone present to ensure it is acceptable.

Purpose of the meeting
- to update and involve the family over the Consultations that have taken place, the strategies planned, the work that has been carried out
- to discuss the family's views on the school's concerns and strategies
- to identify current concerns
- to work out together ways of promoting progress.

Plan of the meeting
1. The work carried out in school so far:
   1.1. The original Consultation took place with .... on ....
   1.2. The concerns expressed then were:
   1.3. Actions, programmes, strategies and methods planned at the Consultation:
   1.4. Progress that has been made in school in implementing these strategies and plans:
   1.5. Effect of the programmes, strategies, methods on the original cause for concern:
   1.6. Parental views and perspectives:
2. Current concerns:
3. Strategies and approaches and how we can work together to make progress as quickly as possible:
4. Any other points or issues that need to be considered:
5. Family + EP discussion/plans for discussion – if needed:
6. Conclusions and action plans:

Figure 7.1: Framework for a meeting in a joint school–family Consultation

At the end of a joint school–family Consultation of a primary-aged child, the child joins the meeting. The final part of the meeting, therefore, comprises the school staff and parents who talk to the child about how pleased they are about the successes they have noticed and about what school and home are planning to do together to help the child further. The successes are written down by the school and handed to the parent for the parent and child to take home.

Older children or young people are usually involved in joint school–family Consultation from the start of the meeting (depending on the developmental stage of the child). The aim with younger children is to ensure that the adults have come to agreements and understandings and have ironed out any misunderstandings so as to present the child with a positive picture of collaborative working between home and school. Taylor (1986) wrote eloquently about how especially important this can be for the families who may be thought of by the school as 'harder to reach' and the children who are then triangulated between school and home and, therefore, unable to do as well in school.

When the concerns about a child's happiness or progress in school that have led to EP involvement have originated from very worried and anxious parents, rather than from school or centre staff, then Consultation may start with joint school–family work. In these situations we would start more explicitly by looking at the best hope of the parents/carers and follow a framework that left space for concerns to be aired before moving on to finding signs of possibilities and of progress and successes.

Multi-agency meetings

The current agenda of *Every Child Matters* (ECM) (DfES 2003) is not new for schools, centres or EPs. Promoting children and young peoples' social development, learning and achievement has always been central to making schooling successful. The ECM simply provides a broadening impetus at a time when schools are overloaded with testing and inspections. However, the multi-agency thrust of ECM and The Children Act 2004 is not quite as straightforward as the architects of legislation and guidance appear to have hoped. Complications in multi-agency working occur because of differing conceptions of the problem and of the possible solution. When people working in education encounter explanations of children based on individual models of the person (still used frequently by health-service professionals), or family dysfunction explanations and family-treatment solutions often proposed by social care, the result can be disappointment, lack of collaborative working and, at worst, accusations of ignorance or arrogance. For teachers and staff in children centres, schools and other similar settings, an important motivating factor is the knowledge that you can make a difference. For health and social care professionals, however, the school is not seen as the context of change for the problems that they as professionals usually deal with, despite moves to more holistic and/or systemic approaches in this field. Pressures on social care workers around child protection and thresholds of involvement are likely to conflict with preventative working and can lead to multi-agency meetings that are predominantly focused around care proceedings. When such multi-agency meetings occur they are often dominated by a problem orientation and a practice of cataloguing in detail the history of problems and the perceived deficits of children and families. This focus can lead colleagues from education and social care to feel alienated one from the other. Such meetings leave very little time for finding strengths, resources or solutions, or for inter-agency solutions. Harker (2001) characterises such meetings as:

> 80 per cent problem talk and 20 per cent solution talk = few solutions found.
>
> 20 per cent problem talk and 80 per cent solution talk = many more possibilities for solutions found.

In multi-agency meetings we hope to encourage inter-agency working and to spend more time on finding strengths and resources, and through that process to find solutions. We have learned that a simple framework is very effective in multi-agency meetings. The framework comprises the following as shown in Figure 7.2:

Principles guiding our discussion and our planning

We are all here because we care about [name of child/young person] and we are concerned to help as much as possible.

The aim of the meeting – discussed and agreed first with all participants is: ....

The plan of meeting is as follows:

1. What are your best hopes for this meeting? How will you know it has been helpful?

2. Worries/concerns: what is happening with the child that is a concern to you at the moment? What needs to change?

3. What is going well at the moment? What is better? How are you contributing to things going better now? How can you help to make things go better for the future?

4. Conclusions

5. Actions: What: Who: When:

6. How useful was the meeting today: on a scale of 0–10

7. Will it be useful to have another meeting: Yes/No. If yes, when:

Figure 7.2: A framework for use in multi-agency meetings

Participants at the meeting are provided with copies of this framework at the start of the meeting, the plan is checked with them and (if everyone is agreeable) each person is asked to address Questions 1 to 3. Following that process, conclusions and actions are drawn up and the meeting is evaluated in terms of its usefulness in relation to the aims of the meeting and the best hopes of the participants, which were established at the outset of the meeting.

The frameworks described above are not the only frameworks that are used but they do provide a flavour of the kind of frameworks used in Consultation.

How can Consultation be evaluated?

The review and evaluation (R&E) of Consultation is a key and on-going aspect of the work and occurs regularly at individual Consultations, and also at an organisational level with the schools and centres that receive a Consultation service. R&E takes place, therefore, at each distinct Consultation meeting. The aim on these occasions is to review and evaluate the Consultation meeting in relation to the participants' best hopes for the Consultation. Consequently, we begin Consultations by asking the participants not only about his or her concerns but also about what would make the meeting a useful meeting. At the end we ask how the meeting has gone for participants in terms of their original hopes for the meeting. We also enquire about how much they feel that the structure and the process of the meeting helped them to contribute.

From the EP perspective, Consultations at the individual level are successful when participants feel able to explore a range of ideas that take them beyond explanations that are internal to the person towards a more Interactionist perspective that provides the person with more possibilities for action within his or her own sphere of influence. For example, this could relate to:

- insights that have developed about the child or young person during the Consultation that open up different ideas for interacting with the child

- aspects of organisation or management of the classroom that have become illuminated, which, if addressed, would improve the situation for the child or young person

- further enquiries with other staff that might help to illuminate key questions regarding when engagement in learning is more successful or when reputation effects might be more or less powerful and

- ideas about enquiries to other agencies about aspects of health or welfare.

R&E also takes place at key points in the year with the schools and centres that we work with. Consequently, we have termly review and annual review and evaluation of the work. Termly reviews are fairly brief and help us to tune the work, using the questions:

- What has gone well?
- What has not gone so well?
- What issues are raised?
- What actions are needed?

The annual review and evaluation of Consultation is designed to check whether positive outcomes are occurring based on the research into what Consultation is intended to achieve, i.e. both remedial and preventive goals as decribed by Gutkin and Curtis (1999). Questions and lines of enquiry in the R&E aim to address specific areas regarding outcomes for children, families, staff and the school/centre as a whole.

Schools have been consistently very clear in the review and evaluation of Consultation over a number of years about the positive outcomes for children and young people over whom they have concerns, as well as the preventive benefits of Consultation for all children, and for staff and for the school as a whole. Feedback to the questions that we ask in our annual review meetings has shown that teachers and staff who are involved in a Consultation service:

- are more likely to generalise ideas and approaches to other children in the same class
- find problems to be less serious
- report enhanced professional skills as an outcome of being involved in Consultations
- are more likely to utilise Consultation skills and approaches in meetings with children and young people, with other staff, with parents and carers and with other agencies – and to report that these meetings are enhanced as a result
- are more likely to shift their attribution for the causation of a pupil-related concern from internal to the child to interactional in nature, recognising the importance of features of the situation in the classroom (such as social climate and groupings, tasks and activities, how learning support and resources can be used more effectively, etc.).

> **Aim of the review** For the EP and school to review, jointly, the work that has been done in and with the school, to examine its effectiveness, to work out developments, and to appreciate and celebrate the successes so that we can build on them.
>
> **Summary of the work of the year** (provided by the EP, plus monitoring of all the work)
>
> **General areas to discuss**
> What has gone well in the content and the process of the school visits?
>
> How effective has the work been?
>
> What does that suggest about how we would like to progress the work further next year?
>
> Any other issues that we wish to raise:
>
> **Summary and conclusions**
> Prompts used to assist in the review:
>
> > Balance in the three levels of work (individual, group/class and organisational)
> >
> > 1. Individual pupil level (overall patterns in the Consultations, transfer of skills, transfer between levels – individual to group, to organisational)
> > 2. Groups of pupils (as above)
> > 3. Organisational/whole-school level: Work with a range of role partners at different levels: individual teachers, groups/teams of teachers, whole staff, parents' evenings, governors meetings, etc.

Figure 7.3: Questions for use in annual review and evaluation of Consultation

SENCos, Inclusion Managers, Senior Managers and Head Teachers tell us that Consultation also contributes towards classroom and school improvement. This feedback matches a range of research on the effects of Consultation (Gutkin and Curtis 1999). In over 75 per cent of studies, Consultation was shown to have yielded positive results (Sheridan, Welch and Orme 1996). Small-scale studies in the UK show a similar promising picture (Larney 2003).

The evaluations (for purposes of accountability) that schools make of the Education Psychology Consultation Service (EPCS) in Kensington and Chelsea are very positive. This has been validated by the Audit Commission's e-survey of schools, which for the past four years has reported that the RBK & C EP Consultation service is the most highly rated in the country (Audit Commission 2006).

An EP Consultation service, when working effectively in a local authority (LA) context, will contribute towards the thinking and action of the LA through participation at the strategic and operational levels of the organisation. We are reported to contribute to an 'outstanding' rating in the authority's Joint Area Review (Ofsted 2007).

How can Consultation be developed?

Consultation is relatively easy to initiate in an EPS since EPs are generally familiar with the ideas of collaborative working and are usually pleased to have the opportunity of working this way – especially if they have been tied to a treadmill of individual assessment work. They usually relish the idea of working more imaginatively at different levels in schools and centres (the individual, group and organisational levels), as well as with other aspects of inter-relating systems, with the local authority and more widely. Teachers and other staff in schools and centres and families are often the first to show their appreciation of Consultation. Working in a collaborative way helps people to take a step back, reflect and work out, individually and together, how they can make a difference to the lives of children and young people whom they work with and care about through direct and indirect work and systems change. Local-authority officers and other agencies with whom EPs work are also generally appreciative of an approach and a style of working that works against the grain of the pressured and pervasive climate of accountability, blame and compliance that has come to dominate many local authorities in the past couple of decades.

Inevitably, a more appreciative style can sometimes challenge strongly held beliefs about development and change in organisations and can create perturbations in the system. We aim to make these as constructive and useful as possible by being open-handed with our colleagues about how we work, where the ideas come from and what the benefits are for children and families, schools and centres and the organisations we work with and in. This is an important and on-going task in developing Consultation in a LA setting, so that it can be understood by other colleagues with whom we work.

The development of Consultation in a service setting requires commitment from the EP team to embrace the evolution of Consultation in the particular service context. Of course, it is easier when EPs are not located as gatekeepers on resources via individual assessment work, but this situation is generally changing.

Consultation will wither and atrophy unless there are active means taken to nurture it and to keep the team focused on the principles, psychologies and practices that are essential to its further development. Without an active and self-reflexive process that engages the whole of the team, it is likely that a gradual regression to more traditional models will occur. Consequently, the study of the psychologies and related practices of Consultation will need to be kept central to our professional development programmes.

There will always be other topics we need to find out about, and with any new development we need to ask the question: 'How does this relate to Consultation?' The challenge is to learn how to become 'multi-lingual' and, at the same time, to make a useful contribution. We need to be able to engage with others in situations in which labels (such as ADHD) or deficit discourse, originating from a medical model, are commonly used. On such occasions we need to be able to connect constructively without becoming oppositional or either losing our way or our sense of what, and how, we can contribute effectively. Nylund (2002) has written superbly on this particular issue.

Consultation is already taught on some EP initial training courses as a unifying theme and an overarching approach, thus avoiding the fragmentation that can result from a more topic-based approach. The key to Consultation is the psychology that is used, and, therefore, Interactionist, Systemic, Appreciative, Solution-Focused and Narrative approaches are all essential on EP training courses. 'Tool-kits' of methods do not feature in such courses, and learning is active and collaborative, with opportunities for application and practice and regular reflection on principles and practice. The approach is one of learning to be helpful without being reactive to be appropriately psychological, without being opaque, and to be essentially respectful of people.

What are the key difficulties with Consultation?

The Consultation process appears simple and this can be deceptive. Such misconceptions have led to descriptions of Consultation as 'having cosy chats', when compared with a highly structured interview schedule. Consultation is intended to be engaging and transparent and in that sense there is an aim and a plan that there will, as far as possible, be a sense of ease in the situation and the interactions. Effective Consultation is, in fact, highly skilful, and one of the skills lies in making it appear easy and helping others to feel at ease, even when the situation is challenging and possibly fraught. Since the key to Consultation is psychology there therefore needs to be an explicit and active development of the psychologies and related knowledge and skills of Consultation over time. This should take the form of a spiral curriculum, which is regularly revisited.

As a profession, EPs tend to be great pragmatists and many initial training courses seem, in the past, to have focused more on methodology than psychology. Consultation invites EPs to reclaim psychology. This can be hard to do when a lot of time in a career has been spent working to satisfy the pressure for gatekeeping on resources, determining resource-worthiness or responding to requests for individual assessment. Some EPs have highly developed individual-assessment skills and for some of those EPs the shift to Consultation can be daunting. EPs may, therefore, feel more comfortable holding on to the individual assessment role and may argue that schools want them to do that. This often occurs when a different approach, such as Consultation, is not seen or understood as being the major contribution of the EP.

Of course, EPs using Consultation do, sometimes, work individually with children or young people, but they are less likely to do this routinely and formally. In individual interviews they enquire about learning, using ideas from Solution-Focused and Narrative approaches or Appreciative Enquiry so as to explore and amplify a child's engagement and success in learning and his/her happiness in school. Schools often say that they find this more valuable than a traditional individual assessment, but in order for this shift to occur it requires that the EP has the training to carry out Consultation in this way. When a service has made a commitment to Consultation, but there is insufficient on-going development of Consultation, the relevant knowledge and skills will fail to develop and in those cases, inevitably, frustration will occur and busy EPs will be likely to revert to previous ways of working.

There are also less considered versions of Consultation, for example, when it is offered as one item on a menu. Another is when so-called Consultation takes place at the beginning of the school year or term with a number of other agencies often involved, and then the EP engages in individual assessment work for the rest of the term or year.

An EPS engaged in Consultation needs to avoid the paraphernalia of referral, while remaining responsive and helpful with expertise at the ready. This does not mean taking anything and everything on, or telling people what to do, but means being prepared to help others to think things through and contribute to a process that leads to the emergence of solutions that are more tuned to the context – and it is this that is the essence of Consultation.

References

Audit Commission (2006) *School Survey Analysis Report for: The Effectiveness of your Council's Educational Psychology Support. Individual Question Analysis: Top-rated Councils.* London: Audit Commission. Accessed 30 July 2007 at www.audit-commission.gov.uk/schoolsurvey/topratedleas.asp

Bateson, G. (1972) *Steps to an Ecology of Mind: Collected Essays in Anthropology, Psychiatry, Evolution and Epistemology.* New York: Ballantine Books.

Berg, I.K. (1994) *Family-Based Services: A Solution-Focused Approach.* New York: W.W. Norton.

Berg, I.K. and Steiner, T. (2003) *Children's Solution Work.* New York: W.W. Norton.

Blumer, H. (1969) *Symbolic Interactionism: Perspective and Method.* Englewood Cliffs, NJ: Prentice Hall.

Bozic, N. (2004) 'Using letters to support consultative work in schools.' *Educational Psychology in Practice 20,* 4, 291–302.

Burnham, J. (1986) *Family Therapy: First Steps towards a Systemic Approach.* London: Routledge.

Caplan, G. (1970) *The Theory and Practice of Mental Health Consultation.* New York: Basic Books.

Conoley, J.C. and Conoley, C.W. (1982) *School Consultation: A Guide to Practice and Theory.* Oxford: Pergamon.

Conoley, J.C., Apter, S.J. and Conoley, C.W. (1981) 'Teacher Consultation and the Resource Teacher: Increasing Services to Seriously Disturbed Children.' In F.H. Wood (ed.) *Perspectives for a New Decade: Education's Responsibility for Seriously Disturbed and Behaviorally Disorded Children and Youth.* Reston, VA: Council for Exceptional Children.

de Shazer, S. (1985) *Keys to Solutions in Brief Therapy.* New York: W.W. Norton.

Department for Education and Employment (2000) *Educational/Psychology Services (England): Current Role, Good Practice and Future Direction – Report of the Working Group.* London: DfEE.

Department for Education and Skills (2003) *Every Child Matters.* London: HMSO.

Department of Education and Science (1978) *Special Educational Needs* (The Warnock Report). London: HMSO.

Gallessich, J. (1972) 'A systems model of mental health consultation.' *Psychology in the Schools 9,* 1, 13–15.

Gergen, K.J. (1994) *Realities and Relationships: Soundings in Social Construction.* Cambridge, MA: Harvard University Press.

Gergen, K.J. (1997) 'The place of the psyche in a constructed world.' *Journal of Theory and Psychology 7,* 31–36.

Gillham, B. (ed.) (1978) *Reconstructing Educational Psychology.* London: Croom Helm.

Gutkin, T.B. and Curtis, M.J. (1999) 'School-based Consultation – Theory and Practice: The Science and Art of Indirect Service Delivery.' In C.R. Reynolds and T.B. Gutkin (eds) *The Handbook of School Psychology* (3rd edn). New York: Wiley.

Hammond, S.A. (1996) *The Thin Book of Appreciative Inquiry.* Plano, TX: Kodiak Consulting.

Hargreaves, D.H. (1972) *Interpersonal Relations and Education.* London: Routledge Kegan Paul.

Hargreaves, D.H., Hestor, S. and Mellor, F. (1975) *Deviance in Classrooms.* London: Routledge Kegan Paul.

Harker, M. (2001) 'How to Build Solutions at Meetings.' In Y. Ajmal and I. Rees (eds) *Solutions in Schools.* London: BT Press.

Hoffman, L. (1981) *Foundations of Family Therapy: A Conceptual Framework for Systems Change.* New York: Basic Books.

Huntley, J. (1999) 'A Narrative Approach toward Working with Students who have "Learning Difficulties".' In A. Morgan (ed.) *Once Upon a Time: Narrative Therapy with Children and Their Families.* Adelaide: Dulwich Centre Publications.

Jacobsen, B. (1985) 'Does Educational Psychology Contribute to the Solution of Educational Problems?' In G. Claxton, W. Swann, P. Salmon, V. Walkerdine, *et al.* (eds) *Educational Psychology and Schooling: What's the Matter?* London: Institute of Education.

Kelly, G.A. (1955) *The Psychology of Personal Constructs.* New York: W.W. Norton.

Kerslake, H. and Roller, J. (2000) 'The development of "scripts" in the practice of consultation.' *Educational Psychology in Practice 16,* 1, 25–31.

Larney, R. (2003) 'School-based consultation in UK: Principles, practice and effectiveness.' *School Psychology International 24,* 1.

Lewin, K. (1946) 'Behavior and Development as a Function of the Total Situation.' In L. Carmichael (ed.) *Manual of Child Psychology.* New York: Wiley.

Meyers, J. (1973) 'A consultation model for school psychological-services'. *Journal of School Psychology 11*, 5–15.

Nylund, D. (2002) *Treating Huckleberry Finn: A New Narrative Approach to Working with Kids Diagnosed ADD/ADHD.* San Francisco, CA: Jossey-Bass.

Ofsted (2007) *Joint Area Review: Royal Borough of Kensington and Chelsea Children's Services Authority Area, Review of Services for Children and Young People.* London: Ofsted.

Ravenette, A.T. (1968) *Dimensions of Reading Difficulties.* Oxford: Pergamon.

Rhodes, J. and Ajmal, Y. (1995) *Solution Focused Thinking in Schools.* London: BT Press.

Sheridan, S.M., Welch, M. and Orme, S.F. (1996) 'Is consultation effective? A review of outcome research.' *Remedial and Special Education 17*, 6, 341–354.

Taylor, D. (1986) 'The child as go-between: Consulting with parents and teachers.' *Journal of Family Therapy 8*, 1, 79–89.

Wagner, P. (1995) *School Consultation: Frameworks for the Practising Educational Psychologist.* London: Kensington and Chelsea EPS.

Wagner, P. (2000) 'Consultation: Developing a comprehensive approach to service delivery.' *Educational Psychology in Practice 16*, 1, 9–19.

Wagner, P. and Gillies, E. (2001) 'Consultation: A Solution-focused Approach.' In Y. Ajmal and I. Rees (eds) *Solutions in Schools.* London: BT Press.

Wagner, P. and Watkins, C. (2005) 'Narrative Work in Schools.' In A. Vetere and E. Dowling (eds) *Narrative Therapies with Children and their Families.* Hove: Routledge.

Watkins, C., Carnell, E. and Lodge, C. (2007) *Effective Learning in Classrooms.* London: Paul Chapman/Sage.

Watkins, C. and Wagner, P. (2000) *Improving School Behaviour.* London: Paul Chapman/Sage.

White, M. (1989) 'The Externalising of the Problem and the Re-authoring of Lives and Relationships.' In M. White (ed.) *Selected Papers.* Adelaide: Dulwich Centre.

White, M. (1995) *Re-Authoring Lives: Interviews and Essays.* Adelaide: Dulwich Centre.

White, M. and Epston, D. (1990) *Narrative Means to Therapeutic Ends.* New York: W.W. Norton.

CHAPTER 8

A Systemic Solution-Oriented Model

Ioan Rees

Introduction

This chapter is the product of my years as an educational psychologist (EP) – and I guess it's the product of even more than that. It goes back to the time I taught in school and, before that, running my own small business in London, and all that I learned by doing these things, and more. All our life stories, about how we got to where we are today, have elements of excitement, challenge, frustration, risk, exhaustion, intrigue, boredom, drama, awe and reward – and for me it's been in pursuit of the answer to a single question: 'How best to effect change?'

As an EP, I believed passionately that the answer to this question was to do with the unlocking of the Solution-Focused (SF) model into becoming a powerful, and effective, Systemic application (Rees 2001a, 2001b). From the start, this has been the vision and pursuit of an organisation I work for, Sycol – to deliver systemic, Solution-Oriented improvement and innovation to public sector services. Armed with what I have learned over the years with that endeavour, this chapter will share with you not only 'how best to effect change' but also how best to do it in a Systemic and Solution-Oriented way.

Many people are familiar with Solution-Focused work and I will explain what is meant by 'Solution-Focused' and why, like others, I have come to call what I do Solution-Oriented. I will also explain what we mean when we use the word 'systems'. Systems will be described as a liberating concept, not a straitjacket, prescriptive entity. Systems serve to open the worker's eyes to the patterns and features that are common within and between good practices, allowing the integration and inclusion of all manner of applications alongside a core, Solution-Focused model. I will draw on my experiences as a researcher, having done a Ph.D. on the subject, but mostly from the hundreds of lessons that I have learnt during the struggle to find the best way of using this simple approach to achieve truly amazing results.

What will be shared will guide those in training, starting out on their journey toward Systemic practice, and also more experienced EP colleagues, by highlighting the process involved in developing a Systemic practice. In addition, for EP the service will provide a clear mapping of how to go about achieving the pervasive application of the Solution-Oriented model across all aspects of delivery, thus fulfilling the promise made to clients.

Origins

You will notice how, during this chapter, as I explain what Systemic practice looks like and how it can be achieved, the Solution-Oriented model emerges from an initial Solution-Focused base. In order to understand this evolution, it will be helpful for me first to describe the origins of both approaches and the distinguishing features.

You'll already know the Solution-Focused (SF) approach started in the therapy room as Solution-Focused Brief Therapy (SFBT). Much has been written about its therapeutic application by very many practitioners, the most prolific of whom was Steve de Shazer (de Shazer 1985, 1988, 1991, 1994). De Shazer was influenced by the early work of Gregory Bateson's team at the Mental Research Institute (MRI) in Palo Alto in the 1970s and went on to become the first to describe the model as we know it today, referring to it as Solution-Focused (Bateson 1972, 1979).

Bill O'Hanlon was also influenced by the work of the MRI and also that of Milton Erickson, a psychiatrist whose work incorporated unique and idiosyncratic methods with the central concept of 'utilisation' to bring about change. O'Hanlon recognised that Erickson would 'use' almost anything the client would bring as a means of eliciting solution patterns out of the existing problem patterns in their lives (Erickson 1954). O'Hanlon continued in this tradition and has written widely on the subject, describing the model as Solution-Oriented (SO) (O'Hanlon 1987, 1998, 2000; O'Hanlon and Beadle 1996; O'Hanlon and Weiner Davis 1989).

The two main differences between the models are simple to explain.

- The first is that the Solution-Oriented model seeks to embrace the problem narrative or concern as a potentially important part of the change process. Acknowledgement of the pain (or whatever is blocking progress) is viewed as an important component in the service of change. The Solution-Focused model considers this to be less important, believing that change can result entirely from building upon competence (O'Hanlon 2007).

- Second, the Solution-Oriented model allows for, and encourages the integration of any other method or technique that will help bring about change – with the proviso that it reflects the key principles of the approach. It is a truly inclusive model. With this in mind practitioners are known to do 'whatever it takes' to help make change happen. Conversely, the strength of the Solution-Focused model lies in its technique, particularly in the use of questions, and, as such, is more 'focused' and contained, as the name suggests (Murphy and Duncan 2007).

In this chapter I intend to share how a Solution-Focused practice can mature into becoming Systemic Solution-Oriented applications, what this looks like and how it works. The cycle of events that occur during this evolution are told as a story – Sam's story. Sam is a fictional EP who represents much of how we think and behave as we grow and get better at what we do. Sam asks all the questions I have once asked – that, indeed, we all ask at some point – in order to discover the answers that I am about to share with you.

The evolution of a Systemic Solution-Oriented model
The Early Stage: All about technique

Sam was a young educational psychologist who decided it was time for her to attend an intensive, week-long training to develop her Solution-Focused (SF) skills, having heard so much about it from colleagues. She returned from the training (as did all who went before her) inspired, motivated and with high hopes. Sam's heart was on fire with SF. 'This is what I've been waiting for, wanting for so long,' she thought. 'As a matter of fact, I now realise this is why I chose to do this work in the first place.' This truly was 'it'. And with this new-found energy, Sam was going to set the world ablaze. She was now on a mission, maybe even a crusade, because, in her mind, she was going to revolutionise her clients' experience of educational psychology from the traditional to SF.

With good intentions, Sam passionately believed that SF would help her achieve amazing outcomes and would even perhaps be evidence enough to persuade her boss (and maybe her service) also to become SF. All this was going to be possible with her strong spirit, determination and enthusiasm – she had bundles of it. Surely, this was all going to be pretty straightforward? 'I've just got to go and do it, model it, show an example, practise what I preach and folk will inevitably follow when they see the results for themselves' is precisely what she said to herself. 'I've just got to go out and use the SF techniques I've learned with everyone.' And indeed for quite a while this was the case and Sam's great SF energy and enthusiasm were truly infectious – and, while it lasted, everybody around her noticed the change in her working methods.

Sam was seized by the power of the technique and had become what is so common – an SF technician. She could see nothing other than her full commitment and hard work in using the techniques she'd learned, the SF questions, the scales, the miracles in as many situations as possible. They appeared in her interviews, consultations, her assessments, meetings and her reports. She'd even gone to the trouble of creating resources such as prompt sheets, script cards and SF forms to assist in the application of all these techniques.

Sam was to be commended for the dedicated hours she'd invested into becoming a very skilful SF technician. Indeed, she'd made a name for herself locally and colleagues were referring 'difficult' and 'stuck' clients to her from all sectors – and she loved it. However, certain things were beginning to bother her and she was realising that operating as a technician would never take her any further than operating as a technician. Although her SF technique was applied systematically in the sense that it ran throughout her practice, it remained on an individual level – reliant on her individual efforts.

When I met Sam her worries on the subject were on her mind and they came as no surprise to me; 'I'm so convinced that I'm doing the right thing – that the SF approach is genuinely respectful of and useful to the clients I work with, but…' she paused. 'But what, Sam?' I asked. 'I actually feel exhausted, lonely and frustrated.'

'I'm not surprised,' I said, 'You've clearly invested your heart and soul in this and it seems to me that you've really tried hard to bring SF to all the people you work with.' Sam nodded and quietly said, 'I have, but it's not working, it's just me doing it.'

'So, okay Sam, let's look at what's happening here to see if we can understand it better and move on. You may be pleased to hear that what's happening here is not unusual, Sam: as a matter of fact it's inevitable. You have become what I call the "perfect technician", and whilst that takes time and effort in achieving, it also means that so long as you stay working as the perfect technician – being able to "do" all the techniques you've been taught – you'll always remain that and always be called to that kind of work. You have seen the demands upon you grow and expectations of you rise, and all because of your great results. People now expect you to do more in less time – a bit like asking a carpenter to saw faster as he becomes more skilled at it. Does that sound about right, Sam?

'Under the growing demand of doing it all, it's understandable that you're starting to tire and notice cracks showing in your once perfect, technical work. You might even have found yourself compromising slightly and dodging some techniques, just to get the job done quicker. No matter how hard you try it seems to start slipping. The meetings you facilitate no longer go to your SF plan and some of them become positively problem-focused. Then one day, your tiredness really shows when you get asked by a colleague, "Are you still doing that SF work, Sam?" and you react defensively.

'So what do you do at this point, Sam? Well, you decide that the best thing to do is go on another skills training course in order to give yourself a revitalising boost of SF. However, once back in work, it soon gets back to where it was – you doing the technique work, you feeling lonely at it and you working very hard. And what about all the people you managed to train in the techniques along the way, where are they now? You get to hear messages that they all think your training was great but they don't have the time, space or money to join with you to carry out the SF work like you do.'

Sam was sitting quietly and said, 'That's exactly what's happened, so what do I do about it, because I don't want to stop, either?'

Sam was going to have to choose between three options in order to make her next move. This is a choice all technicians have to make during the Early Stage of Systemic SO development. Sam's options included the following:

- Option 1: That the technical SF work she conducted be diluted, thus reducing the demand on, and expectation of, her.

- Option 2: That she continues in the same vein, working hard, attending more technical training and accepting that her commitment to SF means that she may continue to feel tired, lonely and frustrated some of the time.

- Option 3: That she moves forward into the next developmental stage – the Intermediate Stages – in becoming a Systemic practitioner of the model.

The Intermediate Stage: Principles as standards

I was pleased when Sam decided on Option 3, that of moving forward. She didn't want to give up or dilute her SF work; on the contrary, she wanted to see and do more of it, but just didn't know how to go about things.

The Intermediate Stage is an exciting phase: it's the introduction to what it takes to become a truly Systemic worker. It follows on from what can sometimes be the exhaustion, hard work, ups and downs of the Early Stage and brings a light, new focus. It is also the first time most of us truly come to realise something about the importance of systems, and how Systems Thinking can make astounding impact on what had previously seemed impossible in our practice. This transitional period comes about when we make a number of observations or realise certain things about how the world works around us. There is so much evidence, every day, everywhere to remind us why we should be moving forward into the Intermediate Stage.

If you are truly interested in finding out how the model can work systemically, then you have to be prepared to move from the SF technician to being Solution-Oriented and the answer to how to do this is to be seen all around you. It's out there, and all you have to do is to go out and look. However, most of us don't do this because we're focused inwardly, on ourselves, interested only in how 'we' do things, rather than being focused 'out', and how things get done well in the world.

If and when we do choose to look and take a real interest in how things work around us – in the shop, in the school, in the restaurant, in the business – then we can see the beauty of how it's organised, its order, its system, the system that makes it work.

At Sycol, we refer to the importance of observing some Fundamental Truths about how the world of work works. These are the starting points for learning about Solution-Oriented Systemic work practice, moving away from just technique to something far greater. Appreciating these truths is important in passing through the Intermediate Stage of Systemic development.

FUNDAMENTAL TRUTH NO.1: THERE ARE COMMON FACTORS DESPITE DIFFERENCES

Most EPs are familiar with going from one school to another – sometimes several in one day, even. From one meeting to another, one consultation to another. It's the same if you are a manager of a service, going from one meeting to another with the probable expectation that you will have the answer.

It's also true to say that the people and organisations we serve, seek answers and for these to be bespoke – to fit perfectly with their unique context. In other words, they're hoping that solutions that the EP provides will be perfectly tailored to solving their unique problem(s).

Whilst, of course, unique problems exist in the world, the imperative of a Systemic worker is not to solely see such difference, but rather to see that which is common across contexts and experiences. This in turn affects the work and is the first Fundamental Truth, that organisations including schools and services (and the people who work in and for them) believe they are very different to all others. But this is not in fact the case - it's not all different and what we need to see is what's in common, whilst acknowledging obvious difference. We need to see what's common about the successful ways they go about doing things, the systems they have for doing things and the patterns of interaction.

As an EP you may hear, 'In our school the children are taller, shorter, more challenging, we have more girls, the socio-economic group is different, it's tougher, there's no grass', and so on, and so on. The message is 'We're different here and you'd better have a bespoke, uniquely fitting solution for us or else it won't stand a chance of working'.

Yes, the children are different, yes, the building is in a different part of town and, yes, there are more girls than boys in the school. But, if you're only looking for what is different between contexts and not what is in common, you'll never be free to work Systemically. Because Systemic practice calls us to look at what's common, then learn from it so that we can potentially replicate the operation over and over.

There are many examples of how looking for what is common works in practice. Take, for example, the Head Teacher who builds a successful school in an affluent part of town, and who, when moved to another school in a less affluent area, in a completely different catchment is successful once more, all over again. How is she able to achieve the same success despite things being so different? How does she do all this, despite the huge contrast in schools? And, what's more, you're unlikely to hear her ever say: ' I can't make this school great, it's in the wrong area of town, the children are too challenging' and so on. The answer is very clear – the Head Teacher is seeing things Systemically and is looking for what's common, what connects everything in the same way, despite the change of context. In doing so, she is cultivating Systems Thinking – thinking about how things work, particularly organisations. It is a natural step from thinking in terms of patterns to then actually seeing the groupings, connections and interactions operating within systems.

FUNDAMENTAL TRUTH NO.2: WORKING 'ON' NOT JUST 'IN'

As mentioned, Sam was a very busy professional. She used her Solution-Focused skills and techniques to the maximum. She believed that only if she did this would she achieve maximum impact on her professional life and the lives of others. But there comes a point, when beyond the initial learning stage, beyond the practice and honing stage, when being busy yields diminishing return. The reality is you being technically brilliant and very busy, it consumes you and, quite possibly, the work you once loved can enslave you. There comes a point where you have to go to work 'on' what you do, in order to improve it – or stay a technician. When you go to work 'on' your team, service, school, organisation to make it the best it can be, you have to leave behind the technician in order to work differently.

It's like the technically excellent chef who decides to open up his own restaurant or the brilliant carpenter who decides to set up on his own. Before you know it they've both named their business after themselves: 'Jo's Bistro' and 'R.J. Watkins Carpentry'. Soon, they are both busy doing what they've always done best; the chef is busy cooking in his kitchen and the carpenter busy sawing in his workshop. In other words, they are both doing what they are good at, and why not? Well, that's fine if that's how they want things to stay forever. However, if they want their business to grow, flourish, and mature beyond them and who they are – so that it does not remain all about them but rather is about great restaurants and carpentry enterprises that do things in special ways – then things will need to change. Both men will have to move from the security of holding onto the busy, technician's mindset to realising a far wider, Systemic perspective of their work and futures; to seeing the bigger picture of how things are organised in their world of work. The chef will need to work 'on' planning his menus, front of house and decorating his restaurant and the carpenter 'on' standardising his work and recruiting apprentices who can do the same.

Sam had just told me that she wanted to move on and face the challenges of the Intermediate Stage. 'So Sam, what we need to look at next is the one crucial element that distinguishes those at the Early and Intermediate Stage. Are you ready?' I paused before moving on. 'During the Early Stage, Sam, all that drives you is you doing the technique well, perfecting the SF method, so that you might become a master at it and able to teach others. Skill and technique become your fuel; they are what keep you going. Going to more training events is like filling your car up with more fuel, and when it runs dry, it's time for another boost. Does this sound familiar?'

'Yes, it does. Please carry on.' Sam was interested in what was being said and was thinking carefully about how all of this was going to have a significant impact upon her work and life.

'At the Intermediate Stage it's something completely different that acts as your fuel, enabling you to go to work "on" what you do, something that every Solution-Oriented practitioner knows and believes acts to transform their work. This fuel is extra to your energy that carried you along as a technician and it's a fuel that will never run dry. This fuel is in the form of a set of guiding, Soution-Oriented principles, and is in addition to understanding the two, Fundamental Truths. The Solution-Oriented Principles are the fuel that will move you out of being a technician, albeit a brilliant one, and into Systemic practice. Yes, at the Intermediate Stage, principles will drive, guide and organise your work, shape your mindset and ultimately influence everything that you do, transforming you into more of a Solution-Oriented Systemic worker.'

'I'd never thought of principles in such a way. So should principles influence everything I do and what kind of principles are you talking about?' enquired Sam.

'Alright, let's look at the first part of your question, how principles might influence all that you do. Principles are often referred to as beliefs or values. We all have them, some are aware of them at a conscious level and others not. They are a product of many things in life – your childhood, your education, and your social experiences, all of which serve to influence how you behave. For example, if you were to believe in the principle of equality then it would not be surprising to hear you address people who have diverse backgrounds equally; your work would reflect this, your communications and commitments. Conversely, if you did not believe in the principle of equality, that too would show in your work. You'd maybe routinely behave in a way that favoured some over others.

'So, what I'm saying is that our principles reflect our view of the world, which, in turn, affect how we behave in the world. One drives the other. How, therefore, do you think you'd behave and act professionally if your principles were Solution-Focused?'

Sam paused, smiled and answered 'In a Solution-Focused way, right?' 'Yes, right', I said 'and not only would these principles guide you in the way you conducted some of your assessments and consultations and most of the techniques you'd use, but the principles would have a pervasive, whole-practice encompassing effect, which affected every single thing you did. They would insist that all of your actions reflected them, consistently and completely.

'The Solution-Oriented Principles that I am about to share with you are ones that can do just that – influence, guide and shape all of your work: in fact all of your being. They are not just to do with technique, they are to do with thinking, feeling, understanding, all of the other parts that go missing when we live without the direction that principles offer. So, this answers the second part of your question, Sam – what kind of principles?'

'Yes, I was going to ask,' Sam said excitedly 'Is this where I'll see a big difference between Solution-Oriented and Solution-Focused?'

'Yes, Sam, and the difference lies in the fact that Solution-Oriented Principles reflect the fact that the approach is broad-based, enveloping and inclusive, culturally sensitive, non-technical, humanistic and embraces of all that works. This principle base means it pays far less attention to technique and specific questions than does SF, which is necessary as you grow from being a technician to being a truly inclusive and successful Systemic worker. Its strength lies in the breadth of its core beliefs, including a profound belief in the necessity for inclusion and utilisation of the full range of the human condition, both pain and possibility. This makes room for all that may contribute to bring about desired ends. It's for you to choose of course, but to move forward in the Intermediate Stage, to embrace the relevance of SO Principles is essential.'

At this point in the conversation I shared with Sam the ten Solution-Oriented Principles that could shape and influence all her practice in future.

The Ten Solution-Oriented Principles

1. IF IT WORKS, DO MORE OF IT; IF IT DOESN'T WORK, DO SOMETHING DIFFERENT
Definition: To listen and look for, seize upon, expand and exploit that which works in order to achieve progress (the caveat being that it needs to be legal,

ethical and respectful). In the same respect, to listen and look for, modify, reduce, shrink, substitute, stop or avoid that which does not work in order to create more space for that which does and to achieve more progress.

2. A SMALL CHANGE IN ANY ASPECT OF A PROBLEM CAN INITIATE A SOLUTION
Definition: Counter to common sense, large problems sometimes require only a small solution. Complex problems sometimes require only the simplest solution. If you only focus on large and complex you will overlook small and simple.

3. PEOPLE HAVE THE NECESSARY RESOURCES TO MAKE CHANGE POSSIBLE
Definition: It's what we all need to hear most about ourselves – our power to change. You'll find what you're looking for in people and, if you believe in this, you will find strength, resilience, energy and hope in the most desperate of situations and people. If you don't believe they exist, you'll never go looking in the first place.

4. A FOCUS ON FUTURE POSSIBILITIES AND SOLUTIONS ENHANCES CHANGE
Definition: Whilst we cannot, must not and do not ignore the past we are always seeking to orientate toward the future in how we work. Although solutions are sometimes to things that have happened in the past e.g. forgiving oneself, we are always concerned with how the future can be and will be positively affected as a result.

5. NO SIGN-UP, NO CHANGE
Definition: This principle reminds us that any given goal is not always enough to motivate somebody to change. The view that it is would be reflected in traditional 'goal-setting' work. However, a good goal will not necessarily get somebody to change; there has to be more. People need to see and believe that the goal is achievable and worthwhile and the benefit from achieving it outweighs the struggle and effort in so doing. We call working with this 'weighing-up' process or 'cost-benefit' analysis that we all conduct spontaneously with goals 'goaling'. If there is no sign-up to participate in goals at the end of a gaoling conversation there is little chance that change will follow.

6. COOPERATION ENHANCES CHANGE
Definition: Working together, finding a way, not giving up – these are all to do with cooperation. Sometimes this principle calls for the maturing worker to allow space for imperfect possibilities whilst continuing to work so that a greater good can be achieved.

7. THE PROBLEM IS THE PROBLEM, NOT THE PERSON

Definition: Remember the person you are dealing with is OK, it's the difficulty, problem or challenge he or she is facing that is of concern. This principle allows for conversations that liberate people from the clutches of restricting and injurious labels such as 'naughty boy', 'bad girl', 'terrible husband' in order that they can begin to regain control over the behaviours that have resulted in such descriptions.

8. POSSIBILITIES ARE INFINITE

Definition: So often the SO approach is confused with being a positive approach when it most definitely is not. This principle invites thinking in terms of possibilities and that they should always be viewed as being present. Indeed, there are two kinds of possibility that co-exist, positive and negative, yin-yang. They live side by side and one cannot survive without the other. This principle calls for the acknowledgement of one and promotion of the other.

9. PEOPLE HAVE UNIQUE SOLUTIONS TO THEIR PROBLEMS

Definition: This principle encourages curiosity and an interest in ideas and ways of moving forward. It's about legitimising people's thoughts and versions about how change should, could and will happen, rather than any pre-planned notion being provided for them.

10. KEEP ONE FOOT IN PAIN AND ONE IN POSSIBILITY

Definition: This refers to the professional balance we must maintain that allows us to accommodate light and dark, pain and possibility, hope and despair. The principle leads to acceptance of the human state, liberating the worker to a place of peaceful tolerance and respect of others.

In order for these Principles to have effect they all need to be seen 'running through' practice, consistently and at all levels. To exemplify this I asked Sam to consider the following scenario in her work.

'Sam, I'd like you to imagine that you were planning to conduct what was regarded by all your colleagues as a "tough" home visit. During the visit you meet with the mother and father of a child who are very concerned about his welfare and disappointed with the efforts of professionals to date. The family are also experiencing unbearable life pressures to do with housing, money and relationships.

'Some time into your visit, you find that your well-planned consultation grinds to a halt, beaten down by the forces created by the family's true stories of suffering and pain. You're stuck. When offered a coffee, you seize the opportunity and take a break. During the break, imagine you manage to call two colleagues for assistance on your mobile telephone. The first colleague you call is an SF colleague who, like you, has developed a sound technical knowledge of the approach. You push him to offer advice that might help you under the circumstances. In response, he suggests you return to the family and ask them a series of questions known to you as scaling, in order that you may proceed effectively. This is something you had not tried with the family as yet, so you are thankful to your colleague and return to carry out the suggestion.

'After ten minutes, however, and having asked the scaling questions, you find yourself continuing to feel stuck, and feel no real movement has been achieved. It's at this point you decide to call your second colleague. Your second colleague has experienced a similar technical, Solution-Oriented journey to that of yours, having been a keen technician at one time. She is now, however, well advanced of this and is a good example of a worker who reflects the virtues of the Intermediate Stage of Systemic development. She has come to appreciate, value and believe in the importance of the SO Principles in guiding her practice. As with colleague number one, you respectfully ask for her guidance in relation to your work with the family. This time, however, the support you receive is very different, as, rather than offering you a script, a question or an observable action strategy to attempt, this second colleague offers you something far greater and quite unexpected. She invites you to tell her what you believe about this family. She asks you if you can see hurt, pain and suffering and whether you've truly heard the story and acknowledged it – "go and really listen" she says. She asks whether you believe possibilities exist for the family, even in a small way – "go and unearth them gently" she says. Then she asks whether you believe the family possess resources, strength, skill, virtue and beauty – "go and help them see it in themselves" she says. She gives you no detail of how to actually go and do any of this, of what questions to ask or how to respond – she simply asks you what you believe in and what you see. You realise that what she has done is call to mind the SO Principles in order that they may be reflected, in your own unique way, with that family.

'You return to the family to discover that your actions are now driven by deeper thoughts, and that you now appreciate "why" you are asking certain questions and saying certain things – it's because you believe in underlying principles. All of a sudden you no longer feel stuck and assisting the family becomes simply a matter of time. Techniques fade in importance for you, giving way to a far deeper level of work – influenced consciously by Solution-Oriented Principles. You find a way forward, you find the words that are needed, they come to you because they simply have to, reflecting each of the principles that you now believe in.'

Sam sat silently and then said, 'That's so powerful. I can see how my over-reliance on technique actually made me a slave to the model and now how the SO principles actually will help free me in all sorts of ways. I can see that it's the principles that count, without these I won't be able to apply my true ability in all areas of my work; I'd just be feeling the need to go on new training all of the time instead!'

I knew at this point that Sam had got it: she could now see for herself how the Intermediate Stage of Systemic Development was all to do with moving from being a SF technician to a SO Principle-based worker. Moving from a reliance on technique to being guided by principles is the journey conducted during the Intermediate Stage. Sam was now ready to consider the third and final phase of development, the Advanced Stage of Systemic Development.

The Advanced Stage: Systems that have only one purpose

Some time passed before Sam and I arranged to meet again in order to discuss how she was progressing and to see if she felt ready to continue her journey in becoming more Systemic.

When I eventually saw her, I could tell that she'd grown a great deal in confidence, especially as she told me about her many applications of the SO Principles within her work. Since we last met, she'd become Head of the Educational Psychology Service (EPS) and was very proud to be leading a great group of colleagues whom she had worked with for years. Before too long Sam made a very bold and exciting statement, 'I want the EPS to be a Solution-Oriented EPS,' followed by the question she'd been eager to ask for a long while, 'Do you think it's possible?'

'Yes, Sam, it's completely possible – so long as that is your vision for the EPS,' I said in return. Sam had grown immeasurably in confidence and her new ambition to build a great service seemed the perfect opportunity to invite her to consider the Advanced Stage of Systemic Development. This would entail becoming truly Systemic by organising all the activities taking place within the service to deliver the big picture and purpose.

It is usually the case that SO Principles are the established drivers of practice well before reaching the Advanced Stage, so what remains now in the final phase is to pull together all of the SO actions, so that they reflect the service principles and take place automatically, predictably and to a high standard, over and over again. This is not achieved by accident, or on an individual basis, but rather by virtue of adhering to a step-by-step organisational process – one that I shared with Sam in order for her to go to work 'on' building a SO EPS.

STEP 1: THE VISION
The first step an organisation like Sam's must take in order to be Systemic is to have a clear vision. In other words a description of the finished picture - no matter what size, be it a service, a team, an organisation, a school, a classroom or department. This description must encompass the functions of the service, team, school and so on.

The description has to be complete, and must provide a vivid picture to others that describes what the finished product will look like, feel like, sound like, smell like and function like. It is just like the importance of the picture on a jigsaw puzzle box – it shows what you're working towards and without it you'd be lost.

This description must include what the experience will be like for all those who come into contact with the finished product, for example, what parents will experience when they come into contact with the EPS. What will it be like and feel like for them? And, significantly, what do you *want* it to be like and feel like for them? And not forgetting how workers will experience the EPS from the inside – what will this experience look and feel like?

'Why do we need all the detail?' Sam asked.

'Because it is so important! You see, you're not only describing what it is you are building as a service, but you are also describing the promise you're making to others. This is called your 'service promise' that as an EPS you are committing to fulfil. It includes, amongst other things, your promise to children and families – that they will be respected, cared for, valued and trusted every single time they come into contact with your EPS, guaranteed. Yes, Sam, you want to be able to guarantee the experience you want people to have so that they expect it from your service and depend on it, and for this to happen your service has to deliver the experience predictably – even if you're not there. If you can't guarantee them that, Sam, then the vision is simply not important enough and you will have a service that operates on luck and chance. It sounds to me like you want to build a SO EPS to guarantee SO experiences, and this will only happen if first you can see it in your mind's eye as a finished vision, a perfect and complete vision.'

Sam had grasped a full understanding of the importance of her service's vision. She sensibly decided that she would consult with colleagues in order to develop the vision, and what resulted was a simple statement that at Sycol we refer to as the 'Core Professional Purpose' (CPP). It described precisely what Sam and her colleagues in her service promised to deliver and how.

The following guide points further assisted Sam in developing her service's CPP.

The Core Professional Purpose:

1. is short and memorable
2. is a vision statement for what will be delivered and how
3. is the promise to service users and staff
4. is central to all professional activity
5. is evident everywhere in sight and sound
6. is the experience a service is determined to guarantee

7. is a product of staff consultation
8. is championed by leadership
9. is known to all staff and actively shared with service users.

STEP 2: APPLY PRINCIPLES AT THE ORGANISATIONAL LEVEL

When the vision is described the next question is all about 'How will it be delivered?'

Sam was asked to recall the ten Solution-Oriented Principles. I asked her 'Now, Sam, how do you think these principles can play a central part in the delivery of your vision, described succinctly as your CPP?'

'I really have no idea,' she replied, 'but I think you're going to say they *need* to, and I think you're going to say they *should*, and I think you're going to say they *can* – am I right?'

'You're right on all three counts: the principles *need* to, *should* and *can* play a central part in the delivery of your vision. First, they *need* to so that you and your colleagues can be guided and reminded by them every day in everything you do as you go about your work. Second, they *should* play a central part because they are now quite literally the standards of your service, the standards by which everything is done and measured by. If ever what you see or hear does not measure up to reflecting these principles, then how on earth will you deliver your vision? Third, they *can* be central because you make them so. You talk them up at every opportunity. They are referred to as central to the vision at meetings, consultations, supervision, appraisals, coaching sessions, recruitment adverts and recruitment activities. They are seen around in the displays, on screensavers, letterheads, compliment slips, reports, booklets, bottom of emails, press and media – quite literally anywhere and everywhere is an opportunity for you to share your service standards, described as Solution-Oriented Principles. At Sycol, we say "Principles need Profile".'

It was further explained to Sam that since her service (as any service will be) is unique in its vision it will be important that service-specific principles are also included, should they apply. For example, some services may feel that the principles of inclusion or equal opportunity need to be stated. Once established, the principles in Systemic practice become what the manager or leader seeks to police – realising that by looking after them, all else will follow because the manager knows that systemically, all actions and systems are determined by principles. It makes sense, therefore, that effective, Systemic managers and leaders deliver the organisational vision by managing principles and systems within that organisation, not people. For the people to consistently perform at their best, the systems that will promote and support such performance need to be in place and understood within the context of the vision and principles.

The following guide points assisted Sam in applying principles at the organisational level.

Service Principles:

1. are developed by staff and are few in number
2. are actively managed
3. drive all staff professionally
4. are the standards by which all systems, protocols, policies and actions are written, developed, measured and conducted
5. are evident throughout the service
6. are accepted by all staff from recruitment and shared with service users.

STEP 3: DEVELOP SYSTEMS IN ORDER TO DELIVER THE VISION

Mention has already been made of systems. In Step 2 of the Advanced Stage of Systemic Development it was said that the best managers and leaders manage principles and systems, not people, in order to deliver the vision. What do we mean by this? Sycol describe three elements to any given system, but what's important is that any system has one function only – to deliver the vision in a way that reflects the principles. System are made up of three elements, Hard, Soft and Information.

Hard elements of a system

These elements are, quite literally, often hard, and inanimate, such as the following;

- letterheads
- report structures
- chairs
- tables
- coffee machines
- tissue box
- colour schemes
- displays
- marketing material
- plants.

Everything on this short list of examples will have to be decided upon, and the process by which these are selected and developed needs to be such that each one of them contributes to the vision and is a reflection, in hard terms, of the principles.

Sam spoke at this point to say 'I see, so even the flowers I saw and smelt as I entered the school I visited the other day, which is a great school, were no accident?'

'Well, they may have been, Sam, I don't know, but if systems are understood in that school then they certainly were not an accident. They had been placed there for a purpose, just as, I suppose, they had a well-kept guest book for you to sign. You see, all of these elements make up their welcoming system, and the welcoming system has been created for you – the visitor to the school.

Furthermore, in order for the systems to truly deliver the vision they need to occur over and over again, even in the absence of the manager or leader. This can only happen, of course, if the vision has been communicated to all staff and their contribution in maintaining the systems is seen as important.'

Soft elements of a system

At Sycol we refer to these kinds of elements as 'people elements'. They are made up of all the ways in which we interact professionally and how we present to service users. They concern all the ways we say, write and do things professionally including how we meet, consult, report, assess, supervise, teach, mentor, coach and so on. These soft elements are no accident either. For example, how one conducts a home visit is a soft element that can reflect Solution-Oriented Principles in order to deliver a vision. To achieve this, home visit protocols require developing, testing and improving continually in order that they keep pace with new ideas, yet still serve to be a system that delivers a vision. For it to be a system, of course, it requires the key features of being able to be described and have the capacity to be taught and shown to others. Only in this way is it possible to disseminate Systemic practice across the organisation. In other words, where possible all operational activity in the form of a system needs to be written down.

This leads, during recruitment for example, to the interviewee being able to see precisely 'how things are done' – and to then later learn them and start contributing to the system delivery.

Information elements of a system

'So, how will we know if all these elemets work or not?' was Sam's next question. The answer to this leads to describing the third type of element that we recognise, Information Elements.

'Information Elements, Sam, are ones that have the purpose of measuring in some way whether or not a system works. These are the elements that as a leader you will want regular access to, because the data will tell which systems require improving and innovating. Let's revisit the example of the welcoming system used earlier. How would a school go about finding out whether all their soft and hard elements of the welcoming system actually worked?

'The answer is that they'd have an Information Element as part of the system as a way of finding out. For example, they might choose to seek anecdotal, qualitative evidence from the people who visited the school by asking them directly about their experience. Or, they might request that when guests sign out, they score the experience of visiting the school in terms of its welcome on a scale of 1 to 5. This would yield quantitative information. Either way, the information would be used to determine whether the system is contributing effectively toward the vision or whether it requires further innovation in order to be improved.'

Sam listened carefully and nodded, showing that it was all making sense to her and that all pieces of Systemic practice methods were falling into place.

The following guide points further assisted Sam in developing systems in order to deliver the service vision.

Systems:

1. are made up of Hard, Soft and Information elements
2. serve one purpose only – to add value and deliver the Vision/CPP
3. reflect service principles
4. are subject to regular review and innovation.

The vision is the unifying purpose that lends tremendous force to the application of SO principled practice. The systems we develop, made up of hard, soft and information elements, enable us to deliver that practice at every level of operation and to provide the means to maintain and deepen the efficiency and effectiveness of our work.

It should be stressed that vision, principles and systems will not be solely Sam's concern. She will need to ensure active engagement by her colleagues at all levels within her EPS, and compatibility between individual ambitions and service vision will be important. She may start small with a selected area of service focus, and it may take time for the service as a whole to come onboard but diligence in shaping her systems will produce the outcomes Sam has chosen to be her organization's special promise to their clients.

Conclusion

In summary, the Solution-Oriented Systemic model described in this chapter can be equally well applied to any team, service, organisation or school. Indeed, this is what the Sycol Solution-Oriented School Programme does (Solution-Oriented School 2007). Schools in various parts of the UK, the Channel Islands and Eire are successfully cultivating effective systems to express the vision they have developed. The inclusive nature of this approach means there is room for all those activities and initiatives that schools and services are obliged to take into account. All that is needed is for them to be woven into the vision. Follow the steps, and the means to fulfil them will emerge. The Sycol framework is simply represented in the Figure 8.1.

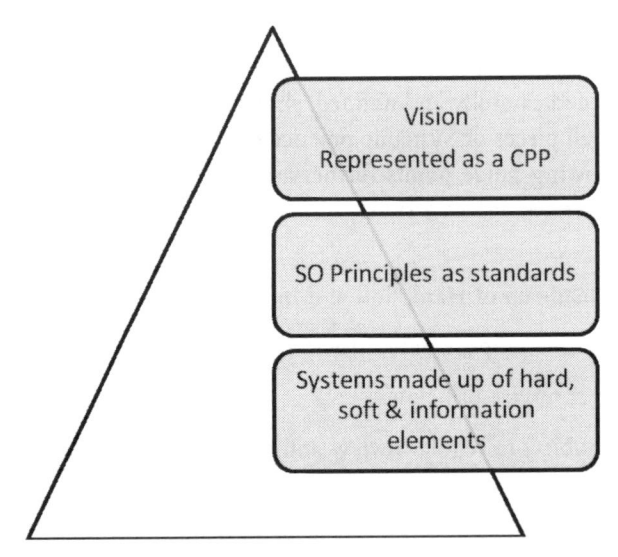

Figure 8.1: The Solution-Oriented Systemic model

Through our conversation and over time, Sam progressed through the phases of Systemic Development in order to understand how she would go about completing her professional wish to build a Solution-Oriented service. She passed through the Early Stage, where she recognised herself as a Solution-Focused technician. Then came the Intermediate Stage, which introduced her to the power and importance of pervasive mindfulness of Solution-Oriented Principles in her practice. Finally, Sam moved to the Advanced Stage where her vision was described as a Core Professional Purpose and she learned how this could be delivered by systems that reflected service principles.

The framework for Solution-Oriented Systemic development can be represented as shown in Figure 8.2.

| Early Stage: Reliance upon technique | Intermediate Stage: Principles guide practice | Advanced Stage: Vision exists / Principles act as standards / Systems developed to deliver the vision |

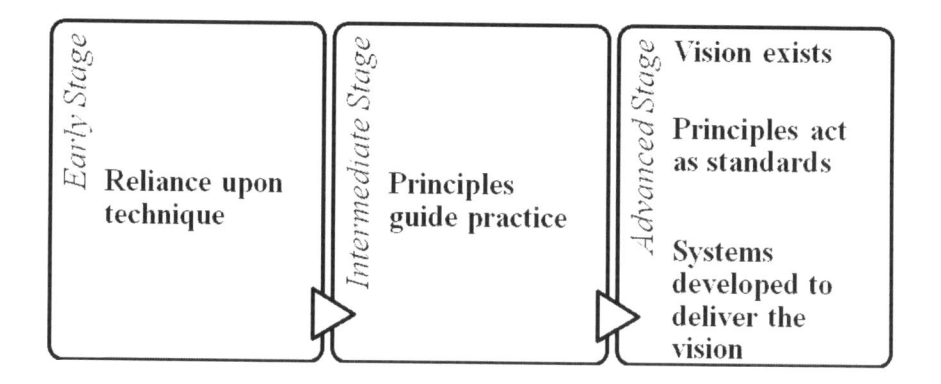

Figure 8.2: The three stages of Solution-Oriented Systemic Development

References

Bateson, G. (1972) *Steps to an Ecology of Mind*. New York: Chandler.
Bateson, G. (1979) *Mind and Nature: A Necessary Unity*. New York: Dutton.
de Shazer, S. (1985) *Keys to Solutions in Brief Therapy*. New York: W.W. Norton.
de Shazer, S. (1988) *Clues: Investigating Solutions in Brief Therapy*. New York: W.W. Norton.
de Shazer, S. (1991) *Putting Difference to Work*. New York: W.W Norton.
de Shazer, S. (1994) *Words were Originally Magic*. New York: W.W. Norton.
Erickson, M.H. (1954) 'Special techniques of brief hypnotherapy.' *Journal of Clinical and Experiential Hypnosis 2*, 109–129.
Murphy, J.J. and Duncan, B.L. (2007) *Brief Intervention for School Problems: Collaborating for Practical Solutions* (2nd edn). New York: Guildford Press.
O'Hanlon, B. (1987) *Taproots: Underlying Principles of Milton Erickson's Therapy Hypnosis*. New York: W.W. Norton.
O'Hanlon, W.H. (1998) 'An Inclusive, Collaborative, Solution-based Model of Psychotherapy.' In M.F. Hoyt (ed.) *The Handbook of Constructive Therapies*. San Francisco, CA: Jossey-Bass.
O'Hanlon, B. (2000) *Do One Thing Different: Ten Simple Ways to Change your Life*. New York: William Morrow and Co.
O'Hanlon, B. (2007) *Frequently Asked Questions: What is the Difference Between Solution-Focused, Solution-Oriented and Possibility Therapies?* Accessed 30 August 2007 at www.brieftherapy.com/faq/whatis.htm
O'Hanlon, B. and Beadle, S. (1996) *A Field Guide to Possibility Land: Possibility Therapy Methods*. London: Brief Therapy Press.
O'Hanlon, B. and Weiner-Davies, M. (1989) *In Search of Solutions*. New York: W.W. Norton.
Rees, I. (2001a) *Pupil Support: A Solution Focused Approach*. Liverpool: Positive Behaviour Management.
Rees, I. (2001b) 'Solution World'. In Y. Ajmal and I. Rees (eds) *Solutions in Schools: Creative Applications of Solution-Focused Brief Thinking with Young People and Adults*. London: BT Press.
Solution-Oriented School (2007) *The Solution-Oriented School Programme. Sycol: Solution-Oriented School*. Accessed 20 August 2007 at www.sycol.co.uk/sos

PART FIVE
Frameworks for Practice for Psychological Theory and Research

CHAPTER 9

Positive Psychology as a Framework for Practice

Stephen Joseph

Introduction

The aim of this chapter is to discuss the application of the Positive Psychology framework to educational psychology, and in particular to reflect on how Positive Psychology leads us to reflect on the fundamental assumptions underpinning practice. Although there have always been psychologists who have been interested in understanding optimal functioning, it has only been relatively recently that the term 'Positive Psychology' has become widely used to describe this field of study. The term 'Positive Psychology' was used by Martin E.P. Seligman in his Presidential Address to the American Psychological Association (APA) (Seligman 1999) in order to describe his vision for the future of psychological science. Seligman realised that psychology had largely neglected the latter two of its three pre-World War II missions: curing mental illness, helping all people to lead more productive and fulfilling lives, and identifying and nurturing high talent. It was with that realisation that Seligman stated: 'The aim of positive psychology is to begin to catalyze a change in the focus of psychology from preoccupation only with repairing the worst things in life to also building positive qualities' (Seligman and Csikszentmihalyi 2000, p.5).

In this chapter I will consider the implications of Positive Psychology for educational psychologists and will begin by discussing, first, practical applications of Positive Psychology to educational psychology – in particular, how Positive Psychology can inform the everyday practice of educational psychology through its explicit focus on the positive side of human experience. I will then go on to consider theoretical perspectives about how Positive Psychology provokes re-examination of the fundamental assumptions underpinning the practice of educational psychology.

The interface of educational psychology and Positive Psychology

Before examining the implications of Positive Psychology for educational psychology, it is useful to reflect briefly on a definition of the latter. The task of an EP is to tackle the various problems experienced by young people in education. EPs aim to enhance a young person's learning, achievement and well-being by drawing on their knowledge of the wider psychological and developmental literature, as well as their understanding of its specific applications to young people, the learning process, and relevant social and cognitive processes.

Although the role of the EP is to tackle problems, the goal of the Positive Psychological approach is not simply to repair the worst but to also build positive qualities. The objectives of a 'positive' EP would therefore be stated in terms of striving toward achieving optimal functioning. Many educational psychologists will nod in agreement since this is what they have always done; however, for others this will be a new way of thinking about their role. This new approach is illustrated in the above definition of educational psychology with its use of the term 'well-being'. So, what is well-being? Traditionally, many psychologists have used this term to refer to the absence of distress, illness, and so on, rather than to the presence of positive states of happiness, satisfaction, and so on. Thus, from a Positive Psychological perspective, the role of the EP is not only about how to alleviate distress, treat illness and repair weakness, and so on, but is also about how to facilitate well-being, promote health and build strengths.

Adopting the Positive Psychology perspective

As I will go on to discuss, the main implication of the Positive Psychology movement for EPs is that it provokes us to re-examine the ideas behind practice. However, before I move on to consider that, I will first give some concrete examples to show how practice begins to change when we adopt the Positive Psychological framework.

The work of an EP can either be directly with a child (for example, through assessment and counselling and other interventions) or indirectly through working with parents, teachers and other professionals. So, how can we begin to bring the Positive Psychological framework to these tasks?

Assessment and intervention

Direct work involves some form of assessment to explore the presenting problem through consultation with professional colleagues, observation, interview, or use of test materials. The Positive Psychology perspective offers new ways of thinking about such assessment. For example, as I've already discussed, the term 'well-being' has been traditionally used in educational psychology to refer to the absence of psychopathology, but from the Positive Psychology perspective it refers to the presence of positive subjective and psychological states. At the most basic level we therefore begin to reconfigure the goals of our practice differently, and thus need new assessment instruments alongside the traditional ones in the armory of educational psychology.

A variety of measures now exist within the Positive Psychology tradition that educational psychologists will find useful here (see Lopez and Snyder 2003). It is beyond the scope of this chapter to go into detail on a range of specific measures, but we can provide here a brief example of one such measure in order to illustrate what can be done. The Children's Hope Scale (CHS) (Snyder *et al.* 1997) is a six-item (e.g. 'when I have a problem, I can come up with lots of ways to solve it') self-report measure for young people aged 7 through to 14 years. The task is to build such measures into intervention plans and to therefore be able to evaluate their success in relation to Positive Psychology goals. We no longer think simply about the alleviation of the problem as the goal, but also about moving beyond this to achieving optimal functioning. For example, strategies for accentuating hope can be of much practical utility and interest to educational psychologists (see Lopez *et al.* 2004).

There is now a need for further research and measurement development related to the practice of a 'Positive Educational Psychology'. As our thinking shifts towards this perspective, our goals for intervention change. Other areas of research activity of particular interest to educational psychologists now include:

- the facilitation of curiousity (Kashdan and Fincham 2004)
- developing wisdom (Baltes, Gluck and Kunzmann 2002; Kunzmann 2004; Sternberg 1998)
- flow (Csikszentmihalyi 1990), and
- how to facilitate emotional intelligence (Salovey, Caruso and Mayer 2004).

Emotional intelligence has received considerable attention already through school-based programmes (see, e.g. Graczyk *et al.* 2000; Topping, Holmes and Bremner 2000). Given the importance of emotional literacy for society in general (not only as a means to increase academic performance, but also to increase positive citizenship), it is surprising that this is not taken more seriously at the level of policy.

Indirect work
The indirect work of an EP involves consultation with others: parents, teachers and other professionals. It is always vital that the contribution of psychology is

seen as relevant. This can be difficult to achieve, especially when others know little about psychology. The Positive Psychology perspective raises additional challenges as the target of working towards Positive Psychological outcomes may not immediately be seen as relevant, and may need even more careful discussion and deliberation. But this is the task that arises from the Positive Psychology perspective: that of promoting to a wider audience ideas about working towards optimal functioning. There is much to be done and EPs have an important role in doing this within a local authority. EPs are often called upon to advise or join working/consultation groups on issues concerned with organisation and policy planning. They are therefore in an ideal and often unique position within the education authority to implement Positive Psychological principles, to influence others in how they think about the application of psychology, and to promote Positive Psychological perspectives. For example, as mentioned, working to promote the facilitation of emotional intelligence programmes in schools would seem to be priority. However, we must also be wary that our involvement in such programmes is genuinely for the advancement of emotional literacy, and does not become usurped into simply becoming a way of increasing socially desirable behaviour in children.

Changing how we think

In addition to challenging us to think differently about what we do, Positive Psychology also raises more deep-seated issues. It is to these that I will now turn. Ultimately, the practice of psychology is an expression of a particular philosophy of human nature. In the following sections I will describe how traditional psychology is grounded in a medical-model vision of the person as requiring expert-extrinsic help in order to overcome his or her difficulties, as opposed to the Positive Psychology vision of the person as possessing potential and intrinsic motivation towards growth and development. Our expressions of how to help others are part of an inescapable moral vision (Christopher 1996) and is certainly true of any practitioner who applies the ideas of psychology to helping another person (Joseph and Linley 2006). Indeed, perhaps it is even more important for EPs since the young people they work with are more vulnerable and powerless in the world than adults and are thus less able to resist oppressive and abusive forces. The power of an EP in the life of a young person in difficulty cannot be overestimated. Since society gives EPs a highly responsible role in relation to the welfare of young people, it is vital that we reflect on what it is we do and, more importantly, why we do what we do, as well as having a willingness to be open to new ways of thinking and working.

When helping others, what we consider constitutes help is ultimately an ideological point of view. This might seem a strange assertion to those who view themselves as evidence-based practitioners but what it means is recognising that data is never neutral but is always collected from a particular viewpoint. How we think ultimately shapes the questions we ask, the data we gather, and therefore the answers that we get. The Positive Psychology perspective is an example of a new viewpoint, and clearly the evidence that we begin to gather from this perspective will tell us different things from what we currently know.

As Seligman (2002, 2003) notes, much of modern psychology has been dominated by the doctrines of Freud, 'the ghost in the machine' of psychology.

> There has been a profound obstacle to a science and practice of positive traits and positive states: the belief that virtue and happiness are inauthentic, epiphenomenal, parasitic upon or reducible to the negative traits and states. This 'rotten-to-the-core' view pervades Western thought, and if there is any doctrine positive psychology seeks to overthrow it is this one. Its original manifestation is the doctrine of original sin. In secular form, Freud dragged this doctrine into 20th-century psychology where it remains fashionably entrenched in academia today. For Freud, all of civilisation is just an elaborate defence against basic conflicts over infantile sexuality and aggression. (Seligman 2003, p.126).

Although Positive Psychology has served to reawaken interest in the underlying philosophical and ideological assumptions, such considerations were also central to the early humanistic psychologists. In considering views of human nature, Horney (1951) delineated three possible positions in trying to understand core human nature:

- The first position was that people are driven by primitive destructive instincts. From this first position, which reflects the Freudian view, the goal of society must be to contain these destructive impulses.

- The second position was that inherent within human nature was both something essentially constructive and something essentially destructive.

- The third position was that inherent within people are evolutionary constructive forces that guide people towards realising their potentialities. From this third position, the goal of society must be therefore to cultivate the facilitative social-environmental conditions that are conducive to people's self-realisation.

When people's tendency toward self-realisation is allowed expression, Horney argued that:

> we become free to grow ourselves, we also free ourselves to love and to feel concern for other people. We will then want to give them the opportunity for

unhampered growth when they are young, and to help them in whatever way possible to find and realize themselves when they are blocked in their development. At any rate, whether for ourselves or for others, the ideal is the liberation and cultivation of the forces which lead to self-realization. (Ibid., pp.15–16)

This constructive force for self-realisation formed the basis of Horney's (1951) therapeutic approach, and this 'growth metaphor' now has resonance with the modern Positive Psychology movement with its conceptualisation of human beings as possessing inherent potential for the development of positive character traits and virtues (Seligman and Csikszentmihalyi 2000). A similar meta-theoretical perspective is also provided by Self-Determination Theory, which has an impressive body of empirical support (Deci and Ryan 1985, 2000; Ryan and Deci 2000, 2001). What this illustrates is that there are broad, meta-theoretical principles that underpin practice; and Positive Psychology has caused us to re-evaluate our fundamental assumptions.

Person-Centred Psychology

Although the term Positive Psychology is increasingly used to refer to a new field of study, there is a clear linkage of its ideas with those of humanistic psychology. Humanistic psychology – and, in particular, the Person-Centred approach developed by Carl Rogers (1959, 1963, 1964) – was also built on the meta-theoretical view that human beings possess a constructive force toward self-realisation. It is this growth metaphor that is the crux of the humanistic Person-Centred Psychology that Rogers developed. In brief, the growth metaphor is that human beings have an inherent tendency toward growth, development and optimal functioning, but that they require the right social environment in which to *self-actualise* their inherent optimal nature. Problems in living are therefore not seen as arising due to psychopathology within the person but as a result of that social environment. Psychological problems arise when the social environment thwarts the inherent tendency toward growth, development and optimal functioning. Although the Person-Centred approach has been criticised for a lack of empirical support, there is now in fact converging evidence from the Positive Psychology and Self-Determination literature that can be read as providing evidence in support of the Person-Centred view (Patterson and Joseph 2006). But, although evidence-based practice is an important consideration, I would argue that it is more important to consider the ethical base and the values underpinning what we do.

Reflections on assumptions

In this section, I will now go on to explore how our approach to practice ultimately rests on which of these two positions we adopt – i.e. the traditional approach of psychology (with its roots in Freudian thought) or the new Positive Psychological approach (with its roots in person-centred psychology). These are two opposing ideological positions through which to view the world, our clients and the goals of our practice.

Maddux *et al.* (2004) identified three primary ways in which the adoption of the traditional medical model and the illness ideology has determined the remit and scope of psychology.

- First, it promotes the notion of dichotomies between normal and abnormal behaviours, between clinical and non-clinical problems, and between clinical populations and non-clinical populations.

- Second, it locates human maladjustment as arising from within the person, rather than without in the person's interactions with the environment and his or her encounters with socio-cultural values and social institutions.

- Third, it portrays people who seek help as victims of intrapsychic and biological forces beyond their control, and thus leaves them as recipients of an expert's care and advice.

In contrast, Person-Centred Psychology resists the ideas behind the medical model and the illness conception of distress. As we have seen, this is because it is based on the alternative meta-theoretical paradigm of organismic growth. Extending this metaphor to understanding human distress gives us a very different way of thinking and working.

- First, it promotes the notion of continuity between normal and abnormal behaviours, between clinical and non-clinical problems, and between clinical populations and non-clinical populations.

- Second, it locates the causes of human maladjustment as arising from outside of the person and in his or her interactions with the environment and encounters with socio-cultural values and social institutions, and not from within the person.

- Third, it portrays people who seek help as the best experts on themselves, and not as recipients of an expert's care and advice.

Thinking about the implications of the above for educational psychology, it should be clear that the Person-Centred approach is antithetical to the medical model. The essential difference is whether practitioners hold themselves to be the expert on the other person, or whether they hold the other person to be his or her own best expert. These are two mutually opposing meta-theoretical views. All psychological practitioners habitually adopt either one or other of these positions in their interactions with clients. How we think we ought to practise ultimately rests on our deep-seated ideological position on these issues – whether we adopt the position that people are motivated by socially destructive impulses that need to be shaped and controlled, or whether we adopt the position that people are motivated by socially constructive impulses that need to be facilitated and released. Which of these conceptions we choose will have profound implications on how we see the role of the educational psychologist.

People's fundamental assumptions are often difficult to introspect upon since they are inevitably formed within a particular social, cultural and historical context (Prilleltensky 1994). Our assumptions provide us with the framework through which we view the world around us and are thus typically implicit. These are, therefore, often uncritically accepted by practitioners and are taken for granted, often assuming the position of the status quo. Often, it is only when there is a challenge to our world-views that our assumptions become highlighted. Positive Psychology has provided one such challenge. An example of this might be as follows:

Jack has difficulties in class, often causing disruption. He is restless, and uninterested in lessons. The EP is called in for a meeting with the teacher and Jack's parents. The teacher wants Jack to stop causing disruption in the class and to settle down to lessons. Jack's parents are concerned that there is something wrong with Jack and they are eager for reassurance that everything will be all right. What does the EP want? As already mentioned, one of the key developments that Positive Psychology has brought about is a re-framing of the questions in which practitioners may be interested. The answer to this question can be sought from a number of different perspectives. Take a few minutes to think about this situation, and what you believe an educational psychologist might want. It is likely that whatever the EP wants there will, in any case, be different agendas in operation: Jack's, the teacher's, the parents', the EP's, the school's. The fact is that they are not necessarily going to be compatible.

It would not be unusual for a child like Jack to receive a diagnosis of a psychiatric problem, perhaps Attention Deficit Hyperactivity Disorder, or Oppositional-Defiant Disorder, and to be referred for help from a psychologist. However, although there will be young people who do require expert intervention, we must be cautious about this process. We can see the child as being either dysfunctional and requiring treatment (as if their difficulties were an illness), or as experiencing difficulties arising from his or her social context. We need here to consider, for example, the likely efficacy of providing one hour of intervention per week to a child with Oppositional-Defiant Disorder who lives in an abusive and chaotic home with an alcoholic mother in a poverty-stricken part of the city. So long as the broader family and social structures remain unchanged, the intervention is not likely to be very successful. In addition, acting as though the child is the one with the problem can be simply 'blaming the victim' when it is his family, and broader social environment, that are actually sick and largely responsible for his problems. As psychologists, not surprisingly, we have a tendency to 'psychologise' problems and to think in terms of interventions at the behavioural and cognitive level. But we must be wary of this because this is not always the appropriate level of analysis. Gillian Proctor (2005), a clinical psychologist, has recently written of how:

> the psychologisation of distress firmly places the cause for psychological ill-health within the individual... Thus deprivation, abuse, oppression and the social and political context of distress can largely be ignored and the practice of clinical psychology can continue to try to mop up problems caused by a sick society. (p.280)

Similar concerns might be expressed about educational psychology. As referred to in passing earlier, school-based programmes that are initiated with the values of humanistic psychology can become usurped so that they end up as little more than techniques for increasing conformity and socially desirable behaviour. We must wonder about the potential efficacy of psychological interventions so long as we remain in a society that is dysfunctional in many ways, including in its educational system. To what extent is our educational system facilitative of children's potential? Of course, how we answer this question depends on how we conceptualise human nature and thus what the function of the educational system should be. Should it exist to facilitate potential? EPs need to be reflective about these issues and be wary that we, too, are not subject to these same criticisms that we are simply mopping up the problems of a sick society.

So, whose agenda is the educational psychologist working to? How does this agenda relate to each of the ideological positions discussed above? Do we assume that Jack's behaviour is symptomatic of some underlying impulses on his part and that it is our job to help control in order to get him to sit at his desk? Or, do we assume that Jack's behaviour is an expression of how thwarted he feels and that it is our job to release his impulses for exploration and activity in a more constructive direction? There is no right answer to these questions. How we decide our answer to these questions will be based on our ideological view of what the roles of EPs are, and whether we adopt a medical model or person-centred model as our core ideology.

This brings us to a related issue of who educational psychologists work for. Who decides on their agenda for practice? How does their agenda fit with our own ideological perspectives? For some EPs, the ideological perspectives of themselves and their employer matches and no conflict is experienced. But for others, there is a conflict. For example, if we believe in facilitating the constructive potential of young people and we perceive ourselves to be employed to restrict and control their tendencies towards actualisation, there is a conflict. How do we resolve such conflict? This is an issue that could be usefully discussed as a small-group exercise, in which the task is to examine ideological positions in relation to expectations of placements and employers in order to identify areas of conflict and tension and how such conflict can be managed and dealt with.

There are also issues around the profession of educational psychology, such as to what extent is it used as an oppressive force for controlling young people? Or, to what extent is educational psychology a facilitative force for releasing the potential in young people? To what extent is educational psychology about changing young people to fit within society, or about changing society? The answers to these questions need regular discussion and debate by the current generation of trainee EPs, who are the future of the profession. It will be they who will increasingly define educational psychology over the coming years.

Questions that I believe all EPs should reflect on are as follows:

- What are my assumptions about human nature?
- What are the assumptions about human nature of my employer and the organisation I work for?
- What are the points of conflict between my beliefs and those of the organisation I work for?
- How do I resolve these points of conflict?

Conclusion: Looking to the future

A Positive Psychological framework to educational psychology requires a different way of thinking than that which is prevalent in current mainstream practice. Positive Psychology challenges us to re-examine our fundamental assumptions about human nature and to understand that it is our fundamental assumptions that determine how we practise. The implications for practice in terms of our value position, the agenda to which we are working, our understanding of human functioning, and the epistemologies that we consider appropriate, all follow on from our fundamental assumptions.

Suggestions for further reading
On Emotional Intelligence
Bar-On, R. and Parker, J.D.A. (eds) (2000) *The Handbook of Emotional Intelligence: Theory, Development, Assessment, and Application at Home, School, and in the Workplace.* San Francisco, CA: Jossey-Bass.

On Humanistic Psychology and its values
Joseph, S. and Linley, P.A. (2006) *Positive Therapy: A Meta-Theory for Positive Psychological Practice.* London: Routledge.

On applied Positive Psychology
Linley, P.A. and Joseph, S. (eds) (2004) *Positive Psychology in Practice.* Hoboken, NJ: John Wiley.

On general Positive Psychology
Seligman, M.E.P. and Csikszentmihalyi, M. (2000) 'Positive psychology: An introduction.' *American Psychologist 55*, 5–14.

References
Baltes, P.B., Gluck, J. and Kunzmann, U. (2002) 'Wisdom: Its Structure and Function in Regulating Successful Lifespan Development.' In C.R. Snyder and S.J. Lopez (eds) *Handbook of Positive Psychology.* New York: Oxford University Press.

Christopher, J.C. (1996) 'Counseling's inescapable moral visions.' *Journal of Counseling and Development 75*, 17–25.

Csikszentmihalyi, M. (1990) *Flow: The Psychology of Optimal Experience.* New York: Harper and Row.

Deci, E.L. and Ryan, R.M. (1985) *Intrinsic Motivation and Self-determination in Human Behavior.* New York: Plenum.

Deci, E.L. and Ryan, R.M. (2000) 'The "what" and "why" of goal pursuits: Human needs and the self-determination of behavior.' *Psychological Inquiry 11*, 227–268.

Gable, S.L. and Haidt, J. (2005) 'What (and why) is positive psychology?' *Review of General Psychology 9*, 103–110.

Graczyk, P.A., Weissberg, R.P., Payton, J.W., Elias, M.J., Greenberg, M.T. and Zins, J.E. (2000) 'Criteria for Evaluating the Quality of School-based Social and Emotional Learning Programs.' In R. Bar-On and J.D.A. Parker (eds) *The Handbook of Emotional Intelligence: Theory, Development, Assessment, and Application at Home, School, and in the Workplace.* San Francisco, CA: Jossey-Bass.

Horney, K. (1951) *Neurosis and Human Growth: The Struggle toward Self-realization.* London: Routledge and Kegan Paul Ltd.

Joseph, S. and Linley, P.A. (2006) *Positive Therapy: A Meta-theory for Positive Psychological Practice.* Routledge: London.

Kashdan, T.B. and Fincham, F.D. (2004) 'Facilitating Curiosity: A Social and Self-regulatory Perspective for Scientifically Based Interventions.' In P.A. Linley and S. Joseph (eds) *Positive Psychology in Practice.* Hoboken, NJ: John Wiley.

Kunzmann, U. (2004) 'Approaches to a Good Life: The Emotional-motivational Side to Wisdom.' In P.A. Linley and S. Joseph (eds) *Positive Psychology in Practice.* Hoboken, NJ: John Wiley.

Lopez, S.J. and Snyder, C.R. (eds) (2003) *Positive Psychological Assessment: A Handbook of Models and Measures.* Washington, DC: American Psychological Association.

Lopez, S.J., Snyder, C.R., Magyar-Moe, J.L., Edwards, L.M., *et al.* (2004) 'Strategies for Accentuating Hope.' In P.A. Linley and S. Joseph (eds) *Positive Psychology in Practice.* Hoboken, NJ: John Wiley.

Maddux, J.E., Snyder, C.R. and Lopez, S.J. (2004) 'Toward a Positive Clinical Psychology: In P.A. Linley and S. Joseph (eds) *Positive Psychology in Practice.* Hoboken, NJ: John Wiley.

Patterson, T.G. and Joseph, S. (2006) 'Person-centered personality theory: Support from self-determination theory and positive psychology.' *Journal of Humanistic Psychology 47,* 117–139.

Prilleltensky, I. (1994) *The Morals and Politics of Psychology: Psychological Discourse and the Status Quo.* Albany, NY: State University of New York Press.

Proctor, G. (2005) 'Clinical Psychology and the Person-centred Approach: An Uncomfortable Fit?' In S. Joseph and R. Worsley (eds) *Person-Centred Psychopathology: A Positive Psychology of Mental Health.* Ross-on-Wye: PCCS Books.

Rogers, C.R. (1959) 'A Theory of Therapy, Personality, and Interpersonal Relationships, as Developed in the Client-centered Framework.' In S. Koch (ed.) *Psychology: A Study of a Science.* New York: McGraw Hill.

Rogers, C.R. (1963) 'The Actualizing Tendency in Relation to "Motives" and to Consciousness.' In M. Jones (ed.) *Nebraska Symposium on Motivation,* Volume 11. Lincoln: University of Nebraska Press.

Rogers, C.R. (1964) 'Toward a modern approach to values: The valuing process in the mature person.' *Journal of Abnormal and Social Psychology 68,* 160–167.

Ryan, R.M. and Deci, E.L. (2000) 'Self-determination theory and the facilitation of intrinsic motivation, social development, and well-being.' *American Psychologist 55,* 68–78.

Ryan, R.M. and Deci, E.L. (2001) 'On happiness and human potentials: A review of research on hedonic and eudaimonic well-being.' *Annual Review of Psychology 52,* 141–166.

Salovey, P., Caruso, D. and Mayer, J.D. (2004) 'Emotional Intelligence in Practice.' In P.A. Linley and S. Joseph (eds) *Positive Psychology in Practice.* Hoboken, NJ: John Wiley.

Seligman, M.E.P. (1999) 'The presidents' address.' *American Psychologist 54,* 559–562.

Seligman, M.E.P. (2002) 'Positive Psychology, Positive Prevention, and Positive Therapy. In C.R. Snyder and S.J. Lopez (eds) *Handbook of Positive Psychology.* New York: Oxford University Press.

Seligman, M.E.P. (2003) 'Positive psychology: Fundamental assumptions.' *The Psychologist 16,* 126–127.

Seligman, M.E.P. and Csikszentmihalyi, M. (2000) 'Positive psychology: An introduction.' *American Psychologist 55,* 5–14.

Snyder, C.R., Hoza, B., Pelham, W.E., Rapoff, M., Ware, L., Danovsky, M., *et al.* (1997) 'The development and validation of the Children's Hope Scale.' *Journal of Pediatric Psychology 22,* 399–421.

Sternberg, R.J. (1998) 'A balance theory of wisdom.' *Review of General Psychology 2,* 347–365.

Topping, K., Holmes, E.A. and Bremner, W. (2000) 'The Effectiveness of School-based Programs for the Promotion of Social Competence.' In R. Bar-On and J.D.A. Parker (eds) *The Handbook of Emotional Intelligence: Theory, Development, Assessment, and Application at Home, School, and in the Workplace.* San Francisco, CA: Jossey-Bass.

CHAPTER 10

Activity Theory and the Professional Practice of Educational Psychology

Jane Leadbetter

Introduction

Interest in Socio-Cultural and Activity Theory approaches has been growing rapidly over the past 25 years. Variously described as Cultural-Historical Activity Theory and Socio-Cultural Activity Theory, it draws upon a range of disciplines including psychology, sociology, political theory and communication studies. It is being studied and used in research all over the world and is increasingly being applied within a range of work settings. Its use within the practice of educational psychology is new and innovative, but, as this chapter demonstrates, the approach has tremendous potential to widen and enrich the work of practitioners.

Within this chapter, the focus is on Activity Theory and how this has emerged as an area of practice distinct from socio-cultural approaches, although the two are still very closely linked and have some shared elements. Activity Theory itself has been extended not only in terms of theoretical concepts but also in terms of its range of application. This chapter explains some of the key concepts within Activity Theory and describes how it has been developed and used in different contexts. The chapter also describes ways in which Activity Theory can be used to enhance and facilitate the practice of educational psychology and describes specific applications: namely, Activity Theory as descriptive framework, analytic device and organisational development tool. Finally, the approach is discussed in relation to other frameworks available for educational psychologists working within current employment contexts.

Origins and history

Activity Theory has developed over the past 70 years from the original ideas of Lev Vygotsky and other Soviet psychologists. This was a time of huge political, social and cultural turmoil, during the Russian Revolution, yet Vygotsky and his colleagues began working within the state education system and developed theories around learning and development, emphasising how these are strongly linked to social and cultural factors. Vygotsky has been described as a 'cultural psychologist' (Daniels 2001) and his work, alongside the work of other notable Russian psychologists working at the same time (for example, Luria and Leontiev), has been studied and extended by many different writers and researchers.

Vygotsky was attempting to understand and explain the links between individual processes of learning and development and the cultural and social contexts within which all learning and development takes place. Such important ideas have been expanded in different directions – with some writers emphasising the importance of culture (Cole 1996), others developing approaches around mediation (Kozulin 1998), and, more recently, the centrality of the concept of activity being emphasised by researchers such as Engeström (1999a).

Activity Theory and Activity Systems

As this chapter is concerned with frameworks for practice that can be used by practitioners and trainee EPs, it is not appropriate to describe in detail how Activity Theory developed over the six decades after Vygotsky's death up until the 1990s when developments and applications increased vastly. Engeström and Miettinen (1999) offer a detailed description of the history and growth of Activity Theory. A key writer and researcher in this field, Yrjo Engeström directs a research centre in Helsinki that is devoted to the development and application of Activity Theory, and he has conceptualised Activity Theory as falling into three generations, which we will now go on to consider.

First, it is necessary to be clear about what a unit of activity is or might be. Vygotsky emphasised the importance of mediation in the process of learning and development. In contrast to the behavioural stance (which suggests that activities can be viewed and analysed as simply an action being taken on an object and an outcome being the result of this), Vygotsky drew attention to the nature of human behaviour and interactions and emphasised that actions are always mediated in some way. Thus a simple behavioural model of:

Subject (acting upon) → Object (to produce) → Outcome

is modified to emphasise the importance of mediation, in the form of tools or artefacts. Hence, a first-generation Activity Theory model can be depicted as in Figure 10.1. This simple model shows that the subject position can be taken up by an individual or it can be viewed as a group or dyad taking action. The object (what is being worked on, acted upon or is the focus of the activity) is one of the most elusive and difficult elements to define within any Activity System. This is because within groups of people, trying to act collectively, there will invariably be a lack of clarity about what the object is, and this object is likely to be interpreted slightly differently depending on a range of factors but particularly upon the motives of the individuals involved. Hence the inclusion of the word 'motive' in the activity system (see Leont'ev 1978, p.64 for further explanation). The top of the triangle represents the mediation that takes place between the subject and the object in order to achieve an outcome. The artefacts (or tools) might be concrete (such as an object, machine or instrument) or may be abstract (the most common being language, but also including processes or frameworks). Included later in the chapter are some examples of how simple relationships work within an Activity Theory model used within psychological practice.

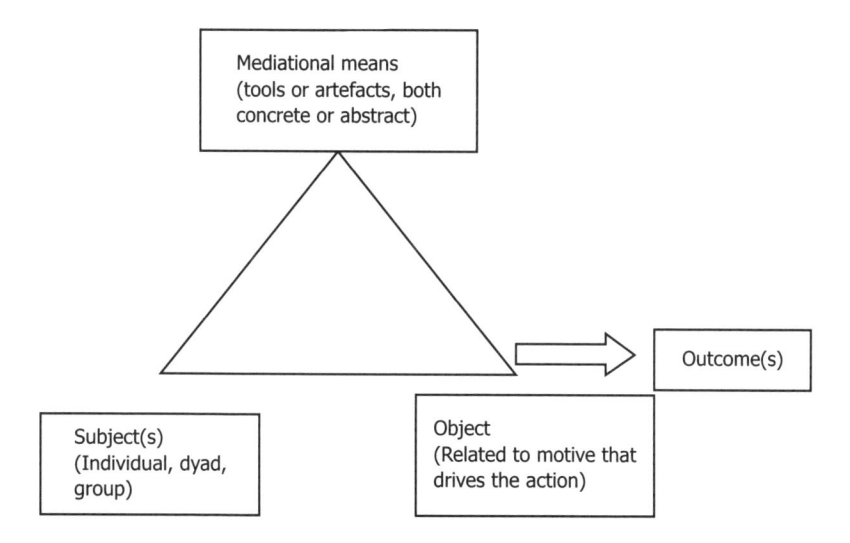

Figure 10.1: First-generation Activity Theory model (Daniels 2001, p.86)

Central to the idea of a simple activity system is the notion of mediation and in itself this is an extremely useful area to explore within any activity. However, Engeström, whilst accepting the importance of mediation, also felt that the relationships between individual actions, the tools used and their outcomes should be related to wider historical, cultural, social and contextual factors. Accepting that no actions take place within a sealed-vacuum-like environment, he stressed that the collective and communal aspects of activities were equally as important as the mediation that was taking place. Thus he extended the Activity System triangle to include these aspects and to ensure that high priority was given to the relationship between the key elements. Figure 10.2 depicts what Engeström has called 'Second-generation Activity Theory'.

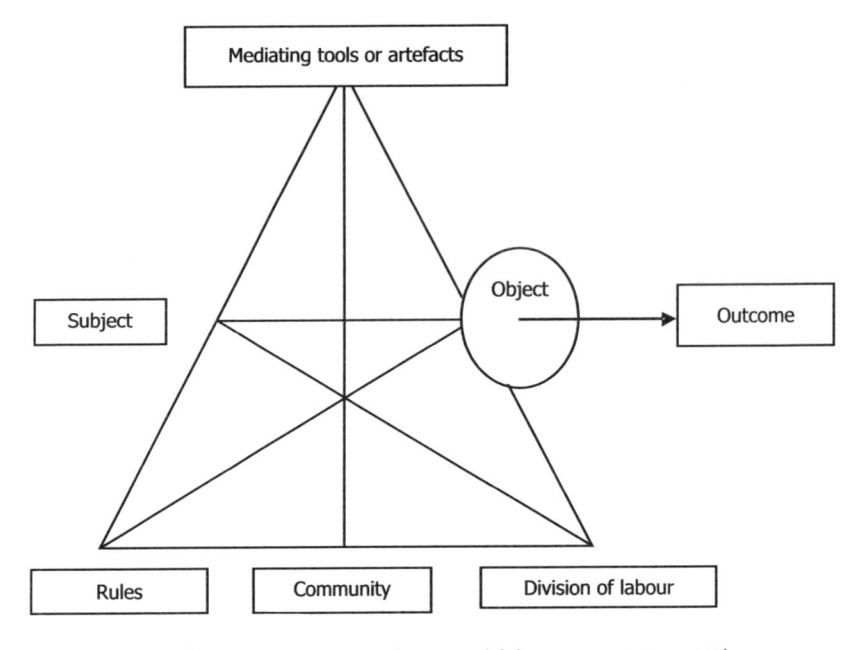

Figure 10.2: Second-generation Activity Theory model (Engeström 1987, p.78)

By using the extended Activity System triangle a range of elements can be elicited and examined and the important relations between wider historical and contextual factors can be considered with respect to the actions being taken, or proposed, and the methods used to achieve outcomes. Engeström's terminology to describe the lower part of the triangle is influenced by Marxist thinking. Hence the rules that impinge on activities are of paramount importance, as are the other people involved or potentially involved in any activities. A useful, but perhaps surprising categorisation is the 'division of labour' point on the triangle, but considerations of role demarcation and role expectation can lead to questions about how work is shared out and why. Later in the chapter, we provide examples to show how this expanded Activity Theory model can be used.

Engeström continues to develop his ideas around Activity Theory and has proposed a further development which he calls 'Third-generation Activity Theory'. Here he introduces conceptual tools to consider the multi-voicedness of Activity Systems (different players viewing and acting within Activity Systems in different ways), the importance of tensions and contradictions within any systems, and the notion that there are networks of interacting Activity Systems. Thus although it is possible to depict and interrogate an Activity System from one perspective, it is important not to forget that it also operates in relation to other Activity Systems. Thus two systems can be viewed as operating, perhaps with different and sometimes competing objects, and it may be that new objects for action need to be negotiated. This new object formation is shown in the diagram of a minimal Third-generation Activity Theory model in Figure 10.3.

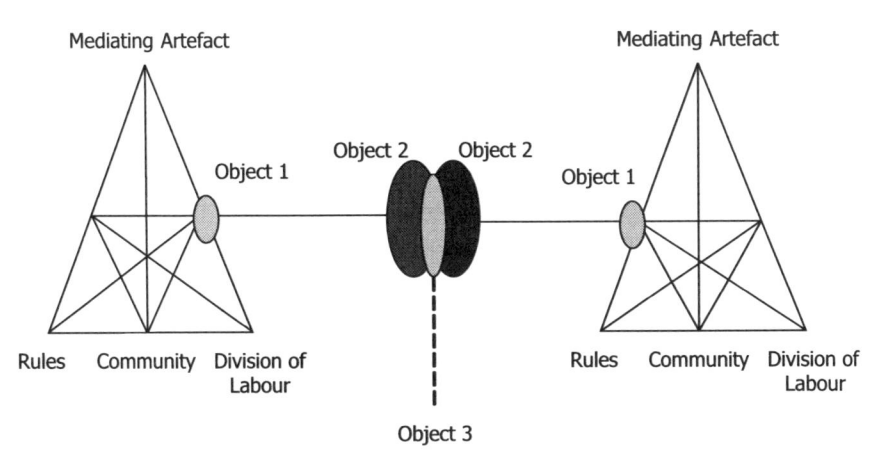

Figure 10.3: Third-generation Activity Theory model (Engeström 1999c, p.4)

It is perhaps important to note that Engeström is not the only researcher developing and using Activity Theory. The approach has seen a rapid expansion, particularly in the past ten years and is now used in many parts of the world, including Scandinavia, Australia, Japan, South Africa and the United States. Engeström has, however, written extensively and has produced seminal papers and ideas that others have taken further and tested in different settings. Thus different emphases are found in the variety of interpretations of Activity Theory. Engeström (1999c, summarised in Daniels 2001, pp.93–94) attempted to define five principles that pertain to Activity Theory and that can help researchers to understand some of the complexities of this approach. These are summarised briefly below.

1. The prime unit of analysis in Activity Theory is 'a collective, artefact-mediated and object-oriented activity system, seen in its network relations to other activity systems' (Daniels 2001, p.93).

2. Activity Systems are usually multi-voiced as there are always a community of multiple viewpoints with differing interest and traditions.

3. The historicity of Activity Systems is extremely important in that they develop over long periods of time and are constantly

transformed and transforming. Through investigating the historical aspects (formation) of systems, new understandings can be brought to bear on current Activity Systems.

4. Contradictions are central to an understanding of Activity Theory as they are sources of tension, disturbance and eventually change and development. By examining contradictions within and between Activity Systems new objects can be created and new ways of working can be developed.

5. Finally, the transformative nature of Activity Systems is emphasised as Engeström maintains that through examination of contradictions participants may question established patterns of working and new motives and new objects may be formed. These transformations may occur over lengthy periods of time and result in a much wider range of possibilities for action. Daniels suggests that these five principles act as a manifesto of the current state of Activity Theory (2001, p.93).

Before concluding this section on the basic elements of Activity Theory it is important to re-emphasise that Activity Systems should not be viewed only as static, descriptive devices. They can act as frameworks for understanding relationships between elements but they can also be used as analytic tools where actions and views can be mapped and recorded and contradictions can be identified and worked upon. This leads to the final important use of Activity Theory: its application to work environments where it is central to a mode of working known as 'Developmental Work Research' (DWR).

DWR, invented by Engeström and his team in Helsinki (Engeström 1999b), has been used as a means of promoting learning within organisations in settings as varied as banks, hospitals, communications companies and law courts (see Engeström 2001 for one example of this type of application). In the United Kingdom, the method has been applied in working with teachers in a range of different schools within a locally agreed project (Daniels *et al.* 2007) and also with multi-agency teams of workers within Children's Services (Leadbetter *et al.* 2007). A description of what DWR is and how it can be used to work with groups or organisations is included later in this chapter.

Activity Theory as descriptive framework, analytic device and organisational development approach

In this section I will explain how Activity Theory can be applied to various aspects of the work of EPs as currently practised. However, given the shifting landscape of EPs' work it is important to consider future applications and the extent to which any theory or framework can be adapted to enable new patterns of work to emerge. For each of the three uses outlined above, you will find below an explanation of how the theory can be applied and then an example highlighting particular elements of Activity Theory.

A descriptive framework

Activity Theory derives from Vygotsky's work centring upon the importance of social and cultural factors in development and learning. Any introduction to pedagogy will undoubtedly include reference to Vygotsky's work and his term 'zone of proximal development', or ZPD, has been well used and sometimes abused. Vygotsky considered the levels of mediation that were necessary in order to help a person to move from one stage of learning to a higher level. Kozulin (1998) examines in detail the psychological tools that can be learned, encouraged and employed to facilitate learning, and this emphasis upon mediation is central to the notion of dynamic assessment.

Building on this approach to examining learning, the notion of 'scaffolding' as coined by Wood, Bruner and Ross (1976) is also in common parlance, although how scaffolding can be used to facilitate learning and inform teaching is less clear. These two concepts have in common the importance of mediation, in relation to extending a child's learning or capability, and this is an area that EPs could, and should, be contributing to in a range of learning interactions and environments. Daniels (2005) in his article 'Vygotsky and educational psychology', elaborates on the range of applications of Vygotsky's work and suggests that this work has radical implications for the work of applied psychologists working in education.

When considering the learning and development of an individual child, whether in terms of assessment or intervention, it is important to consider both individual and environmental factors. Using a Second-generation Activity Theory model, EPs can conceptualise their own thinking and planning around a piece of work and can also share this with others (such as the teachers concerned) in order to ensure that the learning opportunities are maximised. The example in Figure 10.4 shows how a programme can be planned to ensure that appropriate mediators, objects to work on and other resources can be used.

This descriptive, conceptual model has been used as an aid for planning interventions for trainee psychologists, as well as a device for discussing and sharing with staff in schools possible ways of working – and, in particular, the various factors that need to be considered in relation to an intervention. Once the different elements of the Activity System have been clarified, then the relationship between each element can be analysed to identify any contradictions. There are often contradictions between the rules and the object to

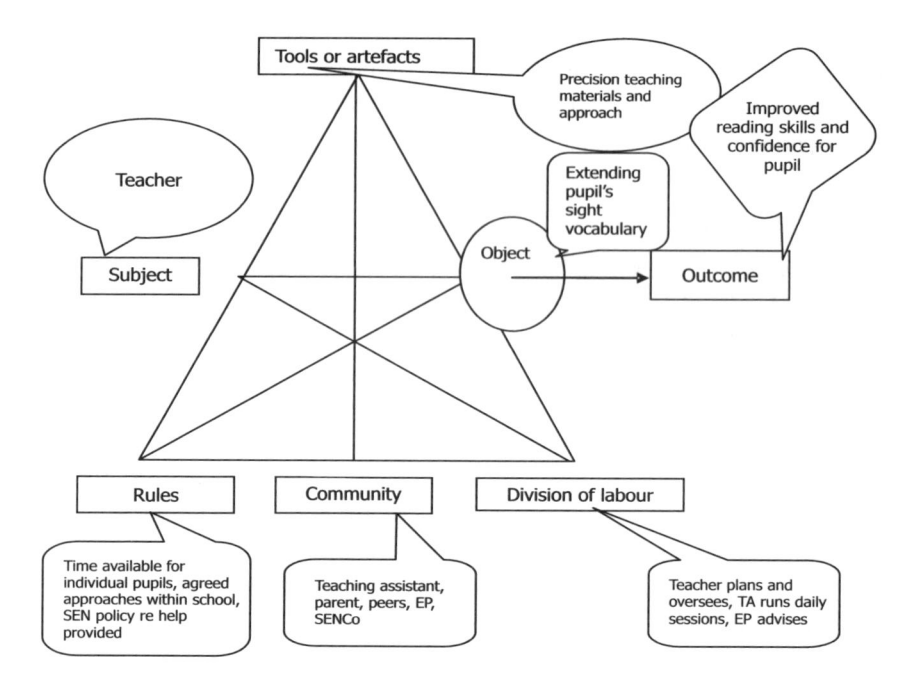

Figure 10.4: Activity System showing a learning programme

be worked upon and in the example in Figure 10.4, time available and/or models of support might not facilitate work on the identified object. Such contradictions highlight areas for further discussion and negotiation between the various participants or stakeholders.

In this example, precision teaching approaches have been used as one of the tools for work on building up sight words. However, there are many other artefacts that could have been chosen. Artefacts can be concrete or abstract: thus other concrete tools could have been used, such as a structured reading scheme, a word-wall or word-tin. Alternatively, or additionally, the teacher could have been trained in a particular way of working and may, thus, have been using a strong internal model or framework, such as 'direct instruction' approaches or 'real reading' approaches. The advantage of clarifying the different elements so that all the actors can comment upon the Activity System, in an open and collaborative way, means that:

- additional artefacts can be suggested
- there can be an objective discussion about whether the chosen artefacts are fit for purpose, whether others can be involved in a support role and whether the work is being divided up in the most efficient way.

Flynn (2005) demonstrates in more detail how Activity Theory has been applied in order to provide an approach to working with children with autistic spectrum disorders (ASD) in mainstream schools. He uses Activity Theory to examine possible barriers to inclusion of children with ASD and proposes a model of situated dynamic assessment in order to facilitate future planning. This model has been used successfully by EPs working in schools with children with ASD.

These examples demonstrate the importance of mediation within Activity Theory and the usefulness of clarifying the relevant artefacts that are being utilised to work on the object.

An analytic device

There is some similarity between the use of Activity Theory as a descriptive device and its use in analysing and making sense of situations and systems. It is likely that once a system has been described or delineated according to Activity Theory categories, the people concerned may want to analyse the relationships between the different elements or evaluate the relative strengths and weaknesses of different aspects of the Activity System. The next example shows how Activity Theory can be applied to a more complex area of work and how analysis and comparison across different systems can provide helpful data. It also shows how Activity Theory modelling can be used to track changes over time by constructing models from data collection, people's views, document analysis and other methods and then repeating the data collection when changes have occurred.

Consider the area of transition between stages of school for pupils of different ages. There is clear evidence of dips in achievement at certain key times (Galton, Morrison and Pell 2000) and this is an area of work in schools that EPs are often, quite correctly, asked to contribute to in terms of knowledge of psychology as applied to school settings. One project (Atkinson 2006) explored pupil transition from a number of primary schools to different secondary schools, mainly from the perspective of pupils, but also taking account of other factors. In particular, the contexts of the receiving schools were viewed as extremely important in terms of the success of the transitions.

Pupils were interviewed in Year 6 (aged 11) prior to their transfer to secondary schools. They were then interviewed again in their first term of secondary schooling (after the 'settling in' period) and again towards the end of their first year of secondary education. Key teachers in the primary and secondary schools were also interviewed about the arrangements, provision and support that were provided to facilitate pupil transfer. The data gathered was analysed using Activity Theory and a number of models were drawn up based upon the categories generated from the responses.

Atkinson identified seven themes emerging from her interviews with the pupils during their transfer periods. These were:

- feeling lost
- the school as a community
- what makes a good teacher
- curriculum issues
- the learning experience
- family involvement
- the wider community.

Five of these themes echoed earlier, similar work undertaken by Tobbell (2003). The pathway of the data analysis followed familiar lines, with the interviews being coded and categorised and then common themes identified and evidenced. However, a further level of analysis was undertaken using an Activity Theoretical approach in order, first, to highlight the tools that were used during the transfers within and across the different schools and, second, the areas of contradiction at the three points in time across the pupils' transfer journeys.

It is not possible in this chapter to show all the differences, as evidenced in the Activity Systems, of the pupils and teachers at different points in time. However, Figures 10.5 and 10.6 show two different Activity Systems based on the evidence emerging from the pupils and the teachers when interviewed towards the end of the first year in secondary school.

The contradictions that emerged, although not evident entirely from these two figures, pointed out clear differences in views and, hence, in possible future actions. Table 10.1 summarises the key contradictions emerging from Atkinson's work with schools in exploring and developing transition work. The contradictions were shared with the schools and provided definite signposts for future work to improve the systems within and between schools.

CONTRADICTIONS

This example demonstrates how Activity Theory can be used to consider contradictions emerging from different subject positions (in this case, pupil perspective and teacher perspective). As mentioned earlier, Engeström emphasises the importance of contradictions within Activity Theory (see the five principles of Activity Theory referred to earlier in this chapter) and views them as having a central role as sources of change and development. They can be analysed between and within Activity Systems and occur especially when an Activity System adopts a new element from outside, such as a new technology.

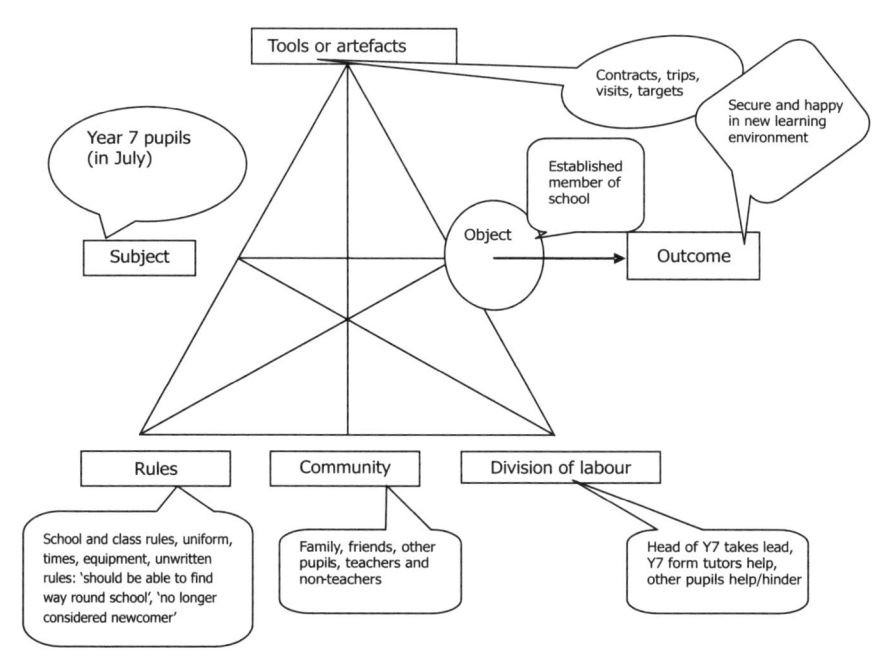

ACTIVITY THEORY AND THE PROFESSIONAL PRACTICE OF EDUCATIONAL PSYCHOLOGY 207

Figure 10.5: Activity System showing pupil views of transition at the end of Year 7 (from Atkinson 2006, p.161)

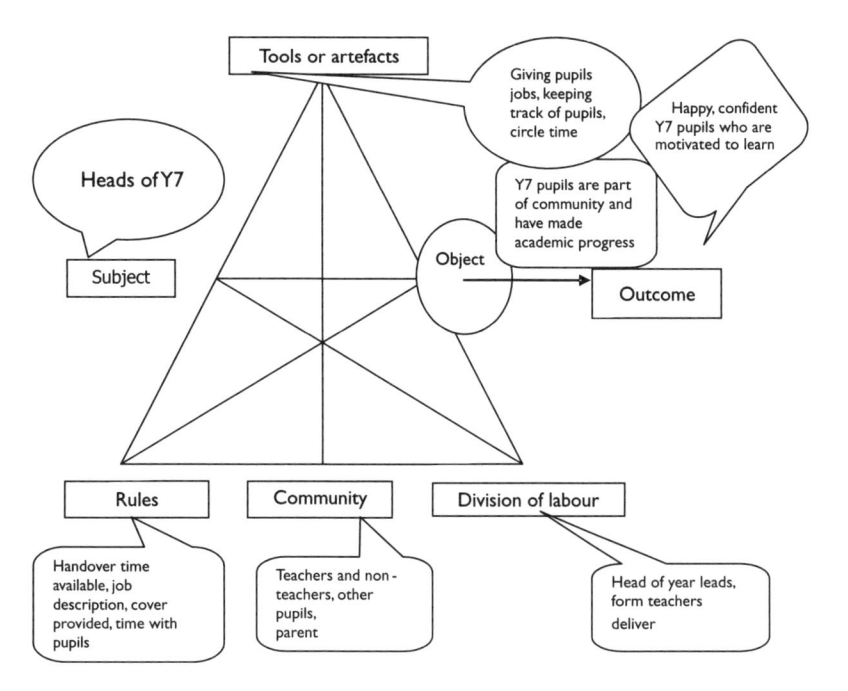

Figure 10.6: Activity System showing teacher views of transition at the end of Year 7 (from Atkinson 2006, p.166)

Table 10.1: Summary of Activity Theory contradictions surrounding pupil transition from Year 6 to Year 7 (adapted from Atkinson 2006, p.170)

Time of interviews	July (end of Y6)	November (start of Y7)	July (end of Y7)
Pupils	The importance of family and friends in providing information and support highlighted and yet they are not reported to be involved by school staff	None of the tools mentioned by teachers address the two biggest concerns reported by pupils during the first term – homework and missing previous teacher	No extended support or allowances made for Y7 pupils beyond the first term, however pupils feel they still require it as they are still anxious about finding their way around school, organising their homework and they continue to miss their old teachers
Teachers	Y6 pupils are passive actors in teachers' preparation of transfer process. They provide no support to parents; much of preparation relies on communication between pupil and teacher, with little flexibility for those who have communication or relationship difficulties	Y7 aims to provide curriculum continuity and be more lenient at the same time. No clear induction programme leads to greater teacher variation. No consultation with pupils who are passive in planning and implementing their induction programme	Head of Y7 no longer involved with current Y7 as their time is now focused on new intake

HISTORICITY

Second, this example shows how using an Activity Theoretical approach can be broadened out to consider wider cultural and historical factors. Although the project designed above was limited in terms of its scope, it could have focused more upon the culture of the different schools and how this influences the processes that are put in place around transfer. Activity Theory is also described by many as Cultural–Historical Activity Theory (CHAT) since the historicity of any Activity System is important as it can provide valuable information about how it came to be functioning in a particular way. Understanding why activities take place as they do can be enhanced by a historical perspective and Activity Theory utilises this. Hence this example of the applications of Activity Theory compared three sets of Activity Systems over time and looked to see how the changes might have resulted in new objects, new tools and possible contradictions.

An organisational development approach

For many years, 30 at least – if Gillham's landmark book *Reconstructing Educational Psychology* (1978) is taken as a signifier – educational psychologists in the UK have staked their claim to work with organisations as well as individual pupils who may be in difficulty. Through research and development work (see, for example, Timmins, Shepherd and Kelly 2003) or through seeking to work with organisations (Stoker 1992) there has been a drive by EPs working with schools and other organisations to apply psychology in its broadest sense. Looking to the future, the growth in organisational psychology qualifications and the proliferation of business psychologists working with organisations suggests this is an area where applied psychologists with contemporary knowledge and experience of educational settings (i.e. EPs) should be focusing.

Activity Theory is not just a static, descriptive or analytic modelling device: it has been developed to be used as a way of engaging with organisations to examine and expand efficient working practices. Again, it is Engeström – working originally in Finland, but also in California – who has used Activity Theory in action in a wide range of settings. As mentioned earlier, he coined the term Developmental Work Research (DWR) to describe the way he began to work with teams of people in banks, hospitals, schools and communication companies. Again, given the focus of this chapter, there is not enough space to describe in detail how DWR methodology operates. However, it is important, yet again, to emphasise that DWR is rooted in Vygotskian thinking. He advocated analysis *of action in and on our worlds* and Scribner (1985) suggests that Vygotsky did not privilege one particular approach to investigations but instead proposed four stages. Engeström (1999a, p.35) summarises these as follows:

1. Observation of contemporary everyday behaviour, or rudimentary behaviour,
2. Reconstruction of the historical phases of the cultural evolution of the behaviour under investigation,
3. Experimental production of change from rudimentary to higher forms of behaviour, and
4. Observation of actual development in naturally occurring behaviour.

These steps have been incorporated into DWR methodology by Engeström in order to consider how knowledge is created and how learning is expanded. His theory of 'expansive learning' is outlined in Engeström (2001) and this aspect of Activity Theory provides useful steps to guide any exploration or intervention of how participants work in groups, teams and organisations.

Daniels *et al.* (2007) describe how the approach was used with a group of schools working together trying to promote and enhance creativity across their individual curricula. He suggests that:

> This form of intervention involves the preparation and facilitation of workshops in which the underlying structural contradictions that are in play in emergent activities are highlighted and articulated in such a way that participants may engage with what may otherwise remain hidden and unexamined tensions. (p.125)

Essentially, DWR uses Activity Theory as a means of modelling what is happening in work settings with teams or groups of people. Hence, data is collected around participants' views, historical precedents and working practices, rules, protocols and constraints. This is achieved through interviews, observations and other ethnographic approaches. After this a series of workshops are conducted where the data is presented using Activity Theory models and participants are invited to comment upon, counter, elaborate upon and engage with the models presented. The workshops are, however, developmental as each workshop is video-recorded and extracts from the workshops are used in subsequent workshops as stimuli that may or may not represent key issues for practice. Again, participants are invited to comment upon what they see and hear presented by the facilitator/researchers and to discuss these in the workshop. In order to ensure participants become familiar with the theory, the models and the terminology, the familiar activity triangle is made enactive through a series of questions. These are often revisited within the DWR workshops and can be seen in Figure 10.7.

These questions are used to guide participants through discussions about past, present and future practices. Although changes to working practices may

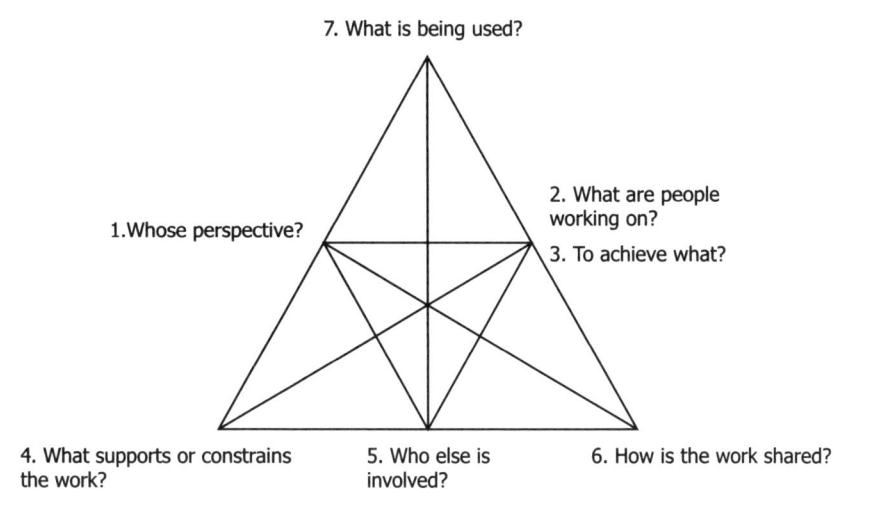

```
                    7. What is being used?
                         /\
                        /  \
                       /    \
                      /      \   2. What are people
1. Whose perspective?/        \  working on?
                    /          \ 3. To achieve what?
                   /            \
                  /              \
                 /_____\
4. What supports or constrains   5. Who else is    6. How is the work shared?
   the work?                        involved?
```

Figure 10.7: Questions used to facilitate Developmental Work Research workshops

not be agreed during the workshops, it is clear from analysis of how the workshops develop that changes *do* occur and participants talk about how the workshops and the new ways of thinking have influenced their work. The following two examples describe how these methods of applying Activity Theory can promote change within groups and organisations.

MULTI-AGENCY TEAMWORK

A large-scale, nationally funded research project studying the professional learning involved in multi-agency work, the 'Learning in and for Interagency Working' (or LIW) project is a theoretically driven study that utilises Activity Theory as a way of understanding multi-agency work (see Leadbetter *et al.* 2007 for a fuller description). It is not, however, a descriptive project, tracking and reporting the work of different teams, but uses DWR methods in order to enable team members to uncover what they are learning through working in multi-agency teams and, further, what they *need* to learn in order to work together more effectively. The teams involved in the project include:

- a Looked After Children team
- a Youth Offending Team
- a Child and Adolescent Mental Health Service (CAMHS) team
- school staff and external support staff working within and around an extended school
- a multi-disciplinary generic team working within a geographical area within Children's Services and

- teams of professionals working together to facilitate cross-school working within a divided section of a community.

For each of these teams a series of workshops (alongside on-going ethnographic data collection) enabled them to examine their practices, reflect on areas that needed further development or work, consider the division of labour and critically evaluate some of the tools they were using. Figure 10.8 depicts how multi-agency work can be modelled, and it was this type of modelling that was used within the workshops to tease out context-related contradictions.

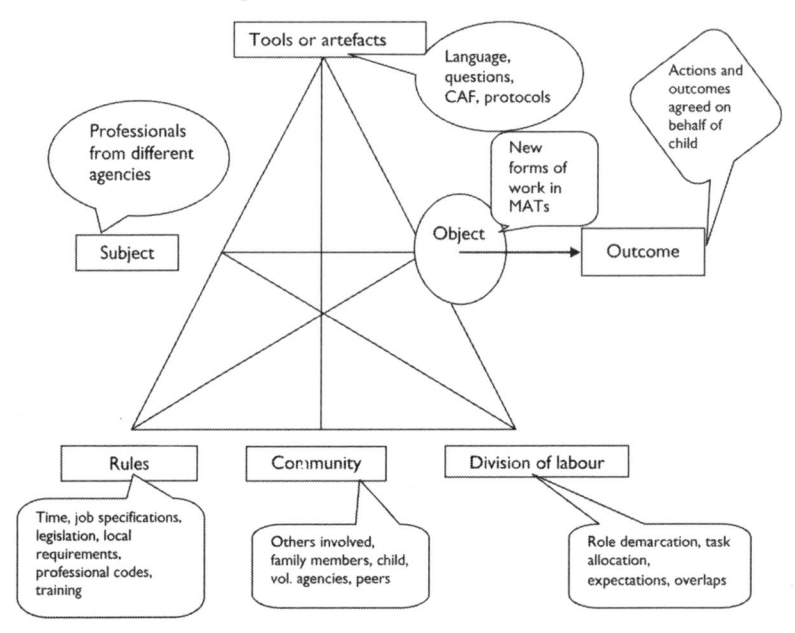

Key:
CAF = Common Assessment Framework
MAT = multiagency teams

Figure 10.8: Multi-agency working viewed as an Activity System

Although it may be unlikely that EPs will be involved in large-scale projects such as that described above, they are called upon to work with groups and to facilitate planning meetings within a range of organisations. EPs:

- help schools with planning actions to promote inclusion in schools
- work with staff in Children's Centres to help them decide on priorities and who to involve and how, and
- work within CAMHS teams, acting as a facilitator to consider how new work is taken on and how differential skills should be deployed.

In such examples, applying Activity Theory in a dynamic way, using DWR methods can provide theoretically grounded, yet practical tools with which to widen the role of the EP.

Although it is not the place of this chapter to describe the findings of the LIW research study, there are some interesting emerging issues that relate to other aspects of Activity Theory hitherto not mentioned. The project focuses on learning, and within each team aspects of learning have been identified.

- Professional identity appears as a clear area where change and learning have taken place for many teams members (see Leadbetter 2006a for description).

- Professional expertise and division of labour are areas keenly discussed and where new learning and new practices are being developed and agreed.

- Whole-child versus categorisation approaches. Learning in relation to new legislation entails negotiating new uses of shared language.

- Horizontal learning across teams is happening but there is a perceived need in many teams for this to be increased.

- Learning which rules can be broken or bent to enable improvements to practice is a common theme across project teams.

- Creation of new tools is happening as old practices are seen to be unfit for purpose. Team members are learning through developing new tools and practices.

Clearly, all the above themes can be viewed as psychological in content. For a psychologist working with a group of professionals there is a rich seam of data, issues and practices that could be developed with the help of applied knowledge and skills in organisational, social and interpersonal psychology. This example highlights the importance of learning within Activity Theory and the application of the theory through DWR methodology.

Service development and service delivery
The final example of the use of Activity Theory pertains directly to the work of individual EPs as Activity Theory has been used to facilitate both small- and large-scale changes within EP services (EPS). Many EP services have needed to realign their practices and the way in which they relate to schools, children and families due to changes in legislation, priorities and desired ways of working within the profession. In particular, the move to embrace Consultation as a core method of engaging with a range of clients or stakeholders has been noticeable

(Wagner 2000; Leadbetter 2000, 2006b). However, in some services not all EPs use Consultation in the same way and as schools move to become extended schools, and nurseries become Children's Centres, there are opportunities for EPs to expand their role and work across areas and clusters in diverse ways.

Using Activity Theory and DWR approaches it has been possible to work with one EPS to examine their use of the term Consultation, the tools they have created to implement their service delivery and the extent to which the changes they have introduced have been effective. This has taken place over a three-year period, during which time team members have become familiar with Activity Theory and the related terminology and it has provided a shared language and conceptual framework around which they can plan and review and evaluate. A final example of an Activity System, used in this organisational development work, is shown in Figure 10.9.

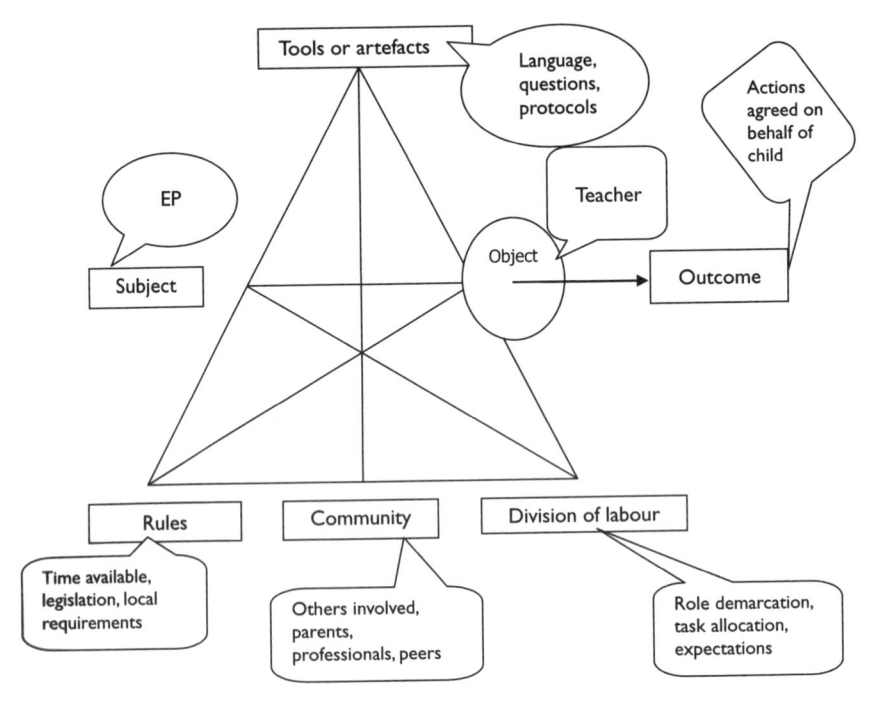

Figure 10.9: Consultation meetings between EPs and teachers viewed as an Activity System (from Leadbetter 2006b, p.26)

Activity Theory as a legitimate tool for enhancing the professional practice of EPs

Kurt Lewin famously said 'There is nothing so practical as a good theory' (1951, p.169) and I would like to endorse this proposition in the context of educational psychology since Activity Theory can be applied successfully to the practice of educational psychology and the tasks undertaken by EPs in a number of important domains. These have been explained and demonstrated in earlier sections of this chapter, but here I would like to emphasise its particular strengths. Daniels (2001, p.83) states that: 'Because of its focus on the irreducible tension between agents and cultural tools which defines mediated action, this analysis stands in contrast with others that focus on individuals or on instruments in isolation.'

Thus Activity Theory is a framework that can be applied to any situation where human action is taking place, as it focuses upon mediation, tool usage and dynamic tensions. In its sophisticated form it can be used to analyse individual action within cultural and historical contexts and through particular methods and approaches (DWR) it can be applied effectively to support learning within organisations.

Other approaches and frameworks for practice described in this book also have their uses and it is important for practitioners to ensure they are well equipped and well informed when they draw upon models and frameworks to guide their practice. Choosing supportive frameworks that are fit for purpose, are conceptually and theoretically sound and are easy to apply are important factors. Activity Theory does not preclude the use of other approaches. Essentially it provides an Interactionist, socially and culturally embedded model through which activities can be viewed, analysed and worked upon. It is practical and it is action-oriented.

As an approach to be incorporated into training of EPs it is to be commended because it reinforces the importance of context and environment when approaching any problem – especially when problems are perhaps depicted, in a limiting way, as residing within the child. It also provides a solid, theoretical underpinning rationale, coming as it does from a widely respected (Vygotskian and post-Vygotskian) approach to cognitive and social psychology. There are regular calls for educational psychology practice to be accountable, transparent and to demonstrate utility. Activity Theory can help EPs meet these challenges and can provide a useful function as part of their conceptual and practical repertoire. In this way it can be seen to provide both conceptual and concrete tools and artefacts.

As with any approaches, there are some areas of Activity Theory that are weaker or underdeveloped. Activity Theory acknowledges the importance of discourse and language (not least as probably the most important artefact in everyday use). However, incorporating methods of understanding and analysing language within Activity Theory are underdeveloped. This is an exciting area for future work. Second, the role of the subject within an activity system and the role the subject takes up is often underplayed in any analysis and, again, this is an exciting area for expansion. Psychology has a huge amount to contribute in terms of our understanding of attitude formation, motivation, construct and value formation, identity formation and more, and all these aspects play a part in the way a subject views and acts within an Activity System.

In 2005 one volume of the *Journal of Educational and Child Psychology* was devoted to this area, entitled 'Sociocultural psychology and activity theory: new paradigms to inform the practice of educational psychology'. This included a wide range of contributions that stretch beyond Activity Theory. In this volume it was suggested that as a new paradigm for use within Applied Psychology, Socio-cultural and Activity Theoretical approaches have much to offer because:

- they are based on sound and important psychological principles and theory
- they take due account of the individual within any simple or complex system
- the role of mediation within learning and other activities is viewed as central and therefore, through developing and using theoretical and conceptual tools that surround mediation, our understanding and applications can be enhanced
- they provide a framework for understanding the sociocultural aspects of organisations and systems without downplaying the importance of the individual within any system
- they emphasise the importance of historicity in understanding why individuals and systems function as they do.

(Leadbetter 2005, p.27)

The variety of contributions and the new perspectives offered by Activity Theory demonstrates that psychologists should not restrict their choice of approach to well-worn traditional routes when new, exciting and encompassing ways of working are becoming available – and are being appropriated by other parties, perhaps non-psychologists.

References

Atkinson, S. (2006) *A qualitative investigation into pupils' views and experiences of the transfer from primary to secondary school in a local authority.* Ed. Psych. D. thesis, School of Education, University of Birmingham.

Cole, M. (1996) *Cultural Psychology: A Once and Future Discipline.* Cambridge, MA: Harvard University Press.

Daniels, H. (2001) *Vygotsky and Pedagogy.* London: Routledge Falmer.

Daniels, H. (2005) 'Vygotsky and educational psychology: Some preliminary remarks.' *Educational and Child Psychology* 22, 1, 6–17.

Daniels, H., Leadbetter, J., Soares, A. and MacNab, N. (2007) 'Learning in and for cross-school working.' *Oxford Review of Education* 33, 2, 125–142.

Engeström, Y. (1987) *Learning by Expanding*. Helsinki: Orienta-Konsultit.

Engeström, Y. (1999a) 'Activity Theory and Individual and Social Transformation.' In Y. Engeström, R. Miettinen and R.L. Punamaki (eds) *Perspectives on Activity Theory*. Cambridge: Cambridge University Press.

Engeström, Y. (1999b) 'Innovative Learning in Work Teams: Analysing Cycles of Knowledge Creation in Practice.' In Y. Engeström, R. Miettinen and R.L. Punamaki (eds) *Perspectives on Activity Theory*. Cambridge: Cambridge University Press.

Engeström, Y. (1999c) 'Changing practice through research: Changing research through practice'. Keynote address, 7th Annual International Conference on Post-compulsory Education and Training. Griffiths University, Australia.

Engeström, Y. (2001) 'Expansive learning at work: Toward an activity theoretical reconceptualization.' *Journal of Education and Work* 14, 1, 133–156.

Engeström, Y. and Miettinen, R. (1999) 'Introduction.' In Y. Engeström, R. Miettinen and R.L. Punamaki (eds) *Perspectives on Activity Theory*. Cambridge: Cambridge University Press.

Flynn, S.A. (2005) 'A sociocultural perspective on an inclusive framework for the assessment of children with an autistic spectrum disorder within mainstream settings.' *Educational and Child Psychology* 22, 1, 40–50.

Galton, M., Morrison, I. and Pell, T. (2000) 'Transfer and transition in English schools: Reviewing the evidence.' *International Journal of Educational Research* 33, 341–363.

Gillham, B. (1978) *Reconstructing Educational Psychology*. London: Croom Helm.

Kozulin, A. (1998) *Psychological Tools. A Sociocultural Approach to Education*. Cambridge, MA: Harvard University Press.

Leadbetter, J. (2000) 'Patterns of service delivery in Educational Psychology services: some implications for practice.' *Educational Psychology in Practice* 16, 4, 449–460.

Leadbetter, J. (2005) 'Activity theory as a conceptual framework and analytical tool within the practice of educational psychology.' *Educational and Child Psychology* 22, 1, 18–28.

Leadbetter, J. (2006a) 'New ways of working and new ways of being: Multi-agency working and professional identity.' *Educational and Child Psychology* 23, 4, 47–59.

Leadbetter, J. (2006b) 'Investigating and conceptualising the notion of consultation to facilitate multi-agency working.' *Educational Psychology in Practice* 22, 1, 19–31.

Leadbetter, J., Daniels, H., Edwards, A., Martin, D., Middleton, D., Popova, A., *et al.* (2007) 'Professional learning within multi-agency children's services: researching into practice.' *Educational Research* 49, 1, 83–98.

Leont'ev, A.N. (1978) *Activity, Consciousness and Personality*. Englewood Cliffs, NJ: Prentice Hall.

Lewin, K. (1951) 'Field theory in Social Science.' In D. Cartwright (ed.) *Selected Theoretical Papers*. New York: Harper Row.

Scribner, S. (1985) 'Vygotsky's Uses of History.' In J.V. Wertsch (ed.) *Culture, Communication and Cognition: Vygotskian Perspectives*. New York: Cambridge University Press.

Stoker, R. (1992) 'Working at the level of the institution and the organisation.' *Educational Psychology in Practice* 8, 1, 15–24.

Timmins, P., Shepherd, D. and Kelly, T. (2003) 'The research and development in organisations approach and the evaluation of a mainstream behaviour support initiative.' *Educational Psychology in Practice* 19, 3, 229–242.

Tobbell, J. (2003) 'Students' experiences of the transition from primary to secondary school.' *Educational and Child Psychology* 20, 4, 4–14.

Wagner, P. (2000) 'Consultation: Developing a comprehensive approach to service delivery.' *Educational Psychology in Practice* 16, 1, 9–18.

Wood, D.J., Bruner, J.S. and Ross, G. (1976) 'The role of tutoring in problem solving.' *Journal of Child Psychology and Psychiatry* 17, 2, 89–100.

CHAPTER 11

Illuminative Evaluation

Bob Burden

Educational psychology is the study of ways in which people, throughout their lives, make sense of and become involved in the process of education in all its aspects. In its applied form it becomes the application of the knowledge and perspectives thus gained to the furtherance of the education of any individual or group in a variety of different contexts, of which schools are just one example.

Although there are likely to be some universal principles emerging from such a study, it is also certain to be influenced by different cultural contexts and by different paradigmic views of the world. It is a 'social' rather than a 'natural' science and owes as much to the arts as it does to scientific methodology. The direction and nature of development of applied educational psychology services in any part of the world will be subject to a dynamic interplay of political influences, which will include people, events, ideologies and economic forces.

Your starter for ten
The above statement represented the foundation of my inaugural address as President of the International School Psychology Association in the early 1990s. Its construction helped me to 'come out' within my chosen profession as someone who was at odds with its received wisdom, and to clarify for myself exactly what I did believe educational psychology had to offer. In retrospect, what surprised me was that I had never before stopped to think through the underlying principles of my work as an educational psychologist (EP), and how helpful it was to undertake such reflection. As far as I am concerned the notion of the EP as 'scientific practitioner' simply doesn't ring true. What I shall try to do in this chapter, therefore, is to provide a historical account of how I came to this conclusion and how I have interpreted this as running parallel to changing

conceptions of educational research and evaluation. My main purpose is to suggest that educational psychologists can, and should, come to see evaluative research as both useful and rewarding, if they can shake off their positivist shackles.

Taking a socio-cultural perspective

As a fresh-faced young psychologist in the early 1960s, I was taught that our relatively young discipline would only ever achieve wide academic acceptance and respectability by demonstrating our credentials as 'hard' scientists. It was emphasised that only by applying the principles of logical positivism and associated experimental methods, with their demand for control groups and the application of statistical analysis to outcome data, would we be able to achieve this aim. As most of our practical work was carried out in the laboratory investigating how lower forms of animal life learned to perform fairly simple tasks, it was relatively easy to convince ourselves that we were in the process of helping to establish coherent theories about how organisms learnt throughout the phylogenetic scale and thereby developing principles of human learning. The ultimate aim, of course, was the accurate prediction and control of human behaviour – an aim that the grandiose claims of Byron Skinner and other behaviourists appeared for a brief period to make perfectly achievable.

In the subsequent extended process of preparation to take on the mantle of an EP, the complex nature of learning within the real world struck home. Although some aspects of the behaviourist approach undoubtedly proved helpful in shaping the behaviour and learning progress of some children with whom most of us worked in the intervening years as teachers, its conceptual and practical limitations quickly became all too apparent. Similarly, it soon became abundantly clear that the experimental study of rats or zebra fish under 'controlled' conditions was a far cry from trying to make sense of how and why children acted in a range of different ways within typical school classrooms.

During our training year – in which the supposedly twin disciplines of psychology and education were brought together in a marriage of convenience – concepts of ability and attainment came to prominence, particularly in the way in which intelligence tests were offered as the key to understanding why some people had more or less difficulty in learning than others. Subsequent disillusion with the social implications of drawing upon atheoretical assessment techniques that clearly disadvantaged those from lower socio-economic backgrounds led me to begin to question the nature of the science upon which my new profession claimed to be based (Burden 1973, 1975). One of my primary concerns at this time was that far too little attention was being paid to the context in which children's learning difficulties were occurring. To my mind, far too much attention was being paid by the educational psychology profession to spurious psychological concepts like intelligence, and far too little to important aspects of the whole educational process. This led to me spending a period of exploration on what came to be termed 'Systems Theory' (Burden 1978, 1981) and my further questioning of the assumption that the root of all learning difficulties lay within the individual.

Meanwhile, a revolution had been occurring in theoretical approaches to learning. Not only had Piaget made it acceptable once more to consider what was going on in children's heads as they became more proficient learners, but the discovery and advocacy of Vygotsky's ideas by Jerome Bruner and others helped to re-emphasise the importance of the historical, cultural and social contexts in which all learning took place. It no longer made sense, if it ever did, to assume that learning took place in some kind of vacuum. The significance of this for the working EP was enormous, although there were many who were very slow to recognise it. At the same time, the post-modern revolution questioned the very notion of 'objective truth' whilst emphasising the relativity of different observers' perspectives. In order to gain some kind of understanding of any one child's learning difficulties, it thus became essential for EPs to take into account the dynamic nature of the interactions between teachers, learners, learning activities and learning contexts and the sense that the different sets of participants were making of those interactions. This led to the important conceptual leap from envisaging the EP as assessor of individual attributes to that of evaluator of learning processes within specific contexts.

A potted history of evaluation

In so far as it is concerned with evaluation, most educational psychology practice can be conceived as fixed within what Guba and Lincoln (1989) refer to as the first generation of evaluation, or what might legitimately be called 'the measurement generation', whereby the terms 'measurement' and 'evaluation' are often used interchangeably. In her role as a 'scientific practitioner', the EP acts essentially as a technician, applying a (fairly limited) range of instruments to measure preordained variables such as intelligence and scholastic attainment. This first – and long since outmoded – form of evaluation was also tied to the perceived strengths of (quasi) experimental methodology, whereby no evaluation was considered to be worth its salt without the application of randomised group designs involving the random allocation of 'subjects' to experimental and control groups. In the language of metaphor, this is often referred to as 'agricultural' evaluation, referring back to its botanical roots and associations with farmers' rotation of crops.

Despite my claim that this form of evaluation has long been outmoded, it nevertheless continues to be widely and unquestioningly used by many psychologists working within the field of education – with its claim to scientific respectability presumably making it invulnerable to criticism. The fact of the matter, however, is that experimental and strict psychometric methods are completely inadequate for elucidating the complex problem areas that confront them in the social context of human interactions. Moreover, as a means of evaluating educational programmes or processes they provide little effective input to decision-making processes.

Some 30 years ago, Malcolm Parlett and David Hamilton (1977) identified several weaknesses of the 'agricultural' approach to educational evaluation. First, they pointed out that the very requirement for large, random samples and strict controls make it costly in terms of time and resources. What's more, proper control groups of individuals are virtually impossible to find, and the random allocation of potential human participants to intervention/non-intervention groups is itself fraught with ethical difficulties. It can easily lead to the evaluator thinking and talking in terms of 'parameters' and 'factors' rather than individuals or institutions. This form of evaluation is not only strictly summative, it also assumes little or no change in the process of a project or programme during the period of study. It can even have the negative effect of discouraging new developments or redefinitions midstream. Artificial restrictions on the scope of the evaluation imposed by this kind of rigid design may well mean that other, potentially even more significant, data is overlooked or neglected. What is sought is generalisability, not individual difference. In Parlett and Hamilton's terms, 'there is an insensitivity to local perturbations and unusual effects'(1977, p.60). Finally, this sort of approach is based on an assumption that the purpose of evaluation is to discover some kind of 'objective truth'. What it doesn't take into account is that there is a multitude of different perspectives, and, therefore, it cannot articulate with the varied concerns and questions of different participant stakeholders.

Evaluation's 'second generation' can be seen in some respects as allied to the behavioural revolution with its emphasis on the assessment of desired learning outcomes in the form of objectives. The emphasis here was on curriculum development, epitomised by such approaches as 'precision teaching' and the now little-used Datapac materials. The notion of 'formative' evaluation was introduced here, but only in so far as it was linked to prescribed 'summative' outcomes. Measurement thereby came to be seen as just one of a range of tools available to the evaluator, but much more related to *in situ* investigation of whether set targets were being achieved (Guba and Lincoln 1989).

Evaluation as illumination

The metaphor preferred by Parlett and Hamilton, and those who took up and built upon their ideas, is that of evaluation as a form of social anthropology. Their introduction of the term 'Illuminative' Evaluation in 1972 was not only a reaction against the 'agricultural' approach, but also an early post-positivist attempt to focus upon the holistic study of educational programmes in order to throw light on what was happening, as it happened, from the perspective of all those involved. Their argument was that the programme's rationale, operations, achievements and difficulties should all be studied within the context in which they occurred.

The primary concern of Illuminative Evaluation is with description and interpretation rather than measurement and prediction (Parlett and Hamilton 1977). As such, it can be seen to have been one of the primary precursors to the interpretative research paradigm.

> The aims...are to study the innovatory programme: how it operates; how it is influenced by the various school situations in which it is applied; what those directly concerned regard as its advantages and disadvantages; how students' intellectual tasks and academic experiences are most affected. It aims to discover and document what it is like to be participating in the scheme, whether as teacher or pupil; and, in addition, to discern and discuss the innovation's most significant features, recurring concomitants and critical processes. (p.61)

Two main concepts underpin the Illuminative approach, the 'instructional system' and the 'learning milieu'. The former refers to the process by which any curriculum is transmitted. Traditionally, it is evaluated in terms of whether it meets specified objectives, for example, improved SATs results, progress in reading scores, etc. Measures are chosen or devised and implemented to check on whether this has occurred. An Illuminative Evaluation, however, works on the assumption that no curriculum is ever delivered in pure, unaltered form. The abstract model or shared idea may remain, but variations will inevitably occur in the way in which these ideas are delivered in each different situation. Thus, for example, the efforts of many 'school effectiveness' researchers to produce a single set of criteria that can predict how to produce an 'effective' school would be seen by most Illuminative researchers as pointless.

The 'learning milieu' refers to the social-psychological and material environment in which teachers and pupils work together. It thus represents a network of cultural, social institutional and psychological variables (Parlett and Hamilton 1977). Any change that is introduced into a school in the form of curriculum innovation (instructional practice), however straightforward this may seem to be (e.g. the introduction of a 'literacy hour' or a new reading scheme), will have a number of knock-on effects. At the same time, it needs to be recognised that within any specific classroom environment there will be:

- numerous constraints (architectural, financial, administrative)
- pervasive operating assumptions (the arrangement of subjects, teaching methods)
- teacher characteristics (teaching style, experience), and
- student perspectives (interests, attributions, ambitions) and characteristics (motivation, learning styles).

Parlett and Hamilton summarise the effects of these succinctly.

> The introduction of an innovation sets off a chain of repercussions throughout the learning milieu. In turn these unintended consequences are likely to affect the innovation itself, changing its form and moderating its impact. (p.62)

Somewhat surprisingly, they claim that one of the chief concerns for Illuminative Evaluation is connecting changes in the learning milieu with intellectual experiences of students. I must say that I find this far too narrow and out of alignment with the notion of throwing light on all that occurs in a school or business organisation, unless the meaning of 'intellectual' is broadened to encompass emotional reactions and social outcomes, and not just those of the students.

Putting it into operation

Parlett and Hamilton were always resistant to providing any standard format for Illuminative evaluations, which were described as coming in diverse forms according to the differences in the innovations and learning milieus studied: 'Illuminative evaluation is not a standard methodological package but a general research strategy'(p.64). Thus, the assumption is that the problem will always define the methods employed, and not vice versa. Nevertheless there are characteristically three overlapping stages, within which the evaluator observes, inquires further and then seeks to explain – drawing, as and where appropriate, on both quantitative and qualitative methods. Malcolm Parlett (1981) makes the point that, unlike more conventional forms of evaluation, Illuminative Evaluation does not begin from a position of seeking to establish whether set outcomes or identified objectives have been reached. In its initial phase, it is essential that considerable care is taken to negotiate exactly what sort of information all parties hope to gain from the evaluation process. In this respect it can, and must, be seen as a form of collaborative inquiry rather than any form of 'inspection'. The main role for the potential evaluator here is to help the client to identify exactly what would be the most helpful outcome of the evaluation process and to make clear just what is within the evaluator's capabilities. It may even transpire, at this stage, that the evaluator is unable or unwilling to meet the client's requirements. It is far better for such an outcome to be decided at the outset than for mismatched expectations to lead later to disappointment and recriminations.

The 'illumination' is most likely to arise from exploring the perspectives of as wide a range of 'stakeholders' as possible. The notion is therefore rejected of any one objective reality, which is replaced instead by an acceptance that perceptions of reality are constructed and multi-faceted. There are as many truths about a school or project or person as there are people connected with them. Somewhat disingenuously, Parlett (1981) has referred to the role of the Illuminative Evaluator as a 'neutral outsider' (p.224), but this really does seem like wanting to have one's cake and eating it, as taking such a stance can clearly be seen as bringing a positivist perspective to bear. A more consistent interpretative approach would be to admit to having one's own values-based construction of people, places and events, and to present this as an inevitably biased narrative in which the characters are invited to identify themselves (or not, should they feel disinclined to do so).

This underlines another important aspect of Illuminative Evaluation, the need to construct a *recognisable reality* for those involved in the project or institution under review. This in itself raises problems because the ideal scenario in which consensus is reached is extremely difficult, some might say impossible, to achieve. Nevertheless, unless a significant majority of those involved are prepared to admit that they recognise themselves and their accounts in any final report, one would need to ask whose light is being shown on the proceedings. This brings out the further point, as indicated above, that people's perceptions of what they think they believe, or even of what they think they do, does not always match up to others' perceptions. The role of the Illuminative Evaluator is not to provide 'evidence' of who is right or who is wrong, but to bring into the public domain the fact that these different perspectives occur. The facilitation of some kind of joint agreement as to constructive ways forward is likely to be the most appropriate next step.

To summarise, Illuminative Evaluation is built upon a number of key assumptions; it is:

- anti-positivist in its orientation
- thoroughly context-bound
- multi-faceted in its perspectives
- illustrative of the mismatch that often occurs between rhetoric and action
- concerned with revealing a recognised and recognisable reality.

The SPARE wheel approach

Although writers like Parlett and Hamilton shun the use of models or frameworks, it has always seemed to me that this was a step too far. A framework will not necessarily restrict one's range of investigation, but can provide a helpful structure to the evaluator's observations and questions. It was for this reason that when my colleague, Marion Williams, and I were asked to evaluate an innovatory curriculum project by the principal of an international school, we constructed the SPARE wheel acronym to provide such a framework.

There is a danger in pushing the analogy too far, but the notion of a wheel was meant to emphasise our belief that evaluations should be cyclical rather than 'one off', and that the connections between the various elements were inter-related as if by 'spokes', i.e. that they were not necessarily sequential. The concept of SPARE was meant to signify that evaluators could carry it around with them to use when necessary, like the spare wheel of a car, but more significantly as a mnemonic for the four key aspects of the approach: investigation of the **S**etting, the **P**lans, the **A**ction, the **R**eactions and the overall **E**valuation.

The *setting* is akin to Parlett and Hamilton's notion of the learning milieu. Here the aim of the evaluator should be to construct a 'rich picture' of the setting or context in which the action is occurring, or about to take place, taking into account historical, cultural and political perspectives. The evaluator(s) meanwhile need to investigate the proposed nature of any innovation (the *plans*) – whose idea it is, why they want to do it and how they intend to bring it about. At the same time, they need to determine what *action* has already been taken or is about to take place, because this is often where a mismatch is likely to occur. However good or revolutionary the intentions of one or more senior managers are, when it comes to translating these into practice, they are never realised in the form originally intended. The task of the Illuminative Evaluator here is to pinpoint exactly where and why these plans go astray as well as identifying areas where they appear to be working successfully.

It is important to discover also the *reactions* of all those who are involved. Basically, what do the participants think and feel about what is going on? What is their level of involvement and commitment to the success of the project? What do they see as its positive and negative aspects? This does not rule out the more structured measurement of outcomes, if this has previously been agreed, but this is used only as one aspect of a much more comprehensive process.

The *evaluation* stage is both ongoing in the sense that evaluators are involved in continuous reflections about what they hear and observe and should be in an on-going dialogue with the main stakeholders about this. It must never be left to a final revelatory denouement at which some kind of unforeseen or unexpected outcomes are revealed. Therefore, a successful Illuminative Evaluation should never spring any surprises at its conclusion. The ongoing collaborative process of collecting information and gathering participants' perspectives should incorporate also feedback and discussion of a regular nature such that the final illuminations are made up of a number of small candles, or even fireworks, that have been lit along the way, rather than one big bang or flash of light. A full description of the different functions of each aspect of the SPARE wheel model, together with just some of the key questions that might fruitfully be asked at each stage, is provided in the appendix to this chapter. However, some examples of how it has been used might help to elucidate matters further (see also papers by Burden and Williams 1996, and Burden and Nichols 2000).

The SPARE wheel in action

One early project involved the evaluation of an innovative scheme by the principal of an international school who intended to organise the teaching of some curriculum subjects in a foreign language – for example, English pupils would be taught geography in French, and French pupils would be taught geography in English. As it happened, the organisational structure of the school would have made it possible to arrange a pre-post quasi-experimental design, but we opted instead for a more open-ended Illuminative approach. Our exploration of the setting made it clear that there were considerable barriers within the school to the successful implementation of such a scheme. The majority of the staff felt that they had not been consulted and were very clearly split in their enthusiasm for the proposed changes. We concluded that if these changes were to be implemented as and when originally planned by the principal, the likelihood of success would be minimal.

In talking to the pupils, we discovered that the enthusiasm for learning foreign languages differed greatly between English and French speakers, as also did their current level of linguistic ability. Moreover, the perceived popularity and competence of the teachers who were most likely to be involved in introducing the changes varied considerably.

In feeding back this information to the principal, we were able to help the staff elucidate their concerns and to work with the main stakeholders in facilitating a joint consultation process whereby an alternative approach towards achieving the same aims was co-constructed.

Instead of trying to measure improvement in language competence, we devised an 'Attitude to Foreign Language' questionnaire with a particular emphasis upon personal motivation. (This later proved to be extremely helpful when we were asked to investigate why students at a local comprehensive school were faring so badly in foreign language examinations – see Williams, Burden and Lanvers 2002 for a detailed description of this research.) This questionnaire was administered before the revised programme was implemented, and again

12 months later, producing results which the principal and school staff found interesting and helpful in determining how best to move forward. Although we were not in a position to monitor closely the action that took place over the project's first year, we were able to pick up the threads quite easily at the end of that period and to identify how well the teachers felt they had been able to accomplish what they set out to do. From the reactions of both the teachers and pupils we were able to evaluate relative successes and failures and to identify what were likely to be obstacles to further progress. The principal declared himself satisfied with what had been accomplished up to that point, and was also in a much clearer position to decide how to act next in order to keep the momentum going.

More recently, the establishment of Exeter University's Cognitive Education Centre has led to a considerable growth of interest in the concept of a 'thinking school', coupled with requests for advice on how to evaluate whether the introduction of thinking-skills programmes into the school curriculum has beneficial effects. In response to such requests, it would have been perfectly feasible to suggest a traditional experimental control group design, as Topping and Trickey have done with what appear to have been impressive results in terms of IQ gains (Topping and Trickey 2007). Our approach has been very different in drawing up a number of criteria based upon the SPARE wheel model (see www.education.ex.ac.uk/cec, accessed 2 June 2008, for further information on these criteria).

The move in this direction was partly triggered by the lessons Louise Nichols and I learnt from our Illuminative Evaluation of one secondary school principal's attempt to introduce thinking skills into his inner-city comprehensive (Burden and Nichols 2000). There we found that the best-laid plans of a forward-thinking Head Teacher were doomed to failure due to incomprehension and natural resistance amongst the majority of teachers, the constraints of an already overcrowded curriculum and the perceived lack of status of the new lessons by the pupils (see Baker 1987 for similar findings with regard to the introduction of Feuerstein's Instrumental Enrichment programme into a Somerset comprehensive school).

In monitoring the implementation of the new programme, we found that although the necessary materials were well prepared and disseminated by the project leader, some of the teachers who were required to present the new programme felt ill prepared to do so. The reaction of many of the pupils to this was shown in their complaint that although they had enjoyed the first few thinking-skills lessons, they had quickly become bored with a constant diet of worksheets. Whilst the majority of more academically successful pupils tended to find the thinking-skills lessons rather a waste of their time, the least successful pupils found it difficult to understand what was required of them. Only those in the mid-range showed signs of responding positively to the project's aims of improving feelings of self-efficacy and developing their general learning abilities.

The lack of allocated meeting time for feedback and reflection meant that these issues were not being picked up by the staff involved on a regular basis and incorporated into planned changes in the process of implementation. In our first round of evaluative feedback, we made sure to discuss these findings with the principal and the key staff involved. Changes were made as a means of overcoming these obstacles which brought about a more positive student response, but it continued to be clear that the students did not feel empowered, on the whole, to transfer their newly developing skills into different areas of the curriculum. When the principal moved on to another position soon after, the project gradually wound down and was eventually dropped. We did not see this as a failure on our part. What we were able to reveal were a number of reasons why the project was not working and what needed to be done if it was to achieve its stated aims. In retrospect, this led to the conclusion that in order for any innovative project to make the kind of impact intended, it is necessary for a critical mass of all stakeholders (teachers, support staff, governors, parents and pupils) to be fully committed to it.

Some implications for the everyday practice of educational psychology

It is my contention that educational psychology as it has been traditionally practised in the United Kingdom – and, indeed, throughout the world – has been largely irrelevant, at least with regard to the big educational issues. This is not to say that individual children and families have not been supported, or that some teachers were not helped to improve their practice. What EPs have not been inclined to do, however, is to act in the broader sense as consultants to the education system at large. When they have attempted to do so, this has often been by means of rhetoric about such issues as the moral imperative towards inclusive practice in schools. What they have shown less inclination to do is to investigate ways in which schools are attempting to implement inclusive practice and identify the advantages and disadvantages of such practice from the perspective of those most closely involved.

If they really want to be considered significant players in the education game, EPs need to become much more involved in carrying out worthwhile educational research; they are in an excellent position to do so. Such research need not be, and, I strongly believe, *must* not be research of the 'agricultural' kind, which will continue to lead them into sterile backwaters. Illuminative Evaluation can offer a viable and exciting alternative, but is not the only one. In the last analysis, it comes down to each individual's personal definition of what it means to be an EP, but also to the profession's preparedness to constantly re-examine its goals and values.

For those who object to what they may see as too grandiose notions for their humble profession, I would nevertheless suggest that there are several fundamental principles that are emphasised by this open-ended approach.

- The role of the educational psychologist is more appropriately that of consultant than that of diagnostic expert.
- One-off interventions are more often than not a waste of time.
- No referred case should ever be considered in isolation, out of context.
- Any individual referred case must be seen as reflective of the ways in which a teacher, school system, parent or family is trying to make sense of a broader phenomenon, such as learning disability or 'inappropriate' behaviour.
- There will always be a multitude of perspectives on any 'case', including the EP's own and that of the referred client, which will reflect each participant's value systems.
- Solutions do not come readily packaged, but need to be constructed consensually by all stakeholders.

Some final thoughts

In its original conception, Illuminative Evaluation was fairly heavily orientated towards a sociological perspective, focusing mainly on the curriculum ('instructional system') and the learning context ('milieu'). What it didn't offer was much in the way of advice on how to go about collecting information needed for reflection and feedback; nor did it place enough emphasis upon the psychological commitment of the individuals involved. Educational psychology has a wealth of possible resources at its disposal to enable such gaps to be filled, ranging from questionnaires to interview techniques and a wide range of alternative approaches that have been tried elsewhere, together with the skills of Consultancy. Nevertheless, what this approach does emphasise is a preference for exploring attitudes, perceptions and attributions over assessing attributes and attainments.

For some, the approach will appear far too subjective and 'unscientific'. The response to this is that the recognition of this fact is a strength rather than a weakness. Pretending to be scientific when one is not is akin to scientology. Awareness of our own values and prejudices, and the way in which they affect all that we do, and preparedness to act accordingly, should help us to be wary of offering 'snake oil remedies' for the problems with which we are presented.

References

Baker, D. (1987) *Changing Tactics: An Illuminative Study of an Educational Intervention.* M.Ed. thesis, University of Exeter.

Burden, R.L. (1973) 'If we throw the tests out of the window, what is there left to do?' *Journal of the Association of Educational Psychologists 3*, 5, 14–19.

Burden, R.L. (1975) 'Meaningful questions or meaningless answers: The educational psychologist in search of an identity.' *Journal of the Association of Educational Psychologists 3*, 7, 15–21.

Burden, R.L. (1978) 'Schools' Systems Analysis: A Project-centred Approach.' In B. Gillham (ed.) *Reconstructing Educational Psychology.* London: Croom Helm.

Burden, R.L. (1981) 'Systems Theory.' In B. Gillham (ed.) *Behaviour Problems in Secondary Schools.* London: Croom Helm.

Burden, R. and Nichols, S.L. (2000) 'Evaluating the process of introducing a thinking skills programme into the secondary school curriculum.' *Research Papers in Education 15*, 30, 293–306.

Burden, R.L. and Williams, M.D. (1996) 'Evaluation as an aid to innovation in foreign language learning: The SPARE wheel model.' *Language Learning Journal 13*, 51–54.

Guba, E. and Lincoln, Y. (1989) *Fourth Generation Evaluation.* London: Sage.

Parlett, M. (1981) 'Illuminative Evaluation.' In P. Reason and J. Rowan (eds) (1981) *Human Inquiry: A Sourcebook of New Paradigm Research.* Chichester: Wiley.

Parlett, M. and Hamilton, D. (1977) 'Evaluation as Illumination: A New Approach to the Study of Innovatory Programmes.' In D. Hamilton, D. Jenkins and C. King (eds) *Beyond the Numbers Game.* Basingstoke: Macmillan.

Topping, K.J. and Trickey, S. (2007) 'Collaborative philosophical enquiry for school children: Cognitive effects at 10–12 years.' *British Journal of Educational Psychology 77*, 271–288.

Williams, M., Burden, R.L. and Lanvers, U. (2002) 'French is the language of love and stuff: Student perceptions of issues related to motivation in learning a foreign language.' *British Educational Research Journal 28*, 4, 503–528.

Appendix to Chapter 11
The SPARE Wheel Model

Descriptor *Function*

SETTING
- to describe in as full detail as possible the context within which the person, programme or project under investigation is operating
- to identify reasons for any perceived need for change in terms of who sees it necessary (or not) and why
- to gain some idea of how ready the system is to bring about and encompass the proposed change
- to identify potential barriers to change within persons and the system as a whole.

Key questions
- Who most wants change to occur and why?
- How far does this represent the mood of the majority of stakeholders?
- How far does this represent the desires of key individuals?
- What (who) are likely to be the forces most supportive of and resistant to change?
- What are likely to be the wider effects of the successful implementation of change or the failure to bring this about?

PLANS
- to elucidate the instigator's plans to bring about change
- to assess the feasibility of those plans with regard to the setting and to the status and/or personal qualities of the person(s) devising them
- to agree upon suitable methods for assessing the anticipated and unanticipated outcomes of the change process.

Key questions
- Exactly how is it proposed to bring about the proposed change?

	• What is the precise nature of the anticipated outcomes of this change?
	• How will anyone know if it has been successful?
	• What suitable methods are available to measure both anticipated and unanticipated outcomes?
ACTION	• to monitor as far as possible exactly what occurs in the efforts to bring about the desired change
	• to identify aspects of the implementation process which appear to foster or prevent the desired change
	• to identify the degree of match and mismatch between proposed plans of action and what actually occurs
	• to apply or suggest assessment procedures which will most readily reflect the project's aims.
Key questions	• What is actually happening on a day-to-day basis?
	• How well is the project director/change agent monitoring the implementation process?
	• How adequate were the original plans in directing this process?
	• What degree of match/mismatch is there between the plans and what actually occurs?
	• Have the agreed assessment procedures been successfully applied?
	• If not, why not?
	• Have others been added/substituted en route?
REACTIONS	• to identify outcomes at specified points in time, e.g. by means of a comparison of quantitative and qualitative data collected from a representative sample of participants at different intervals
	• to relate these outcomes, where possible, to the intervention process
	• to determine which changes could have occurred for reasons other than the intervention under review
	• to decide whether other data might have been more usefully gathered or other assessment techniques more gainfully employed.
Key questions	• What data has been collected?

	• What does it tell us that can be directly attributed to the intervention?
	• Could any of the results have been due to other reasons?
	• How useful were the assessment techniques employed?
	• Are there other available techniques that might have been more helpful?
EVALUATION	• to draw together information gathered under each of the previous headings
	• to look for connections and possible causal pathways between this information
	• to identify points at which plans had not been implemented due to unforeseen or other obstacles within the setting
	• to comment upon the perceived successes and failures of the intervention up to a specified point in time
	• to speculate on most likely reasons for those successes and failures
	• to suggest positive ways in which successes might be enhanced and failures minimised in the next phase of the project
	• to help decide on whether it might be preferable to (temporarily) abandon the project in view of the strength of the negative forces weighed against it.
Key questions	• Which aspects of the information gathered are of particular relevance to the success of the project?
	• What is the likelihood of direct causal links between one set of data and another?
	• What appears to be preventing the successful implementation of the project?
	• Are there obvious steps that can be taken to increase the likelihood of success and remove impending obstacles?
	• Where, if anywhere, do we go from here?

PART SIX

Developing an Integrated Methodology for Training and Practice

CHAPTER 12

Developing a System of Complementary Frameworks

Barbara Kelly and Lisa Woolfson

As argued in Chapter 1, because educational psychology has a complex historical relationship with regard to its theoretical underpinnings a major problem for the profession over the years has been to articulate the complexity of its intentions. The Summerfield Report (DES 1968) was a turning point in the role confusion and professional dissatisfaction expressed by educational psychologists. Their difficulty, as we saw, was directly related, on the one hand, to the realisation that Social Constructionism had profound implications for their profession, and, on the other, to the lack of timely frameworks to allow this theoretical model to be expressed in applied terms. There has been no clear evidence of educational psychology keeping a weather eye on developments in Social Constructionist Theory in order to help overcome the fundamental problems of embedding it effectively in professional practice, and academic training has been seen to be seriously out of step with such theory. Where attempts have taken place to embed such theory in practice they have been isolated responses to parts of the theoretical jigsaw with little applied power (Stobie 2003; Wolfendale *et al.* 1992). Debate, for example, about the relative merits of systemic versus individual casework has suggested a slow evolution in accessing and realising both the nature and scope of contemporary, academic Social Constructionist models (Stobie 2003). Similarly, while the British Psychological Society (2006) has helped to articulate and direct the wider perspective of the educational psychologist by creating training guidelines in ecological assessment and in endorsing the teaching of problem-solving frameworks for trainee educational psychologists, it can be argued that these do not provide sufficient direction to link role with theory in a coherent and systematic way that enables practitioners to feel confident in making practice choices and decisions (Stobie 2003).

This lack of coherent academic and professional guidance was discussed as long ago as 1992 as being a key factor in explaining slow professional developments in response to radical changes in perspective (Wolfendale *et al.* 1992). Wolfendale and her colleagues offered a very positive, critical review of core skills in educational psychology, looking at advances in practice in individual work, changing organisations, influencing the community and the organisation and management of educational psychology services. Although not explicitly stated as such, the areas reviewed did, indeed, reflect Constructionist and Eco-Systemic Theory but the book mainly highlighted the tendency for educational psychology to focus on and grapple with the lack of a coherence in professional identity, methodology and objectives.

While Wolfendale *et al.* set out only to offer a descriptive, discursive and contextual account of the range of activities that EPs carried out, 16 years on we have set ourselves a different challenge in this book. Two areas of concern emerge from the current text as fundamental to developing the unity and rationale of the profession:

- first, the nature of the psychology practised by educational psychologists, in particular, its clarity, distinctiveness and value and

- second, a dissonance between the status and role of academic psychology and that of applied, practitioner-based psychology.

These concerns were identified by Wolfendale *et al.* and still seem to us to be representative today of key areas of difficulty that underpin the profession's on-going, self-reported lack of coherence. As we have noted in exploring the role of academic theory in Chapter 1, there is a gulf between educational psychology and its academic roots that is, arguably, greater than in other areas of applied psychology (Whittrock and Farley 1989). In a historical overview Wolfendale *et al.* highlighted accusations of irrelevance and inaccessibility by practitioners towards academically inspired approaches, on the one hand, and charges of irresponsibility by academics towards the loose paradigms employed by practising educational psychologists, on the other. This is symptomatic of the historically problematic relationship between Social Constructionist Theory in educational psychology and its relevance, applicability and contextual responsiveness to the reality of the practitioner role. The loose approaches used in the field can be linked to the slow emergence of applied Constructionist paradigms and, as we have seen, to the child-deficit approaches in educational contexts (Gray and Lunt 1990).

A central theme of Chapter 1 was the exploration of contemporary developments in Social Constructionism and how, if at all, these are reflected in training and educational psychology practice today. Developments in Constructionist Theory – in particular, modern scientific approaches exemplified by Critical

Realism – were identified as being key in creating coherence in applied and academic educational psychology. A number of issues and themes emerged that relate to the exploratory and historical discussions in the introductory chapter. They prompt the following questions:

1. To what extent has educational psychology moved away from traditional, positivist theoretical perspectives and embraced Social Constructionism?

2. Do theories and practice exist that reflect contemporary developments in Social Constructionism, for example, Critical Realism?

Since substantial developments are, indeed, evidenced across the chapters, it is also important to ask questions about the relative utility and effectiveness of the frameworks described. We would frame these as being:

3. How flexible and robust are current frameworks in reflecting and addressing the complexity and diversity of contemporary theory and practitioner tasks?

4. What measures of effectiveness might be applied to frameworks for practice?

Educational psychology and contemporary developments in Social Constructionism

In relation to our first question regarding evidence of a move away from traditional theoretical perspectives we have seen that the frameworks presented here work at a complex array of levels. None is an exclusive answer to Constructionist Theory or real-world demands but all draw on Social Constructionist roots in applying psychology. To varying degrees, each one can be seen to weave together the role of overarching, Constructionist Theory with frameworks for training and practice. Certainly, there can be very little dispute that academic theory and training perspectives have developed considerably, particularly over the past decade. All the chapters, particularly Chapters 4, 5, 6 and 7, reflect this in providing highly developed, comprehensive and versatile frameworks adaptable to varying degrees across academic and applied contexts. Moreover, these chapters suggest that progression and advancement in applied Constructionist paradigms has been taking place, both in terms of the content and direction of academic training for practitioners and in the innovative, practice-led developments in the field.

The rhetoric of 'no change' reported in practice journals (Stobie 2003) and discussed in Chapter 1 does not stand up well to the evidence of Constructionist and context-specific work described here and, indeed, in practitioner journals. Recent explorations of the impact of the academic training framework developed by Monsen *et al.*, and the related, applied practitioner framework developed by Woolfson *et al.* suggest that these are both transferable to and perceived to be effective in the practice context (Kelly 2006; Lane and Corrie 2006). The static perceptions of the profession and the survival of the traditional, child-deficit practitioner reported by Stobie may reflect, to some extent, practitioner anxiety about the continuation of direct individual work *per se*. However we would argue that this model of work, focusing on the individual, can be transformed and rationalised by the value systems, theoretical models and practice frameworks supporting it. It sits comfortably within most of the frameworks for practice represented here which draw on contemporary Constructionist Theory and are informed by professional, statutory and ethical frameworks. Individual work is a legitimate part of the practitioner response to Constructionist analysis of the context. In fact, without individual work it is arguable that purely Systemic or rigidly detached Consultative approaches would fall prey to increasing irrelevance and perhaps charges of unethical practice. In addition, psychological services are also involved in creating and directing their own training and on-going professional development. They are generating and achieving objectives relating to a more rigorous and clearly articulated role definition with linked professional development, planning, and self-evaluation (MacKay 1999).

In their chapter on the historical and emerging legislative and statutory backdrop to educational psychology (Chapter 2), Boyle, MacKay and Lauchlan found the legislative context increasingly diversified, more demanding and less able to support a narrow investment in a traditional practice matrix. Accountability, transparency, continuous improvement, best value, ownership and evidence of effectiveness stand alongside shifts in wider values and beliefs about the nature of psychology and the helping professions. Legislative shifts reflect changes in perspective, increasingly seen as compatible with Constructionist orientations; they might be interpreted as taking account of contextual influences and moving away from the positivist tradition that endorsed the traditional child-deficit model in both education and educational psychology.

Ethics and values also provide a system of imperatives to shape both training and practice. They can be seen as reflecting Critical Realism by acting to ensure the emancipation of young people and families of children with additional educational needs. They also inform the ethos of education itself, placing increasing emphasis on consulting directly with pupils and fostering the concepts of holistic education. These developments are balanced by a range of factors and processes (not least research using Constructionist paradigms) that are increasingly informed by educational psychology theory and practice.

There is clear evidence of change at the level of both theory and practice. The challenge for contemporary educational psychology, it seems, then is not related after all to evidence that the profession is standing still or looking backwards, but rather to the need to develop the means to express (and to experience) more coherently, and with justifiable conviction, what it is actually doing and why. This brings us full circle to the purpose of this book: the development of a coherent approach to assimilating, understanding and applying necessarily complex theoretical perspectives with equally complex practice methodology. That there is evidence of significant development in theoretical models, applied frameworks and practice itself makes coherence easier to develop.

However, our first question also asked about the extent to which contemporary training and practice frameworks have reflected *advances* in Constructionist theory and research. Although there is evidence that training and practice frameworks have adopted Constructionist perspectives, some reflect modern scientific or Critical Realist developments more clearly than others. Critical Realism provides a contemporary, explicit scientific basis for professional practice and relies on a social and interpretative evidence-base for action. The Monsen *et al.* and Woolfson *et al.* frameworks draw explicitly on approaches derived from Social Constructionism and both can be subsumed within a Critical Realist perspective.

Questions 1 and 2: Flexibility of the frameworks for practice

In practice terms this means that the actions in the frameworks are not only derived from, or located within, Critical Realist approaches but also apply these actively in practice. They:

- ensure that problems or issues are considered in an interpretative, collaborative context with those involved
- direct the gathering of different levels and types of evidence, and
- consider and guide resulting action in the light of psychological and psycho-social theory and evidence.

They also respond to criteria and directives based on professional and statutory guidelines. These are Constructionist frameworks based on advanced social-scientific theoretical models and applying the principles of Critical Realism in practice.

Others frameworks, in particular those derived from humanistic and therapeutic roots, do reflect the broad tenets of Social Constructionism very faithfully – taking account of the language, value systems, experiences, feelings and beliefs central to the fulfilment of individual or organisational potential. In Chapters 7, 8 and 9 Wagner, Rees and Joseph outline frameworks for practice (albeit very different ones) of how to incorporate therapeutic or well-being perspectives and specific aspects of psychological and psycho-social theory and research in a service-delivery format. However, they are less explicit in dealing with the scientific elements and processes reflected so clearly in the Monsen *et al.* and Woolfson *et al.* frameworks. In the former, the guidance for action is derived directly from the dominant themes of the theory behind the framework. Consultation, for example, involves the role of the educational psychologist as facilitator, not expert, and directs his or her input away from collaborative, multi-stranded evidence-gathering and more towards the development of Consultation skills *per se*. Consultation also has as a major goal the emergence of preventative strategies in the context via experiential methodology and generalisation from the processes and outcomes of the collaborative relationship itself. Chapters 7 and 8 on Consultancy and Solution-Focused frameworks can be seen as reflecting Social Constructionist Theory quite clearly, with an emphasis on the interpretative and negotiable nature of reality and the avoidance of individual-assessment approaches or casework as an ideal. But in contemporary contexts this may not be enough to support and justify critical aspects of professional involvement and judgement in, for example, research or planning, policy development or resource management, and training – which, arguably, are enhanced by the broader social scientific rigour of Critical Realism. In developing a Critical Realist evidence-base, the expertise of the psychologist may need to be more obvious in order to satisfy the call for transparency, effectiveness and ethical considerations.

In reflecting Critical Realism closely, the training framework of Monsen *et al.* and the professional, applied framework of Woolfson *et al.* have the potential to offer substantially more to the practitioner in terms of scope, objectives and methodology than largely interpretative, therapeutically derived approaches. In establishing a series of *executive steps* they effectively put Critical Realism into practice. These frameworks systematically set out to clarify roles, explore various sources and types of evidence, disconfirm hypotheses, interpret and justify perceptions, negotiate and collaborate over actions and interventions and evaluate the impact of interventions. This broad executive approach is flexible across many contexts and is sensitive and robust in supporting the modern scientific approach, blending qualitative and quantitative strategies. It also helps to support the psychologist in a wide array of functions – from consultant to researcher, adviser and therapist – creating an efficient system to support the emancipatory shifts that can be a powerful characteristic of professions linked to value systems, political imperatives and ethical considerations.

Anwers to questions 3 and 4
The answer to Questions 3 and 4 seems to be that although they can be considered in isolation, few frameworks can be applied successfully (or, indeed,

ethically) in isolation from each other. For example, Chapters 10 and 11 on Activity Theory and Illuminative Evaluation both address the issues of psychological, social and organisational processes from a Constructionist perspective. They do not in themselves take account of ethical issues, accountability, legislative pressures or political initiatives. These have to be incorporated and taken into account by service-delivery policy and practice and informed by academic and professional training.

The majority of practice frameworks presented here are not mutually exclusive instruments or conceptualisations. Instead, they can and do represent a *system of approaches*. However, in order to demonstrate effective and defensible professional standards, practice in educational psychology requires the support of a network of *essential* frameworks (theoretical, applied, ethical and statutory), but the choice of approaches needs to be guided by clearly defined measures of effectiveness.

As we have seen, the Constructionist roots of modern applied social science and psychology make the quest for traditional objectivity in terms of child-deficit issues redundant. Instead, we are required to consider a complex interaction of needs, perceptions, data and directives in exploring and addressing issues. These issues are wide ranging; they might involve individual pupils with complex individual needs and difficulties, or organisational development and community initiatives.

It seems to us that there can be little choice about whether we substantiate the scientific and professional basis of the profession in line with modern scientific thinking and advances. This means we have to go beyond the broad perspective of Social Constructionism and establish processes in teaching and practice that clearly reflect the more specific modern scientific demands of Critical Realism. This is essential if we are to understand, explain, develop and, crucially, evidence our role. Frameworks must allow for different levels of enquiry and intervention and must also allow for continuous evaluation of impact. How might each framework be seen in relation to these contemporary yardsticks in terms of contributing to professional accountability and effectiveness?

The frameworks that have been identified as 'executive' – those of Monsen *et al.* and Woolfson *et al.* – offer a number of advantages to trainee and practitioner and also help in creating and directing sound service-delivery policy. First, they reflect primary Critical Realism in blending relativism with a widespread qualitative and quantitative evidence-base. They guide the practitioner to attend to external imperatives in establishing close collaboration and in meeting professional and ethical demands for input that is demonstrably least intrusive and has the strongest evidence-base. The thorough search of an evidence-base systematically reflects psychological and Realist Theory. The executive frameworks do not preclude the application (or derivation) of other theoretical considerations or practice but are designed to support the practitioner to find the best fit in terms of interventions. For example, these frameworks do not preclude the use of Solution-Focused work or a Consultancy approach if these are appropriate to the specific issues to be explored, addressed and evaluated. They would not obstruct organisational work using Activity Theory as a framework for change nor would they prevent individual therapeutic work or casework. In addition, their range of impact is very wide in that they are easily adapted to incorporate issues that may be more abstract – for example, the development of educational policy.

We give particular importance to the emergence of these particular executive frameworks because the role they play is one of effectively orchestrating a range of practitioner and service-delivery choices, whilst at the same time applying a series of checks to the quality of the processes involved. As a developing whole, it seems that the framework methodology does justice to the complexity of our contemporary role. The executive frameworks based on the concepts and approaches of Critical Realism and Eco-Systemic theoretical models offer sound meta-frameworks for applying psychology in the field of education. In contrast, the therapeutic and consultative frameworks are based on the development of broad Constructionist principles and are mobilised via therapeutic and interpersonal techniques. They may, however, be restricted in terms of the range of functions demanded in contemporary educational psychology and in the application of its conceptual and theoretical basis. In particular, these approaches would not directly support the more rigorous, evidence-based approach of the Critical Realist paradigm.

In Chapter 7, Wagner described the Consultation Framework as seeking (largely) to *prevent* difficulties arising, and thus reflects the early objectives outlined by Gillham in *Reconstructing Educational Psychology* (1978): to give psychology away by training teachers and parents to identify difficulties and promote change from a more detached, non-expert consultation role. The major difficulty in this approach in the contemporary context might lie in its (restricted) role in the *direct* evaluation of impact and in ethical considerations related to the possibility that indirect Consultancy might not result in appropriate, effective and skilled intervention.

In Chapter 9, where Positive Psychology as a framework for practice is described, Joseph offers a specific conceptualisation and range of input that is based on re-framing the deficit-value system via evidence and practice based on well-being objectives. This might well fit with Consultancy and Therapeutic frameworks in providing a largely preventative value system with the support of more advanced research paradigms and a developing evidence-base.

The Monsen *et al.* and Woolfson *et al.* executive frameworks have sometimes attracted the criticism from trainees and others that they lack the scope to highlight the socially constructed reality that they claim to explore and change (Kelly 2006). There is no doubt that, in order for these particular frameworks to operate effectively, the educational psychologist must be well versed in a range of areas – not least of which is the role of hidden goals and agendas in influencing interpersonal and organisational contexts. This is particularly important where change and development hinge on effective collaboration. In Chapter 11, Burden expands on these processes, providing an approach to exploring the most inaccessible and potentially very powerful processes in our professional contexts. Without the subtle scientific, Constructionist framework Burden offers and without the interpersonal and negotiating skills learned via Consultation and therapeutic approaches, the executive frameworks would, indeed, be mechanistic and ineffective.

The chapters presented in this book describe a range of frameworks for practice. With the exception of the ethical and legislative frameworks (although these, too, are influenced by Social Constructionism to some extent), all are derived from Social Constructionism. However, as we have seen, they have different roots and vary in terms of their flexibility and power to support and reflect a meaningful, broad-based applied model of Social Constructionism. In terms of professional practice, if the frameworks described are to play effective, integrated practice roles, individually they have to meet the demands of a Critical-Realist evidence-base and support best professional practice.

Our concluding discussion so far has highlighted the following themes:

- First, that a coherent backdrop to educational psychology can be provided by advanced, contemporary Social Constructionism, e.g. Critical Realism. Understanding of how this theoretical model can be mobilised directly and effectively in applied frameworks for practice is at presentweakly evidenced in both practitioners and trainees (Kelly 2006; Stobie 2003). An emphasis on the determining role of scientific realism and, in particular, Critical Realism in educational-psychology training programmes would help make the professional remit clearer – the educational psychologist as *scientist* and *constructionist*. This would also enhance and clarify role definition and perception.

- Second, executive frameworks are most closely aligned to the demands of the Scientific Constructionist remit and to the demand for external and internal measures of professional effectiveness. The Monsen *et al.* and Woolfson *et al.* frameworks for practice meet these very specific criteria most clearly.

- Third, the executive frameworks are not prescriptive but are selectively (in terms of reference to a sound evidence-base) informed by skills and approaches derived from other practice frameworks, from psychological theory and from the evidence-bases provided by research, Consultation processes and therapeutic skills.

- Fourth, ethical and legislative frameworks shape practice in the direction of values and beliefs about what is fair and right in educational and wider contexts. Their influence is not *one way* but can be seen to be open to the evidence provided by educational psychology via a Critical Realist perspective. This particular role – educational psychologist supporting emancipation – is already a highly developed academic role for social scientists working within in the Constructionist Theory and research paradigms.

Future directions: Developing an effective system of complementary training and practice frameworks

In conclusion, what are the implications of these frameworks for trainee educational psychologists and for practitioners? How might the profession utilise, apply and develop these further?

Educational psychologists need a clear view of where and how the underlying psychological theory and philosophy of science functions and affects their day-to-day work. We need to ensure that we offer clients a distinctive contribution as psychologists, one that is different from the involvement of educational administrators, teachers and social workers. Although there is some overlap in the skills required across these professional groups, a range of effective practice frameworks (along with their conceptual underpinnings) secure the centrality of psychology and the distinctiveness of our contribution in our professional interactions with schools and families. Figure 12.1 suggests a format for developing a system of frameworks for practice.

Clearly, the various frameworks discussed are each very different and, in a profession where scientific methodology ideally must inform training and practice for the future, an essential step is to clarify their boundaries, scope and focus as well as assessing their relative strengths and weaknesses. The principal concepts and paradigms in Figure 12.1 are those discussed in Chapter 1 and in this concluding discussion. They are highlighted in Figure 12.1 in terms of how they are represented, characterised and applied by each of the frameworks, i.e. the figure shows:

- whether the frameworks are derived from Social Constructionism and whether this dimension is represented mainly by therapeutic and interpretative approaches or by scientific realism

DEVELOPING A SYSTEM OF COMPLEMENTARY FRAMEWORKS 247

	Woolfson et al.	Monsen et al.	COMOIRA	Consultation	Positive Psychology	Solution-Focused	Activity Theory	Illuminative Evaluation	Ethics/values	Statutory/legislative
Critical Realism	✓	✓						✓		
Interpretative Constructionism			✓	✓	✓	✓	✓		✓	✓
Executive approach to service delivery	✓	✓							✓	✓
Designed for practitioner use	✓			✓		✓	✓	✓	✓	✓
Designed as training tool	✓	✓	✓							
Psychological theory prescribed				✓	✓	✓	✓	✓		
Therapeutic/ humanistic roots/ focus				✓	✓	✓				

Figure 12.1: Key parameters of the frameworks discussed in this book

- whether the framework is designed for practitioner use or for training
- whether the primary role is executive or whether psychological theory is prescribed by the framework itself.

In order to be a complementary system and to meet the demands of the yardsticks considered earlier, frameworks for training and practice need to be selected on the basis of a range of criteria. In terms of the frameworks discussed here, Critical Realism is seen to be a guiding theoretical model and the executive frameworks are most closely aligned with this paradigm – they can operate as training and practice frameworks, they do not prescribe any specific psychological theory or approach and are designed to allow the EP to select appropriate evidence-based psychology and interventions.

It seems that the necessary scaffolding for the growth of professional educational psychology is best provided by advanced Critical Realism forming a base from which contemporary knowledge, skills and theories can root and flourish. The implication for professional educational-psychology training courses is to make the determining role of scientific realism – and, in particular, Critical Realism – explicit and central in our training programmes, thereby creating a clearer professional remit for the educational psychologist as scientist, constructionist and critical realist.

In Figure 12.1 ethical and legislative frameworks are seen to have a major role in ensuring effective service delivery for practitioner use. While they shape practice in the direction of values, beliefs and cultural interpretations about what is fair and right in educational and wider political contexts, their influence is not merely top-down, since as practice frameworks themselves, they can be seen to be derived from, and responsive to, the evidence provided by educational psychology via a Constructionist–Interpretative perspective. This highlights the importance of the role of the EP in developing and informing emancipatory shifts, an already developed academic role for social scientists working within Constructionist Theory and research paradigms. EP research into accessing the views of children and using these to influence changes in practice, ethical standards and legislative policies are good examples of this emancipatory role in professional practice.

The Woolfson *et al.* and Monsen *et al.* approaches seem to provide advanced Critical Realist frameworks that optimise the potential for professional and academic growth and development, and facilitate the application of the full range of theoretical perspectives across the broad scope of work in which the EP might be engaged. These approaches may be focused on individual casework, systemic work with classes, schools or local authorities, or in-service training and policy development.

Furthermore their range of application extends comprehensively across the EP tasks of assessment, intervention and evaluation. These frameworks are not prescriptive in terms of any one psychological theoretical perspective but, instead, provide a series of scaffolding steps to inform and structure the sequence and focus of EPs' interactions and enquiries with their clients. It is left up to the individual EP or the psychological service to substantiate and prescribe the content and nature of these interactions, to populate the framework with relevant and robust psychological theories and interventions, to apply psychological skills and up-to-date subject knowledge, and to determine what is the appropriate evidence to gather. The executive frameworks can incorporate theoretical approaches for which there is a substantial evidence-base, guiding and informing the theoretical preferences of the individual EP, the agreed theoretical focus of a psychological service, or current, new and topical theoretical areas of interest. In this way, the Woolfson *et al.* and Monsen *et al.* frameworks can be seen to differ from the other executive frameworks presented in Figure 12.1.

The Critical Realist paradigm should not only be explicitly taught on training courses, but should be in evidence throughout all aspects of trainee professional work. It should not be perceived selectively as something that applies to some pieces of trainee work but is suspended for others, or something that only applies to submitted written work for trainee EPs but not to 'real' work in the field by practitioners. We are suggesting that it should be pervasive throughout EP service delivery and EP practice, whether enacted by trainee or practitioner. Such an emphasis on utilising theoretical and evidenced perspectives offers psychology practitioners the potential to align themselves more closely with academic psychology rather than perpetuate the unconstructive dissonance between practitioner and academic psychologists' viewpoints reported in the past. Not only do the executive frameworks increase the academic coherence of enquiry approaches across the community of psychologists, they also ensure that practitioners implement the professional requirements to address external and internal measures of professional effectiveness.

The role of other practice frameworks is, arguably, clarified and potentially developed more coherently by using Critical Realism as an overarching theoretical model. The key factor in this is the nature of the Critical Realist evidence-base as opposed to the Social Constructionist evidence-base. The COMOIRA, for example, is a complex, analytical and process-related training tool based primarily on Social Constructionism combined with a selective range of additional theories. These additional theories are subject to the negotiable and fluid nature of an undifferentiated, Social Constructionist *overarching* model. In common with other frameworks – Consultation, Solution-Focused, Positive Psychology and others – the nature of the evidential process and of the evidence-base is largely iterative. We would argue that Critical Realism offers a more rigorous system of checks and balances, which is likely to enhance each approach as well as the evidence-base it generates by highlighting its strengths and weaknesses. EP research and analytical skills can be better informed and more differentiated by allowing the rigour of Critical Realism and executive frameworks to guide actions.

Educational psychology is a developing profession, and one that is unusual in the complexity of its theoretical underpinnings and in its preferred range of impact. Historically, in aligning itself with Social Constructionist Theory it has generated a challenge requiring the creative development of complex, flexible and robust approaches. This challenge has been daunting, as we have seen. We set out in this book to demonstrate that these approaches are available but also to suggest that they require to be integrated at both the level of training and of practice, allowing a more effective interaction of theory, skills and social imperatives to shape the profession of the future. To use the full array of theories, frameworks and models available selectively and effectively requires coherent and creative training combined with reflective and responsive practice, each informing and developing the other. Increasingly Western society values and reflects the complexity and the emancipating potential of modern scientific realism; we can see evidence of this in shifting ethical and value systems, refined and complex concepts of rights and entitlement and, not least, in the acceptance of psychological processes and theories in education that aim to expand individual and group potential. Educational psychology has a major role to play in pioneering and demonstrating the value and impact of embracing and exploring complexity via its advanced and complex frameworks for practice.

References

British Psychological Society (2006) *Core Curriculum for Initial Training Courses in Educational Psychology*. Leicester: Division of Education and Child Psychology.

Department of Education and Science (1968) *Psychologists in Education Services* (The Summerfield Report). London: HMSO.

Gillham, B. (1978) *Reconstructing Educational Psychology*. London: Croom Helm.

Gray, P. and Lunt, I. (1990) 'Training for professional practice.' *Educational and Child Psychology* 7, 3.

Kelly, B. (2006) 'Exploring the usefulness of the Monsen problem-solving framework for applied practitioners.' *Educational Psychology in Practice 22*, 1, 1–17.

Lane, D.A. and Corrie, S. (2006) *The Modern Scientist-Practitioner: A Guide to Practice in Psychology*. London: Routledge.

MacKay, T. (1999) *Quality Assurance in Educational Psychology Services: Self Evaluation using Performance Indicators*. Edinburgh: Scotish Executive Education Department.

Stobie, I. (2003) 'Processes of change and continuity in educational psychology. Part 1.' *Educational Psychology in Practice 18*, 3, 214–237.

Whittrock, M. and Farley, F. (1989) *The Future of Educational Psychology*. London: Lawrence Earlbaum.

Wolfendale, S., Bryans, T., Fox, M. and Sigston, A. (1992) *The Profession and Practice of Educational Psychology*. London: Cassell.

Subject Index

academic selection 35–6
Activity Theory 19, 29, 115, 197, 214–16, 243, 244
   Activity System showing a learning programme 204
   Activity System showing pupil views of transition 207
   Activity System showing teacher views of transition 207
   Activity Systems 198–202
   Activity Theory as framework, device and approach 202–3
   analytic device 205–6
   Consultation meetings between EPs and teachers viewed as an Activity System 214
   contradictions 206–8
   descriptive framework 203–5
   First-generation Activity Theory model 199
   historicity 209
   multi-agency teamwork 211–13
   Multi-agency working viewed as an Activity System 212
   organisational development approach 209–11
   origins and history 197–8
   Second-generation Activity Theory model 200
   service development and service delivery 213–14
   Summary of Activity Theory contradictions surrounding pupil transition 208
   Third-generation Activity Theory model 201
Advisory Council on Education in Scotland 44, 45
Affect 83, 91
agencies 139, 144
   multi-agency meetings 152–4
   multi-agency teamwork 211–13
American Psychological Association (APA) 34, 185
   code of practice 54, 55, 56
Anger Management 99
Appreciative Inquiry 115, 145, 146, 147, 149, 158, 159
artefacts 204, 205
assessment 186–7
   Common Assessment Framework (CAF) 38–41
   Framework for Psychological Assessment 114, 116
assumptions 191–4
Attachment Theory 105

Attention Deficit Hyperactivity Disorder (ADHD) 106, 158, 192
Australia 201
autistic spectrum disorders (ASD) 205

Bateson, Gregory 163
Beattie Report 47
Behaviour 83, 91
behavioural problems 75–6, 78
Behaviourism 36, 219
Biology 83, 91
Board of Education 35
Boyle, James 9, 240
British Psychological Society (BPS) 61, 70, 98
   code of practice 52, 55, 64, 65
Bruner, Jerome 220
Burden, Bob 29, 245
Burt, Cyril 34

Cardiff University 98, 115, 117, 118
care-givers 87, 90, 93
   joint school–family Consultation 150–2
Causal Modelling Approach 82
change 110–12, 171
   changing how we think 188–90
child abuse 90
Child and Adolescent Mental Health Service (CAMHS) 211, 212
child clinical psychology 40
Child Guidance 35
Child Study 34
child-deficit 21, 23, 36, 140, 158, 238, 240, 243
children 21, 26, 40, 41, 90, 122–3, 125, 134, 140, 157, 159, 186, 188
   evaluation of Consultation 154, 155
   involving children 149–50, 151–2
   schools 143, 144–5, 147–8
   social context 192–3
Children Act 1989 38, 123
Children Act 2004 38, 152
Children (Scotland) Act 1995 123
Children's Centres 212, 214
Children's Hope Scale 187
Choice Theory 105
Circle of Friends 100
Circle Time 99, 100
Code of Practice (Special Educational Needs) 37
Cognition 83, 91

Cognitive Behaviour Therapy 100, 102
Cognitive Therapy 110
Common Assessment Framework (CAF) 38–9
   Lead Professional 40–1
COMOIRA 16, 94–5, 100, 117–18, 249
   background and contextual issues 98–100
   construct and clarify key change issues 111–12
   construct and explore hypotheses 109
   Enabling Dialogue 104, 106
   evaluate the change 110
   explore ability to change 111
   explore intention to change 110
   facilitate change 110–11
   Informed and Reasoned Action 104–5
   main functions of core principles 105–7
   main functions of eight key decision points 107–12
   reflect, re-frame and reconstruct 108–9
   review the process 109
   Social Constructionism 101–2
   strengths and weaknesses 113–17
   structure and processes 95–7
   Systemic Thinking 102–3
   Visual representation of COMOIRA 95
   ways in which COMOIRA has been used 112–13
competence 57
confidentiality 56, 60
Constructionist Model of Informed and Reasoned Action *see* COMOIRA
Constructionist Theory *see* Social Constructionism
constructs 90
Consultancy *see* Consultation
Consultation 18, 19, 100, 114, 139–40, 213–14, 229, 240, 242, 244, 249
   Consultation meetings between EPs and teachers viewed as an Activity System 214
   Consultation with teachers and staff 147–8
   development of Consultation 140–2, 157–8
   frameworks for Consultation 146

251

Full Consultation 147
  involving children or young
    people 149–50
  joint school–family Consultation
    150–2
  key difficulties 158–9
  multi-agency meetings 152–4
  principles for practice 142–3
  psychologies of Consultation
    143–6, 158–9
  *Questions for use in annual review and
    evaluation of Consultation* 156
  review and evaluation (R&E)
    154–7
Coordinated Support Plans 43
Critical Realism 10, 24–5, 26, 28, 83,
  238–9, 240, 241, 242, 243,
  244, 245, 246, 247, 248, 249
Critical/Accessible Dialogue
  framework 73
Cultural-Historical Activity Theory
  (CHAT) *see* Activity Theory
curiosity 187
curriculum 35, 225, 226, 227
Currie Report 22

Darwinism 34
De Shazer, Steve 163
deficit *see* child-deficit
Department for Education in Northern
  Ireland (DENI) 41
Developmental Work Research (DWR)
  202, 209–11, 213, 214, 215
  *Questions used to facilitate
    Developmental Work Research
    workshops* 211
dignity 56–7
Disabled Person (Services,
  Consultation and
  Representation) Act 1986 44
dyslexia 144

Eastern Europe 55
Eco-Systemic Theory 27–8, 83, 238,
  244
Ecological Theory 10, 18, 26–7
Education Act 1944 35–6, 41
Education Act 1981 36, 141
Education Act 1993 37, 123
Education Act (Northern Ireland)
  1947 41
Education (Additional Support for
  Learning) (Scotland) Act 2004
  43, 44
Education (Mentally Handicapped
  Children) (Scotland) Act 1974
  43
Education (National Priorities)
  (Scotland) Order 2000 46
Education (Northern Ireland) Order
  1996 42
Education Reform Act 1988 142
Education Reform (Northern Ireland)
  Order 1989 42
Education (Scotland) Act 1946 42–3
Education (Scotland) Act 1969 43
Education (Scotland) Act 1980 43–6
Education (Scotland) Act 1981 43, 44

Education (Special Educational Needs
  Code of Practice) (Appointed
  Day) (Northern Ireland) Order
  1998 42
educational psychologists (EPs) 9, 10,
  10–11, 33, 52, 53
educational psychology 33, 48, 52–3,
  237–9
  characteristic problems 75–6
  developing expertise in
    problem-solving 78–80
  history 33–6
  relationship between theory and
    practice 19–20
eleven plus (11-plus) 35, 36
emotional intelligence 187, 188
Enabling Dialogue 100, 104, 106
Engeström, Yrjo 198, 199, 200, 201,
  202, 209, 210
England 33, 35, 42, 43, 142
  legislation 36–41
Environment 83, 91
Erickson, Milton 163
ethics 52–3
  European Federation of
    Psychologists Associations
    Meta-code 55–63
ethnography 34
eugenics 34
European Federation of Psychologists
  Associations Meta-code 55, 64,
  65
  competence 57
  integrity 62–3
  respect for rights and dignity
    56–7
  responsibility 58–61
evaluation 92
  COMOIRA 110
  Consultation 154–7
  Integrated Framework 131
  see also Illuminative Evaluation
Every Child Matters (ECM) 38–9, 152
Excellence For All Children 37, 38
Exeter University 98
expertise, developing 78–80
externalising 145

families 122, 123, 125, 134, 139,
  143, 246
  joint school–family Consultation
    150–2, 157
Family Therapy 144
Feuerstein 227
flow 187
Framework for Psychological
  Assessment 114, 116
frameworks *see* practice frameworks
Fraser, Douglas Kennedy 34
Freudian psychology 189

Galton, Francis 33

Hadow, Sir Henry 35
head teachers 60, 87, 156, 168, 227
Helsinki 198, 202
heuristic approaches 97
humanism 19, 189, 190, 193, 241

hypotheses 77–8, 88, 109, 124,
  125–6
identified problem dimensions 90
Illuminative Evaluation 29, 218–19,
  229–30, 243
  evaluation as illumination 222–3
  history 220–1
  implications for educational
    psychology 228–9
  putting it into operation 223–4
  socio-cultural perspective 219–20
  SPARE Wheel 225–6, 226–8
  SPARE Wheel model 231–3
  see also evaluation
Inclusion Managers 156
inclusive education 53–4, 59
information-gathering 87, 125–6
information-processing theory 73–5
Informed and Reasoned Action 100,
  104–5
Instrumental Enrichment programme
  227
integrated children's services 38–9
integrated conceptualisation 90–1
Integrated Framework 16, 28, 114,
  121–2
  Integrated Framework diagram 124
  key influences 122–4
  Phase 1: establishing roles and
    expectations 125
  Phase 2: guiding hypotheses and
    information-gathering
    125–6
  Phase 2/3 summary proforma
    127–8
  Phase 3 problem-analysis 130
  Phase 3: joint problem-analysis
    126–30
  Phase 4 action plan proforma 132–3
  Phase 4: joint action plan for
    implementation 130–1
  Phase 5 summary proforma 134
  Phase 5: evaluate, reflect and
    monitor 131
  *summary of Phase 3 problem
    dimensions* 129
  uses 131–5
integrity 62–3
Interactionism 158, 215
Interactive Factors Framework 82–3,
  88, 106, 114
  *Interactive Factors Framework
    Diagram* 89, 91
International School Psychology
  Association 218
Interpersonal Problem-Solving
  Approach 114
intervention 91–2, 186–7
IQ tests 35
Iterative Model of Fieldwork Enquiry
  98–100

Japan 201
Joseph, Stephen 28, 241, 244
*Journal of Educational and Child
  Psychology* 216

Kelly, Barbara 9–10

SUBJECT INDEX

Kensington and Chelsea, Royal Borough of 157

language teaching 226–7
Lauchlan, Fraser 240
learning difficulties 21, 145
Learning in and for Interagency Working (LIW) project 211, 213
learning milieu 222–3
legislation 47–8, 240
    England and Wales 36–41
    Northern Ireland 41–2
    Scotland 42–7
Leontiev 198
letters 148, 149–50
local authorities 60–1, 63, 98, 139, 157
Luria 198

MacKay, Tommy 240
maladjustment 35, 36
Manchester University School of Education 39
Marxism 200
medical model 191–2
Mental Research Institute (MRI), Palo Alto 163
Ministry of Education 35
Models of Consultation 100
monitoring 92
    Integrated Framework 131
Monsen, Jeremy 121, 240, 241, 242, 243, 244–5, 248, 249
Motivational Interviewing 110
Munsterberg, Hugo 34

Narrative Thinking 145, 146, 149, 158, 159
Neale Analysis of Reading Ability 90
New Labour 58
NHS trusts 39
Northern Ireland 33
    legislation 41–2
Norwood Report 35

O'Hanlon, Bill 163
Oppositional Defiant Disorder 106, 192, 193

parents 22, 87, 90, 93, 186, 187
    Consultation 147
    joint school–family Consultation 150–2
Pathfinders 47
Person-Centred Psychology 190, 191–2
Personal Construct Psychology 143
Piaget, Jean 220
Positive Psychology 19, 24, 28–9, 185, 194, 244, 249
    assessment and intervention 186–7
    changing how we think 188–90
    indirect work 187–8
    interface with educational psychology 186
    Person-Centred Psychology 190
    reflections on assumptions 191–4

practice frameworks 9, 10, 15–16, 17–18
    ethical basis 54–63
    ethical problem-solving 63–5
    future directions 246–50
    Key parameters 247
Problem-Analysis Framework 16, 19, 69, 70–1, 80–1, 114
    characteristic problems in educational psychology 75–6
    developing expertise 78–80
    hypothesis-testing 77–8
    information-processing theory 73–5
    Phase One 77, 87
    Phase Two 77, 81, 88–9
    Phase Three 81, 90
    Phase Four 81, 90–1
    Phase Five 81, 91–2
    Phase Six 81, 84, 92
    Problem-Analysis Framework 82
    Problem-solving frameworks 72
    progression-by-steps approach 71–3
    reflective commentary 92–3
    subsequent developments 81–3
    summary 76–7
problem-owners 87, 93
progression-by-steps approach 71–3
psychology 9, 10, 17, 18, 139, 142
    Activity Theory 216
    psychologies of Consultation 143–6
psychometrics 35
pupils 93, 143, 205–6, 226–8

reading difficulties 58–9
re-constructionism 36
Record of Needs 43
Rees, Ioan 28, 241
Relativism 24
Research and Development in Organisations (RADIO) 115
responsibility 58–61
Review of the Functions and Contributions of Educational Psychologists in England and Wales in light of ECM 39–40
rights 56–7
Rogers, Carl 190
Russia 198

scaffolding 203
scaling questions 145
Scandinavia 201
schemata 78–9
schools 21, 37, 35, 36, 39, 122, 123, 135, 139, 246
    children 143, 144–5, 147–8
    evaluation of Consultation 154, 155
    joint school–family Consultation 150–2, 157
    SPARE Wheel in action 226–8
    transition between schools 205–6, 207, 208
Scotland 33, 34, 35, 48, 121, 142
    legislation 42–7

Scottish Children's Hearings 45
scripts 142, 146
Self-Determination Theory 190, 191
Seligman, Martin E. P. 185
SENCos 87, 156
Senior Managers 156
Skinner, Byron 219
Social Constructionism 10, 15–16, 17, 18, 20–1, 22, 23, 28, 29, 83, 144, 146, 238, 239, 246, 248, 249
    COMOIRA 100, 101–2
    contemporary developments 239–46
    divergence in professional debate 20–3
    Eco-Systemic Theory 27–8
    Ecological Theory 26–7
    flexibility of the frameworks for practice 241–2
    implications for practice frameworks 23–6
social context 192–3
Social Research Theory 19
Social Skills Training 99, 100
Social Work (Scotland) Act 1968 45
social workers 125
Socio-Cultural Activity Theory *see* Activity Theory
socio-emotional issues 90
Soft Systems 111
Solution-Focused work 16, 17, 100, 131, 142, 144, 145, 146, 147, 149, 158, 159, 244, 249
Solution Oriented 163, 164, 165–6, 167, 169, 170, 180
Solution-Oriented work 19, 100, 110, 116, 163–4, 180–1
    advanced stage 174–9
    common factors 167–8
    Core Professional Purpose 175–6, 179, 180
    early stage 164–6
    intermediate stage 166–74
    origins 163–4
    Solution-Oriented Systemic model 180
    ten principles 170–4
    three stages of Solution-Oriented Systemic Development 181
Solution-Oriented: working 168–70
South Africa 201
Soviet Union 197
SPARE Wheel 114, 225–6
    SPARE Wheel in action 226–8
    SPARE Wheel model 231–3
special educational needs (SENs) 36–8, 141–2
Special Educational Needs and Disability Act 2001 (SENDA) 38
Special Educational Needs and Disability (Northern Ireland) Order 2005 (SENDO) 42
Special Educational Treatment (Scotland) Regulations 1954 43
Spens, Sir Will 35
stakeholders 123, 124, 125–6, 130, 131, 134, 213, 224, 226, 228, 229

Standards in Scotland's Schools etc.
    Act 2000 46
Statements 37, 39, 41
Stewart, Angela 121
Strathclyde University 121
Sully, James 33–4
Summerfield Report 21, 237
supervisors 93
Swansea University 98
Sycol 163, 167, 175, 176, 177, 180
Symbolic Interactionism 143, 158
Systemic Thinking 21, 123, 240
    COMOIRA 100, 102–3
    Consultation 143–4, 145, 146,
        158
    hard elements of a system 177–8
    information elements of a system
        178–9
    soft elements of a system 178
    Solution-Oriented work 162, 163,
        164, 166, 167, 168, 173,
        174, 176, 177
Systems Theory 102, 103, 105, 106,
    132

Tarasoff v. *Regents of the University of
    California* 56
Taylor and Francis (UK) Journals 121
teachers 22, 75–6, 77, 78, 87, 125,
    145, 186, 187
    Consultation 141, 147–8, 157
    head teachers 60, 87, 156, 168,
        227
Theory of Planned Behaviour 110
Therapeutic frameworks 244
Trainee Educational and Child
    Psychologists (TECPs) 80
training 16–17, 41, 52, 53, 56, 57,
    62, 65
    COMOIRA 98–100, 112, 113,
        115, 117, 118
    Problem-Analysis Framework
        80–1, 81–3, 87, 88, 90–1,
        91–2, 92–3
triangulation 88
tribunals 37, 38, 42
tutors 87

United Kingdom 33–6, 156, 202,
    209, 228
    current developments in legislation
        47–8
United Nations Convention on the
    Rights of the Child 39, 123
United States 35, 201

values 53–4
Vygotsky, Lev 197–8, 203, 209, 215,
    220

Wagner, Patsy 28, 241, 244
Wales 33, 42, 43, 142
    legislation 36–41
Warnock Report 36, 44
websites 115
well-being 186
Whaling, Ruth 121
Williams, Marion 225
wisdom 187

Wood report 58
Woolfson, Lisa 9, 240, 241, 242, 243,
    244–5, 248, 249

young people 140, 147, 159, 188,
    194
    evaluation of Consultation 154,
        155
    involving young people 149–50,
        151–2

zone of proximal development (ZPD)
    203

Author Index

Adams, M.J. 59
Ajmal, Y. 100, 145
American Psychological Association 56
Anastas, J.W. 24, 25
Anderson, J.R. 73
Anderson, M.C. 73
Anderson, R.C. 73
Annan, J. 69, 70
Apter, S.J. 17, 141
Argyris, C. 70, 73
Armitage, C.J. 110
Ashton, R. 22
Atkinson, S. 205, 206, 207, 208
Audit Commission 157

Bailey, D. 124
Baker, D. 227
Baltes, P.B. 187
Bateson, G. 139, 163
Baxter, J. 38, 39, 47
Beadle, S. 163
Benn, R.T. 23
Bennett, P.L. 38
Berg, I.K. 144, 150
Berger, P.L. 21
Bersoff, D.N. 56
Bigge, M. 105
Blumer, H. 143
Board of Education 35
Bowlby, J. 105
Boxer, R. 37
Boyle, J. 48, 131
Bozic, N. 148
Bremner, W. 187
British Psychological Society 26, 65, 70, 237
Bronfenbrenner, U. 26, 83, 122, 123
Bruner, J.S. 203
Buck, D. 37
Burden, R.L. 57, 97, 114, 219, 220, 226, 227
Burnham, J. 144
Burr, V. 101
Burt, C. 35
Businessballs.com 116

Cameron, R.J. 22, 48, 70, 73, 122, 129, 131
Cameron, S. 69
Campbell, D. 103, 105
Canadian Psychological Association 56, 64
Caplan, G. 140
Carlson, A. 73
Carnell, E. 149

Carr, A. 97
Caruso, D. 187
Cato, V. 59
Chalmers, A.F.K. 24
Charness, N. 79
Checkland, P. 17
Chi, M.T.H. 78
Christopher, J.C. 188
Clarfield, L.E. 83
Clarkson, P. 60
Cline, T. 82, 106, 114
Coard, B. 61
Coldicott, T. 103
Cole, M. 198
Cole, T. 58
Colley, A. 52
Collins, A.M. 76
Connor, M. 110
Conoley, C.W. 140, 141
Conoley, J.C. 140, 141
Corrie, S. 83, 240
Cranwell, D. 62
Crozier W.R. 73
Curtis, M.J. 155, 156
Csikszentmihalyi, M. 185, 187, 190

Daniels, H. 198, 199, 201, 202, 203, 210, 215
Dawson, M.R.W. 73, 74
Deal, A. 123
Deci, E.L. 190
DECP (Division of Educational and Child Psychology) 97, 114, 116
Denham, A. 100
DES (Department of Education and Science) 21, 36, 37, 57, 141–2, 237
de Shazer, S. 144, 163
Dewey, J. 71, 72, 73, 80, 83
DfEE (Department for Education and Employment) 37, 38, 39, 142
DfES (Department for Education and Skills) 37, 38, 39, 152
DHSSPS (Department of Health, Social Services and Public Safety) 42
Dowling, E. 103
Duncan, B.L. 164
Dunst, C. 123

Efran, J.S. 83
Eisenhauer, L.A. 70
Ellis, J. 36
Elstein, A.S. 78, 79
Engeström, Y. 198, 200, 201, 202, 209, 210

Epston, D. 149
Erickson, M.H. 163
Ericsson, K.A. 74, 77, 79
European Federation of Psychologists Associations 55

Farley, F. 238
Farr, M.J. 78
Farrell, P. 9, 33, 39, 40, 41, 134
Fincham, F.D. 187
Flynn, S.A. 205
Forward, D. 97
Frederickson, N. 17, 38, 39, 47, 69, 70, 78, 82, 100, 103, 106, 111, 114, 12, 131
Frith, U. 82

Gallessich, J. 141
Galton, M. 205
Gameson, J. 16, 70, 95, 96, 100, 104, 105, 107, 108, 112, 113, 115
Garbarino, J. 123
Gendrop, S. 70
Gergen, K.J. 101, 139, 142
Gersch, I. 48
Gillham, B. 20, 21, 22, 23, 33, 36, 97, 144, 209, 244
Gillies, E. 144
Glaser, R. 76, 77, 78, 79
Glasser, W. 104, 105
Gluck, J. 187
Graczyk, P.A. 187
Graham, B. 69
Gray, P. 28, 238
Green, J.M. 145
Greeno, J.G. 76
Guba, E. 220, 221
Gutkin, T.B. 155, 156

Hain, D. 115
Hall, C. S. 54–5
Halliday, J. 70, 76
Halpern, D.F. 80
Hamilton, D. 221, 222, 223, 225
Hammond, S.A. 145
Hargreaves, D.H. 143
Harker, M. 144, 153
Hearnshaw, L.S. 35
Herbert, M. 98
Hestor, S. 143
HMIE (Her Majesty's Inspectorate of Education) 46
HMSO (Her Majesty's Stationery Office) 123
Holmes, E.A. 187
Horney, K. 189–90

House of Commons Select Committee on Education 61
Howarth, I.C. 70
Huntley, J. 145

Jacobsen, B. 142
Jimerson, S. 33
Jonassen, D.H. 74
Joseph, S. 188, 190

Kagan, T.K. 34
Kashdan, T.B. 187
Kelly, B. 28, 69, 70, 80, 81, 240, 245
Kelly, G.A. 143
Kelly, T. 209
Kennerley, H. 100
Kerr, C. 80
Kerr, G. 35
Kerslake, H. 146
Kinsella, K. 103
Kirk, J. 100
Kirkaldy, B. 35
Kozulin, A. 198, 203
Kunzmann, U. 187

La Gro, N. 77
Lane, D.A. 83, 240
Lanvers, U. 226
Larney, R. 156
Leadbetter, J. 115, 202, 211, 213, 214, 216
Leahy, R.L. 110
Lebiere, C. 73
Lehmann, A.C. 74, 77, 79
Leont'ev, A.N. 199
Lewin, K. 143, 214
Leyden, G. 37, 70
Lichtenberg, J.W. 78, 79
Lincoln, Y. 220, 221
Lindsay, G. 52, 53, 54, 55, 56, 58, 60
Lines, D. 100
Linley, P.A. 188
Lodge, C. 149
Lokke, C. 37
Lopez, S.J. 187
Lown, J. 100
Luckmann, T. 21
Lunt, I. 28, 238

MacKay, T. 43, 45, 47, 48, 240
McCallum, M. 35
McGee, S. 74
McKnight, R. 42
Maddux, J.E. 191
Mayer, J.D. 187
Mellor, F. 143
Mennin, S. 80
Meyers, J. 47, 140
Miettinen, R. 198
Miller, A. 36, 62, 70, 97, 98, 114, 116
Miller, W.R. 104, 106, 110
Ministry of Education 36
Mithaug, D.E. 56
Monsen, J. 16, 19, 22, 69, 70, 73, 80, 82, 114, 121, 122
Morris, J.N. 23
Morrison, I. 205
Morton, J. 82

Moss, D. 101
Munsterberg, H. 34
Murphy, J.J. 164

Nastasi, B.K. 47
Neimark, N.F. 116
Newell, A. 74, 75, 76, 78, 83
Nichols, S.L. 226, 227
Nieboer, R. 101
Northern Ireland Commissioner for Children and Young People 42
Norwich, B. 38, 47
Nylund, D. 158

Oakland, T. 33
Ofsted 157
O'Hanlon, B. 97, 163
Orme, S.F. 156
Osborne, E. 103
Outhwaite, W. 24
Oxford Reference Online 97

Parlett, M. 221, 222, 223, 224, 225
Partridge, K. 101
Passmore, J. 115
Patterson, T.G. 190
Pearson, L. 70
Pell, T. 205
Phillips, P. 98
Power, M.J. 23
Prilleltensky, I. 192
Principal Psychologists of Scotland 44
Prochaska, J. 97
Proctor, G. 193

Ranyard, R. 73
Ravenette, A.T. 143
Reder, L.M. 73
Rees, I. 162
Resnick, L.B. 76
Rhodes, J. 100, 145
Rhydderch, G. 95, 113
Roberts, E. 22
Robinson, V. 70, 73, 74, 76, 77, 80, 81
Robson, C. 24, 25
Rogers, C.R. 104, 107, 190
Roller, J. 146
Rollnick, S. 104, 106, 110
Rose, S. 73, 76
Ross, G. 203
Ryan, R.M. 190

Salovey, P. 187
Sampson, O. 35, 42
Schmidt, H.G. 80
Schön, D.A. 73
Schraagen, J.M. 74, 75, 79
Schwartz, A.S. 78, 79
Schwartz, P. 80
Scottish Education Department 44, 45
Scottish Executive 22, 44, 46, 476
Scribner, S. 209
Selekman, M.D. 111
Seligman, M.E.P. 185, 189, 190
Shepherd, D. 209
Sheppard, J. 43
Sheridan, S.M. 156

Shermis, S.S. 105
Shin, N. 78, 79
Shulman, L.S. 79
Sigston, A. 70
Simon, H.A. 74, 75, 76, 78, 83
Smith, E. 80
Snyder, C.R. 187
Solution-Oriented School 180
Spiro, R.J. 73
Sprafka, S.A. 79
Steiner, T. 150
Stern, W. 34
Sternberg, R.J. 187
Stewart, A. 121
Stobie, I. 15, 22, 47, 122, 131, 237, 239, 240, 245
Stoker, R. 209
Stratford, R.J. 70
Svenson, O. 73

Taylor, D. 152
Tesch, R. 24
Thacker, J. 114.
Thompson, L. 22
Timmins, P. 115, 209
Tobbell, J. 206
Topping, K. 187, 227
Trickey, S. 227
Trivette, C. 123
Turner, J. 100

UNCRC (United Nations Convention on the Rights of the Child) 123

Van Berkel, J.M. 80
von Bertalanffy, L. 122

Wagner, P. 100, 114, 123, 143, 144, 145, 146, 214
Warren, L. 100
Watkins, C. 100, 114, 143, 145, 149
Webb, G. 80
Webster, A. 17, 70, 78
Wedell, K. 37, 97, 116
Weiner-Davies, M. 163
Welch, M. 156
Welsh Assembly 41
Wenger, J.L. 73
Westbrook, D. 100
Whaling, R. 121
Whetton, C. 59
White, M. 145, 149
Whittrock, M. 238
Wilden, S. 77
Wiley, J. 79
Williams, M.D. 226
Witmer, L. 34
Wolfendale, S. 237, 238
Wood, D.J. 203
Woods, K. 134
Wooldridge, A. 34, 35
Woolfson, L. 16, 69, 70, 80, 81, 114, 121, 122, 131
Wright, A. 17, 70, 78